THE **CON** MEN

STUDIES IN TRANSGRESSION

STUDIES IN TRANSGRESSION

SERIES EDITOR: DAVID BROTHERTON
FOUNDING EDITOR: JOCK YOUNG

The Studies in Transgression series presents a range of exciting new crime-related titles that offer an alternative to the mainstream, mostly positivistic approaches to social problems in the United States and beyond. Books in the series raise awareness of key crime-related issues and explore challenging research topics in an interdisciplinary way. They allow the global voiceless to have their views heard, offering analyses of human subjects who have too often been marginalized and pathologized.

THE CON MEN

HUSTLING IN NEW YORK CITY

TERRY WILLIAMS AND
TREVOR B. MILTON

COLUMBIA UNIVERSITY PRESS   NEW YORK

Columbia University Press
Publishers Since 1893
New York   Chichester, West Sussex
cup.columbia.edu

Library of Congress Cataloging-in-Publication Data
Williams, Terry M. (Terry Moses), 1948–
The con men : hustling in New York City / Terry Williams and
Trevor B. Milton.
pages cm. — (Studies in Transgression)
Includes bibliographical references and index.
ISBN 978-0-231-17082-6 (cloth : alk. paper) —
ISBN 978-0-231-54049-0 (e-book)
1. Crime—New York (State)—New York. 2. Criminals—
New York (State)—New York. 3. Police—New York (State)—
New York. I. Milton, Trevor, 1976– II. Title.
HV6795.N5W55 2015
364.16'3097471—dc23

2015009581

Columbia University Press books are printed on permanent
and durable acid-free paper.

This book is printed on paper with recycled content.

Printed in the United States of America
c 10 9 8 7 6 5 4 3 2 1

Cover design: Marc Cohen
Cover image: © Mr Doomits/Shutterstock

CONTENTS

ACKNOWLEDGMENTS

There are many people to thank in any book, and it is too much to hope that no one is left out. Two people were central in my early graduate work: Professor William Kornblum and Lindsey Churchill. Churchill became interested in the con-game dialogue and encouraged me to write about the con-game language in his class on ethnomethodology, and this course paid attention to the discursive elements in everyday worlds I was exploring. Kornblum's insights into city ecology opened my eyes to a world of sociological possibilities using a Chicago School lens.

Special thanks to the following people who helped with this book in one way or another: Mario Serrano Marte, whose fieldwork and writing in my ethnography class were central to our text on Maria the numbers operator and who generously gave his permission to use the material. I greatly acknowledge the wisdom and intelligence afforded us by Elmo Johnson, who provided much of the information about street hustling and other games of chance in the text; Dr. Sarah Daynes, my indefatigable colleague, whose intelligence and steadfast assistance is inestimable; Hakim Hasan, my dear friend and intellectual mentor whose suggestions, criticisms, and assistance regarding the draft was extremely important and timely. I wish to express my especial thanks to Jules Lipow, who, along with Natalia Filippova, provided expert knowledge and sagely wisdom of the market; and to my New School University graduate assistants, Ganji Rezvaneh and Guillermina Altomonte, whose hard work and diligence in the library were admirable; Zacch Yemi Olorunnipa, a Princeton student whose fine ethnographic work was extremely helpful; one of my graduate students, Bryan B., whose work on panhandling was instructive; Dr. Lucille Perez, for a conversation that was extremely helpful in understanding the life of teens in the con-game scene; my sisters, Sandra Smith, Janice Williams, Cynthia Pippins, and Jennifer MacDougal, for their lifelong intellectual and loving assistance in all matters of life, love, and food; my cousins, Wallace Dillon, Edward Dillon, Rodney (Stick) Williams, Jenene Bush, Audrey Brown, Linda Hannah, Caron Williams, Donnie Williams, Mack Bethea, Jerry Williams, Denise Williams, Sharon Williams, Penelope Cade, Sally Cade, Vernon Cade Jr., Edwin Moses, Barbara Ann Dillion, and Jean Williams; and my aunt Velma Anderson. Thanks also to New School University Dean Will Milberg, President David Van Zandt, Provost Tim Marshall, David West, Sonia Salas, and Jessie Sze; and thanks to Maria F. Heyaca for her special assistance when needed the most. Special thanks to Charles Winick, Robert Merton, and to Jason Maxwell and his co-barber in the appointment shop, Trevor Bethel, for their wisdom and exciting word display. The Boogie Woogie boys—Jessie Day and Yates Austin, Daron Howard, Paul Craig, Leo Craig, Cookie, Robert Simels, Martin Stolar, Sam Frazier, Jay, and Madeline—for their continued support during the writing of the manuscript. And special thanks to Elsie Chandler, Royce Wilder, Rick Jones, and other courageous staff at the Neighborhood Defenders Service of Harlem office. Their magnificent work on behalf of the people in the city, especially minority kids in trouble, is greatly appreciated. The Defenders staff took their precious time to discuss with me their experiences with young people in Harlem. I have changed or altered some names and locations to respect a desire for anonymity on the part of certain people in the narrative. Thanks also to the editors at Columbia University Press: Jennifer Perillo, Stephen Wesley, Eric Schwartz, and Robert Fellman.

And lastly kudos are due to Alibi, Herlene, Mrs. Wilson, Ace, Skip, and Quick, though reluctant and recalcitrant at times, but without whom this book could not have been written. In the final analysis, if there are errors and issues of interpretation, they are the sole responsibility of the authors.

Terry Williams

* * *

I would like to thank Aubrey Bonnett for being a friend and a wise and trusted colleague and for pointing me in the direction of the Public Criminology Series at John Jay College for Criminal Justice; David Brotherton for suggesting our text to the editors at Columbia University Press; Jock Young, who selected our text for the Public Criminology Series shortly before his passing and whose scholarship is invaluable to the field; Joseph Culkin, Joann Rollo, and all the faculty at Queensborough Community College, for providing a warm, family-friendly, and truly collegial environment in which to work; my officemate, Don Tricarico, who fielded numerous random/unrelated questions; my students at Queensborough and SUNY Old Westbury, who provided invaluable feedback on the text; Jonathan Schiffer, who led me to important contacts; Martin Caba, for linking me up with Ramon; my beautiful wife, Natalia, for her love, hard work, emotional support, and tolerating my sporadic jaunts into the city for ethnographic observation; my children, Zhyom and Zhyara, for making me smile and laugh when I got home; Jan Holland, for being a friend and trusted colleague that I could always come to for advice; all of my respondents, J.T., Otis, Lee, Daniel, Angelina, Frank, Ramon—thank you for making this such a colorful text; the editors at Columbia University Press, Jennifer Perillo, Stephen Wesley, and Eric Schwartz, for being true professionals and excellent wordsmiths; a special thanks to Terry Williams, for being a teacher, mentor, master ethnographer, critic, colleague, compatriot, and friend; and also M. Grabosky and other reviewers for their insightful assistance in making the manuscript the best it could be. But after all is said and done, if there are errors and issues of interpretation, they are indisputably our own.

Trevor B. Milton

THE CON MEN

INTRODUCTION

The hypocrisy of the confidence man and the painted woman did not lie simply in a discrepancy between what they practiced and what they preached. Their art as depicted in the conduct-of-life literature was far more subtle: they could manipulate facial expressions, manners, and personal appearance in a calculated effort to lure the guileless into granting them confidence.
—Karen Halttunen, *Confidence Men and Painted Women*

Walk down any street, in any city; gaze into pool halls or drug dens or dingy dives, any after-hours spot; pause on any corner where men gather, lounging, talking, chatting, playing dice, or just "shooting the breeze," and any of them might be Alibi Jones.[1] Alibi is tall, middle weight, not too skinny, not too fat, about forty-something. Whenever asked about his age, he would say, "You don't want me to lie to you, do ya?" He never did reveal it. One time when Alibi was high, I (Terry Williams) asked again, thinking he would catch him off guard. "Now, don't start me to lying," Jones said. So I left it alone.

Alibi sometimes looks younger than forty and sometimes a bit older. His dark skin is radiant. His hair, now Afro shaped, was processed or "conked" for years back in the day, and now he has a small bald spot (caused by the chemical treatments) near his temples, which he covers with a dark-colored spray. His eyebrows arch at the center of his proud face, and they frame his wide nose, giving him a strong, daring look.

He holds a stare for much longer than is required, and the skin underneath his eyes is taut, not puffy. There is a small scar, almost unnoticeable until his head rises, which runs from the lower part of his right ear to the edge of his left ear. His hands are rough, fingers long, nails manicured. He steps with a slightly pigeon-toed gait, moving side to side, quick paced, always in a hurry, always somewhere to go. Alibi is tough looking and tough sounding. He once said, "I've made more money from motherfuckers giving me their money than twenty of the best stick-up bandits ever got in a lifetime."

As I got to know him, Alibi shared with me his philosophy of running cons. Con games in New York City are sophisticated maneuvers, often complex and unwieldy, and the successful con artist is smooth and tricky. Yet the "hook" in the game, according to Alibi, is not sophistication or smoothness but something else entirely: greed, or what he calls "larceny." "All I need to see is whether the motherfucker got larceny in his heart. That's all I need to see." Larceny is defined by the New York penal code as "intent to deprive another of property or to appropriate the same to himself or to a third person, he wrongfully takes, obtains or withholds such property from an owner thereof."[2] But here, Alibi means something entirely different: a kind of inner thought process wherein the victim of a con is thinking of how he or she might steal from the con artist. According to Alibi, this urge is what often ensnares the victim and makes the con successful.

This is also a convenient philosophy to help con artists justify their own actions: the victim is greedy and deserves whatever he or she gets. Alibi's theory of larceny is a major weapon in the con man's arsenal of deceitful tactics, rationalizations, and opportunistic derring-do that makes the con game operational. "I never robbed nobody that didn't deserve to be robbed, and I never been caught," adding, under his breath, "that many times." "I've always wanted to have money, women, and a warm place to shit, and I've had all of that and more."

Alibi has lived most of his life as a con. He was born in Kenner, Louisiana, a stone's throw from New Orleans, where he spent most of his time as a kid hustling drunks, stealing bicycles, and running away from the police. This, too, he justifies. "Where I come from not a single cop is a good cop. They're all corrupt, crooked, rotten to the core. Cops would even take money from school kids and old ladies, they were totally fucked up. Everybody will tell you about new Aaawlins cops as the worst, most corrupt in the country." His parents were farmers; his father ran a strawberry farm near Slidell, Louisiana, and sold chickens. When he left home, he came to New York and stayed in an apartment in Harlem near Convent Avenue, where he could be seen shooting dice across from the post office, only a block or two from the Apollo Theater.

A CITY SO NICE . . .

I don't believe in reality, or life, just in the imagination because reality is just the stories we tell each other. Some good stories, some not so good.

—Francois-Henri Soulie

New York City is rugged, aggressive, and competitive, yet it is also one of the most desirable cities in the world, with broad boulevards, tree-lined avenues, yellow and lime-green cabs darting hither and yon, and frantic crowds moving along busy streets. And though New Yorkers constantly complain about trash, traffic, trains, and any number of other hassles, most of them readily acknowledge that they live in one of the greatest cities in the world. Among its many finer points, New York offers access to the best museums and cultural institutions and an intelligentsia unmatched anywhere. New York, New York: a city so nice they named it twice, as the disc jockey Frankie Crocker used to say on his 1970s radio show.

The lyrics to the classic 1977 song "New York, New York" assert, "If I can make it there, I'll make it anywhere." The operative word is "if." And, as Alibi Jones often says, "If a frog had a muddy appetite and a square ass he'd shit bricks." This dream of "making it" has been repeated for decades in barber shops and street corners, in social clubs and candy stores, in churches and bodegas, but the reality is that it is hard to make it here—and getting harder. In this city success is defined by the most famous among us, movie stars and superstar athletes, presidents, moguls, and Wall Street millionaires. It would be much more fair to compare your success to that of your peers, those you grew up with, your street buddies, or your neighbors, but that's not how it works.

Those coming to New York seeking great fortune or world-class fame quickly learn the hard way that living in this city is a daily struggle; it requires a tireless work ethic in order to keep up, just to make ends meet. Every aspect of city life can be a grind, from the competitive job market, to the exhausting daily commute, and even to demanding relationships. New York City—massive, crowded, dirty, teeming with bodies—can be a nightmare for the human spirit. It is also a dream location for scientists looking to study the human condition. This towering metropolis or concrete jungle (whichever way you choose to view it) is the end result of centuries of social liberalism, capitalist expansion, herd migration, artistic experimentation, and the rampant street entrepreneurialism that stems from the constant struggle to survive.

As of this writing, the city burgeons with 8.2 million people, and more arrive every day. Massive numbers of new immigrants and migrants work in every conceivable industry: South Americans and Central Americans sell flowers and fruit; Chinese workers hawk knickknacks on the sidewalks; South Asians drive cabs and run newsstands; undocumented Irish construction workers dangle from scaffolding, building new high-rises; little Africas and little Mexicos sprout up in the outer boroughs.

At the other end of the economic spectrum, a new breed of millionaire and billionaire is leaving its imprint. Industries of the past, such as the garment business or other manufacturing concerns, are going, going, gone. Now, finance, insurance, technology, and real estate rule; Wall Street leads the way. Inequality is built into the capitalist system; the catchphrase "the rich get richer" is not a cliché. The growth in the U.S. economy favors the wealthiest individuals (the 2 percent), and, as the economist Thomas Picketty argues in *Capital*, the richest Americans increase their wealth (through inheritances or other means) more than five times faster than the average American does.[3]

The city is full of the "haves" and the "have-nots." For the con man, if you cannot "have," then you take. The con artist's feelings toward this city are complex. Most con artists don't so much hate the city as feel betrayed by it because it beckons with a dream but provides no realistic means to obtain it. In a sense, the American dream itself is a masterful con that suckers people in. So some come to realize that the only way to reach this mythological dream is to not play by the rules of the game but to devise a different game, a game of chance, a gambling game, a hustling game, a conning game, a pretender game, a now-you-see-it-now-you-don't game. To understand the art of deception, you must see that it is essentially about changing the rules of the game and misdirecting the audience in order to "get over." (We should note that the "game" can be played or performed anywhere, in any city, at any time, though large cities are preferable because density and anonymity are part and parcel of the ruse necessary for a successful con to work.)

Thus, laced into city's economy alongside the wealthy, the working classes, the struggling, and the tourists, some New Yorkers have created a quasi-professional niche built on misinformation and seduction. Some are tireless salespeople, illegally trading and bartering goods. Others use sleight-of-hand to distract naïve spectators while swiping their riches. These crafty opportunists of New York City use their well-honed skill set to wring money out of New York's informal economy. They wait for the moment when their target's guard is down—or "sleeping," as they say—and then they strike. These are who we mean when we refer to the con artists and hustlers of New York City.

CON ARTISTS AND HUSTLERS

Confidence artists—those who deceive in order to procure money or goods from unsuspecting strangers—perform a type of street theater that capitalizes on the fluid structure of the dense, diverse, and mobile city. They use their cunning to draw in the unsophisticated and then deploy a practiced anonymity to sneak away with the prize. These skilled craftspeople often take years to learn how to dazzle a crowd in one instant and disappear into the same crowd in the next.

The term "con man" originated with a New Yorker named William Thompson. In the 1840s, Thompson was famous for approaching wealthy strangers, pretending to be an old acquaintance, engaging in conversation, and then asking something to the effect of, "Do you have confidence in me to trust me with your watch (or money) until tomorrow?"[4] Of course, he would never return with the watch or the money, and eventually he was caught. During his trial in 1849, the *New York Herald* dubbed him the "confidence man," thus coining the term.

More recent practitioners of the art, like Sante Kimes or David Hampton, rely on similar skills of ingratiation and disguise to run their cons. Sante Kimes's lifelong career of grifting included forgery, shoplifting, arson, fraud, and theft, and it reached its apex when she attempted to steal the identity of a wealthy heiress, Irene Silverman, to gain access to Silverman's Manhattan mansion. (Kimes and her son were ultimately convicted of murdering Silverman.) David Hampton was a teenage con artist who was famous not so much for the amount of money he received but who he was able to con—the so-called limousine liberals, upper-class patrons of New York society. Hampton was said to have classic con-artist qualities; he was good looking, well groomed, and charmingly articulate. He was able to convince wealthy (and otherwise savvy) New Yorkers that he was the son of the actor

Sidney Poitier and a Harvard friend of their children. They welcomed him into their homes and offered him lavish meals and hospitality; eventually, they discovered that he was not who he said he was. Sidney Poitier did not even have a son.

The French sociologist Loic Wacquant, who has researched ghetto life and culture (but is better known as a radical theorist of the state) defined the actions of the con artist as "a field of activities which have in common the fact that they require mastery of a particular type of manipulation [symbolic capital], namely, the ability to inveigle and deceive others, if need be by joining violence and chicanery and charm, in the pursuit of immediate pecuniary gain."[5] Symbolic capital refers to the value of a person's reputation, in other words, the kinds of resources an individual has at his disposal based on his position in society. Attributes like honor, power, and prestige all have a certain value that can be utilized.

In his 1851 classic *London Labour and the London Poor*,[6] the British journalist Henry Mayhew called con artists "street artists," also known as grifters or back-alley hustlers, all with their own individual skills yet also with much in common. They used their verbal ability and charm to manipulate people into being victims. The con game is a social act and a social event that follows a predetermined series of steps. C. R. D. Prus and Robert C. Sharper, two noted sociologists of the hustling scene, list those steps: finding a suitable victim, gaining the victim's trust, persuading the victim to commit to a scheme that will benefit him or her, getting money from the victim, and, finally, placating the victim in order to quell any uneasy feelings about the situation.[7]

The New York penal code defines conning as "fraudulent accosting . . . when a person accosts a person in a public place with intent to defraud him of money or other property by means of a trick, swindle or confidence game."[8] This is a Class A misdemeanor in New York and is taken seriously by the courts. As compared to con artists, hustlers are the seasoned entrepreneurs of the city's informal economy. They hold down jobs like most anyone else, but their jobs tend to be self-made, self-enterprising, and, of course, illegal. Hustlers are the self-employed vendors of legally purchased goods—or illegally made substances—sold through unauthorized means. Hustling includes a variety of activities that violate numerous penal codes. Such activities can include manufacturing and peddling homemade cocaine in after-hours clubs or on the street; selling stolen ("hot") merchandise; selling counterfeit goods, such as handbags; selling wholesale merchandise, such as electronics, at retail prices; betting on games of chance (cards, dice, pool) in ways forbidden by the law;[9] and participating in the underground lottery of the ghetto, known as policy or numbers. At the more felonious end of the scale, they can include petty pillage and theft; stealing cars; break-ins; scavenging materials such as bricks, copper pipes, windows, and door frames from abandoned buildings; mugging; stickups; pimping; racketeering; extortion; and the wholesale and retail trade in drugs. The sale of "loose" or "untaxed" cigarettes (in violation of New York State Tax Law §1814) is one of the more popular hustles in New York City. It is estimated that 59 percent of all cigarettes consumed in New York State have been smuggled in from other states in order to avoid the state's hefty $4.35-per-pack tax.[10]

Hustling and con artistry differ in a few key respects. A hustler is a kind of con artist, but the category of hustling is expansive and includes individuals who simply work hard to make extra money (by legal means). And then there are "gorilla hustlers" who make a livelihood from more violent acts. A true con artist usually does not resort to physical violence; his most potent weapon is his smooth, articulate conversation. Many con artists are quick to admit that if you must use violence to get a mark's valuables, you are not a con artist but a common criminal, a gorilla hustler. Ironically, con artists do not see themselves as common crooks; as Alibi rationalizes, "I'm only doing what the mark would do to me. You see, an honest man could not be conned."

Local law-enforcement officials restrict, regulate, and squeeze those who want to make fast money by selling illegal goods, yet experienced hustlers, if they are skilled enough to evade surveillance, can make a good living. Hustling is lucrative because the city is saturated with tourists (thirty-five million per year at last count) and locals alike who may want a new t-shirt, a knockoff handbag, or some other good priced slightly or, in some cases, significantly below market value.

Bettylou Valentine, in her book *Hustling and Other Hard Work*, notes that hustling "refers to a wide variety of unconventional, sometimes extralegal or illegal activities, often frowned upon by the wider community but widely accepted and practiced in the slums and ghettoes."[11] Valentine was an important anthropologist who conducted research in poor black neighborhoods in the northeastern United States for half a decade. Her most famous location was the fictitious city of Blackston, a multiethnic community of one hundred thousand in Massachusetts, where she conducted an in-depth analysis of three families and how they survived through "creative lifestyles" such as hustling, public assistance, and other ways of making ends meet. Valentine reasoned that given the intricacies, aggravations, trials, and tribulations these people faced in trying to survive, hustling was essentially "hard work." Her full-immersion method of doing fieldwork was especially notable because it required a more meaningful and sincere collaboration between social scientists and the communities they studied.

Valentine goes on to note:

> People also hustle by buying or selling "hot" goods, whose source is often unknown but correctly assumed to be stolen or otherwise illegally obtained; gambling (most often card games, pool or billiards, craps); bootlegging liquor after hours or Sunday; stealing cars and/or stripping them for salable parts; stripping abandoned buildings of salable parts such as copper tubing and fixtures; shoplifting; looting; hijacking; running con games; and trafficking in narcotics.[12]

Hustling is a complex phenomenon that transcends race, class, and ethnicity. It has both legal and extralegal components. Items can be purchased legally and then resold illegally on the "gray market," or illegal items can be sold. The Madoff Ponzi scheme, the Enron scandal, and the Tyco International Koslowski case all demonstrate that hustling can be perpetuated by the best and brightest, but it is also perpetuated on a daily basis by the common man or woman. Think of the housewife pilfering extra money for her family, the cop fixing tickets for extra pay, or the street kids selling bogus and real drugs. These examples point to a kind of behavior that almost everyone engages in when they "cut corners" (even fudging a bit on taxes could be thought of as a hustle). Thus the definition of hustling should be viewed along a continuum, running the gamut from low to high, legal to extralegal, nonviolent to violent. At the low end is the worker who takes a side job to make extra money. A middle-range hustle might be someone who works at a butcher shop or restaurant and takes meat or produce to sell on the side. At the higher end is the street gambler who acquires crooked dice and inserts them into the game to assure a win. The highest-end hustler would be the Ponzi scam artist who rakes in millions from unsuspecting friends and family members.

But the world we are about to enter involves a more exacting definition of hustling, a more elaborate and lifelong example of what it means to hustle, a vocation that has been around since the beginning of mercantilism. Prus and Sharper, in their book *Road Hustlers*, offer another take on what they refer to as a career hustler:

> Career hustling is much different from occasional involvement—where many persons will "take an edge" if the situation presents itself, it is most unlikely that anyone attempting to make a career or lifework of hustling could rely on chance opportunities alone. A career hustler has to create his own opportunities; he will not only capitalize on circumstantial opportunities but will also set up targets for his hustles. In this sense it matters little whether one is a robber, prostitute, dope pusher, or confidence man, or whether one's hustle is assaultive or sociable, obvious or subtle. Career hustlers cannot simply wait for their opportunities; they are continually "on the make."[13]

The criminologists Ronald Clarke and Donald Cornish claimed that crime and deviance are influenced by opportunities created by circumstance, neglect, or public policy. According to their rational-choice theory, opportunities for crime "may tempt an otherwise law-abiding person into occasional transgressions."[14] According to the tenets of rational-choice theory, an average individual—someone not actively seeking to engage in crime—may do so if, say, a stranger accidentally drops a cash-filled wallet on a sidewalk or a power outage in a major retail store renders the security system impotent or a loophole in unemployment insurance allows to the recipient to work "off the books" while continuing to receive unemployment benefits (a very popular strategy during the recent Great Recession). Clarke and Cornish claim that most crime in society is not committed by a unique, deviant brand of evildoers but rather that increased opportunity and lack of punishment will drive the average (mostly law-abiding) person to commit crimes that seem "rational" in the moment. We will return to rational-choice theory throughout this book.

This now classic theory essentially applies to inexperienced criminals, but New York's con artists and hustlers, such as the ones profiled in this book, are far from average. This book offers a new take on how structure and opportunity influence crime; the average rational person could not engage in the cons and hustles featured here. The con artists and hustlers in this text possess a rare set of utilitarian values and have an unmatched knowledge of the city's landscape and a sophisticated skill set that has taken years (or a lifetime) to acquire. We think of them as sage opportunists because they are able to match their abilities exactly to the opportunities presented by the city's shifting economy. And while many sociologists tend to view their subjects as "victims" of circumstance, we recognize our respondents as very lucid craftsmen (and -women). Together they all represent a unique brand of New Yorker: those who have mastered the art of deception and the science of persuasion.

TERROIR AND THE CITY

The New York City landscape plays an important role in the con game, though its part can be latent and passive. Just as drug dealers and sex workers find hidden spots—behind certain buildings or in warehouses along the waterfront, for example—con artists and hustlers use busy transportation hubs (such as Union Square, Times Square, or Grand

Central Station), crowded city streets, or, in some cases, deserted side streets as part of their plots. Regardless of the locale, this city *terroir* is important in the con strategy.

The term *terroir* originated in thirteenth-century France, referring to agricultural land and, more specifically, to wine making.[15] Several centuries later, it has become a widely used term in the wine world and is understood wherever wine is made, from Napa to Rioja.[16] In French, its definition has diversified to include the idea of "regional space" or even "culture"[17] and to apply to any agricultural product thought to be specific to a given area. More recently, the term has become a staple among social scientists and "foodies" alike, used when describing everything from unpasteurized cheese producers to the slow—or local—food movements.

Terroir is a complex term. It does not solely refer to scientific facts that concern the influence of soil or climate on vines and the grapes they produce, facts that can be tested, proved, or disproved. The notion of *terroir* has been hotly debated and variously considered a cultural specificity, social construct, political object, economic tool, imperialist regulation, and scientific fact.

New York City's climate, landscape, and biodiversity all play a role in whether the con artist's labor will produce a successful yield. The architecture, the buildings, and the street layout also play an important role in the con strategy. A successful con artist must first investigate a site, such as a certain clock or street, before the con or hustle is actualized. A kind of presurveillance has to be done before the mark is decided upon; a series of advanced actions must be arranged. The city is the backdrop for the con artist, and its architecture, buildings, street furniture, and layout provide a mechanism for the con game.

The city can also be a valuable component, even partner in crime, for the game to succeed. The subway tunnels, for instance, have always provided a hideout for con artists and hustlers and a place where a stash is often kept, a "backstage" and escape hatch. The common park bench provides respite for ordinary New Yorkers but is also used by con artists as a strategic spot to watch for potential victims, count cash, and meet other con artists. There are 560 miles of sewers in the city, and they can also act as accomplices in the crime of conning. Back in the 1950s the sewers were used in a common con: A woman wearing what appeared to be real diamonds would step out of a cab over a sewer drain and drop her jewels into a grate, in an attempt to defraud the insurance company.

THE CAST OF CHARACTERS

Here, we introduce the reader to the players in our text, those who volunteered their stories and shared their secrets with us.

Alibi

Alibi has a grift's sense and knows many things, and, unlike most people who might also take notice, he acts on this knowledge.[18] Alibi is our main informant, main contact, and essential sponsor: he provides both the intellectual keys to the con artist's world and a practical day-to-day understanding of conning and hustling. He is our philosophical frontman for the hustle and con game. He is the existential and overarching voice of the text, and chapters 1 through 3 follow the exploits of Alibi and his con crew.

Otis

Otis is a well-known local hustler and public character in the Bedford-Stuyvesant neighborhood of Brooklyn. Skinny and middle-aged but a youthful dresser, he sells bootleg anything. He is a typical street salesman with the verbal game to match. His specialty is pirated DVDs, but as soon as some other gadget comes on the scene, he's on it. Otis is part grifter, part charmer, part man about town, and part crook.

He is a kind of a Robin Hood, too, since he brings to the poor items that would normally be too expensive for them to buy at full price. The sidewalks of the city are replete with informal street vendors like Otis, from teenagers selling candy for a make-believe basketball league, to the middle-aged Caribbean men selling fruits and vegetables from hand-drawn carts, to dreadlocked Rasta boys selling incense and oils. It is difficult to avoid the continuous open-air salesmanship that men like Otis display. Chapter 5 demonstrates how Otis and men like him attempt to make a living off of pirated DVDs.

Lee

A slim, handsome, twenty-three-year-old with a mustache and goatee, Lee works the traffic lights on major throughways selling water. In his uniform—a white t-shirt, shorts, white socks, shower shoes, and a straw hat—he's ready for work. He wishes he could make some "real" money doing other things but knows this is all there is for young men like him. Most of his homies are either locked up or locked down with girlfriends who support them. All of them are trying to "cop that dream everybody be clocking. You feel me?" Jobs are nonexistent unless you make work for yourself, and Lee believes "making work" is about all he can do for now. In chapter 5 we see how hard Lee works on his bottled-water hustle.

Daniel

Daniel is a creature of Canal Street in lower Manhattan. Handsome, tall, and slightly overweight, he works the street selling what may be described as "bogus goods." He is a master at convincing you to buy something you do not want. He can sell you anything and can get you whatever you want—electronics, watches, computers—at a moment's notice.

Daniel—who is proud of his hustles on Canal Street—and his people take products that would usually be discounted and mark them up beyond what you would pay for them if they were brand new. He shows no remorse after ripping off tourists—in chapter 6, you will see how he is able to take some for hundreds of thousands of dollars. His shenanigans support Alibi Jones's existential assessment that the con game is an intrinsic aspect of not only the business life of America but of America itself.

Maria

In the numbers (gambling) business, one person is the designated operator of a "bank," and that person is in charge. In chapter 7 you will meet Maria, who is involved in a popular numbers operation. She earns less than a thousand dollars a week but oversees employees, collects bets, and works until the place closes. She is a gambler, too, and spends a lot of her money on the numbers, trying to achieve the American dream. She says she knows the system is rigged but plays anyway because she's addicted. "I know it's a game of luck, but so is life, no? You take a chance with love, you take a chance with men, you take a chance with everything, so why not take a chance with the number?" At forty years old she is not about to stop doing what she does: "This is all I have right now until I go back to my country."

Lorena

Lorena—middle-aged, Latina, about five feet tall, with black hair, thick makeup, and an engaging smile—is the landlord's worst nightmare. Her main hustle is rent cheating and defrauding landlords by exploiting New York's occupancy-rights laws. Lorena believes that if a tenant plays her cards right, she can live rent-free for years, with full utilities, and sue the owner for civil damages without ever having to prove that their tenant rights had been violated.

In chapter 8 you will watch Lorena succeed at her tried-and-true method of conning: she signs a lease, pays a couple of months rent, and then refuses to pay any more by invoking her tenant rights. She reports numerous code violations to tie the city's housing department in knots. As city inspectors review the claims, she can live rent-free for up to twelve months. In thirty-two years, Lorena has only paid rent for an estimated sixteen months.

Ramon

Ramon is a Puerto Rican man in his midforties with a warm smile and a pleasant disposition. He began his search for the American dream as a salesman in midtown Manhattan, but instead he discovered crack cocaine both as a profit-making venture and, later, as a devilish addiction. In chapter 9 Ramon describes how he was pulled in and nearly pulled under by the drug he calls the "radiant thing."

Frank

Frank is a retired police officer, about forty-five years old, who worked twenty years and never fired his gun. He admits to not being a "cowboy"—a cop who is the first to respond to a violent scene. In chapter 10, Frank speaks candidly about con artists and hustlers—both street criminals and police officers alike. Some of the best hustles, as you'll see, are perpetuated by the NYPD.

J. T. Gartner

J. T. Gartner is a Wall Street trader with a seat on the New York Stock Exchange. He got into the business the old-fashioned way—through the buddy system. Back in the 1980s when "greed was good," J. T.'s college connections helped him secure his seat. Now a retired Wall Street sage, he worked in finance when whole economies could be broken or deeply affected by shenanigans on the "Street." But his ethics kept him from participating in more nefarious deals. The insider knowledge he shares in chapter 11 is more valuable than any business guru's memoirs or financial-regression analysis.

DOING ETHNOGRAPHY

I was once told that ethnography is what everyday people do to make sense of their world; they ask questions, probe for answers, listen, and figure out what's going on around them. Basically, ethnography is a member of one culture studying, observing, listening, conversing, and trying to discover the intricacies of another. To know about con games requires getting to know the people who carry out these various acts on a more or less regular basis. Getting into their world is not simple or easy and demands years of trying to understand who these individuals are, trying to learn what exactly it is they do, trying to figure out whom you are getting to know.

Ethnography developed out of the field of cultural anthropology via noted scholars such as Bronislaw Malinowski and Claude Lévi-Strauss. The discipline of ethnography began in the United States with the so-called Chicago School of urban sociology in the early part of the twentieth century. Ethnography is considered a marriage of the art of fieldwork and the science of cultural description, and its techniques are applied in many disciplines besides sociology and anthropology, for example, business, fashion and design, nursing, and law.

Foremost in ethnography is a commitment on behalf of the ethnographer to "be there." Paul Willis, a noted ethnographic theorist, has argued that there are four key requirements in doing successful ethnography: bodily presence (being there), bodily traction (living through the events being studied), bodily interaction (face-to-face contact, i.e., always going half native), and bodily implication (having access to the action). Ethnographers pick up meaning as it happens and write about the world they see and feel, using their personal contacts and five senses to understand what is around them. In a sense, the ethnographer's very body is a research instrument.

What the ethnographic approach brings to research that other methods do not is the ability to participate and engage in the daily lives of people, usually over a long period of time. The ethnographer is always observing, listening, and asking his subjects about what they do and why they do it. This engagement strategy also adds a certain temporary phenomenological strength because the ethnographer is able to see, for a fleeting moment, the world as other people might see it. You can understand how definitions of the situation are arrived at and how these definitions result in certain patterns of behavior. So as you witness people in these various venues you are reminded of how each of these situations are defined by the people who live in them. As an ethnographer you have an abiding interest in not only providing a descriptive account but also in the processes that form urban social worlds, how these worlds come together, how people live together, and how they stay together under various conditions.

This is what ethnographers do, and it, too, is a form of hustling: "ear hustling," listening to other people's conversations and writing them down and getting paid for the information, selling it to the university, contracting out to publishers, getting paid to lecture to the public. Ear hustling is part and parcel of the ethnographer's trade. In the street, this is how hustlers see what the sociologist-ethnographer does. In other words, no one escapes, no one gets out alive. We are all in the game together. Hustling is life. Yet many of the hustles in this volume are rather harmless and not terribly odious: selling water to thirsty motorists, getting a customer to pay a higher price for discounted goods, convincing someone to buy a shoplifted item, placing a dollar bet on the numbers. Who are the people who hustle, and what does it mean to hustle in the city? Does everyone do it, or is it something only certain groups do? Providing responses to these rather basic questions is what drives the sociologist's intellect, motivates the imagination, and stimulates the desire to discover answers.

GETTING IN

If he think he can just come in here and write what he wants about us, then he's got another think coming.
—Helene, one of the women in Alibi's crew, speaking of Terry Williams

The methodology of this book could be called "collage ethnography" because of the way the text is structured: interviews, reconstructions of events from interviews, and casual observations of the cityscape are all intertwined. The stories in the text unfold in pieces so that the reader is spectator and eyewitness to the events as they happen. We tried to minimize but not entirely dismiss academic considerations (and avoid using too much jargon), yet, at the same time, interpretive frameworks (criminological, sociological, psychological, and economic) are all woven quiltlike into text. We used various means to capture what was happening as we researched this text: our memories, notes, tape recordings, and, in the case of Alibi Jones, his written memoirs.

Some of Alibi's female associates were distrustful and disliked the idea of note taking in their presence. This is worrisome on many levels, not just methodologically, as criminals kill or harass witnesses to crimes because of what they see and hear. In such a case, when the ethnographer feels uncomfortable writing or recording events as they happen, memory must serve. There were times when I (Terry Williams) felt that I might be hurt during our research, though this was less about thinking that the con artists might do me harm and more about me being in the wrong place at the wrong time or being mistakenly identified. At any rate, this lingering feeling of unease did keep me from recording certain information. In such cases, the mere presence of the ethnographer is the sociological/anthropological equivalent of a notebook.

Ethnographers and sociologists rarely focus the ethnographic gaze on family and friends as John Edgar Wideman did when he wrote candidly about his brother and son, both of whom are in prison.[19] Our writing is about people we have known for a time through family connections or met recently while doing this research. This is not unprecedented; even successful professionals and academics have family members and friends who are involved in all sorts of "deviant" (in sociological parlance) activities. There is always an attempt to whitewash family histories and look for sociological analysis "out there."

My (Terry Williams's) family was important to the research because they helped facilitate access to people and social worlds I might not have been able to penetrate as easily without their assistance. Family members who were drug dealers or owners of after-hours clubs made it possible for me to do research within these arenas, where many contacts in the underground were introduced.

Why do people involved in these petty hustles and cons talk to ethnographers? The short answer is that people want to tell their stories, or at least that is what we found to be the case. People will eventually tell you what you want to know if you stay with them long enough. The other point greatly depends on how you meet your initial contact or informant (called a sponsor) and who introduces you. The initial informant usually explains to the ethnographer what's happening on the scene as long as the ethnographer promises not to reveal who the informant is. The ethnographer has to promise anonymity and must be trustworthy.

Ethnography involves trying to provide a detailed portrait of people by staying in their own setting or world for as long as possible to learn about what they do and why and how they do it. You become a participant. You learn about the friendship network, the social interrelationships, and, if you are lucky, you get some things right, and people begin to allow you to record their world because they trust you to record it as accurately as they would. For me (Terry Williams), not all of the people I met in this study came to trust me fully, and this was the first time I'd felt mistrusted by those I wrote about. Part of the problem was that

I was never really the person they thought they knew; for example, I never had anyone over to my apartment except Alibi.

There were times when I preferred to be asked questions rather than ask them of others. This is especially true in this particular group of individuals because I felt that if they asked me questions they would discern more of who I was and perhaps feel more comfortable sharing with me. Yet I also sensed that they did not want to ask me more questions because they did not want me to ask them deeper questions about themselves.

Trevor Milton encountered some respondents who were overeager to share their stories, especially knowing that they would be recorded in literary history; others preferred double and triple layers of anonymity (changing not only names but also details such as age and neighborhood) and sought to meet in "neutral" locations. Yet still they felt the desire to do the interview because their information "needed to be out there."

The act of the so-called informant talking to an ethnographer is partly psychology and partly the historicizing of one's life. As Hakim Hasan wrote in the afterword to Mitch Duneier's *Sidewalk*:

> In my own case (*Sidewalk*), talking to the ethnographer was an act of "revenge" against the larger corporate (read: White) world and everything that I had to endure. The idea of giving form and substance to my life in the form of a book was a way of legitimizing my existence and, furthermore, letting the world know what happened to me.[20]

Mitch Duneier is one of the premier sociologists in the field and has written several books using the ethnographic method, including *Sidewalk*, a remarkable text on street life and culture, which originated when he came upon Hakim Hasan selling books on a street corner in Greenwich Village in the early 1990s. He solicited Hasan's help in getting other vendors to discuss their lives. In time Hasan became more than an informant; he became a valued collaborator in the research and wrote the book's afterword. (The first draft of the manuscript, in fact, was called "Hakim's Table.") "I was keenly aware," Hasan says, "that I had no connection to the cultural apparatus—the legion of editors and publishers at the top of the cultural food chain in New York City. Most, if not all, people from the lower social orders have no connection to the cultural apparatus, the people who decide what is actually written and what we read, hear, and see."

Hasan wanted to let the world know what had happened to him as an employee at a prestigious law firm where he was summarily dismissed without warning, which is how he ended up selling books on Sixth Avenue when Duneier first met him. Hasan explained: "This was my way of putting a face on what sociologists call 'structure.' There are actual people in control of systems and companies who oppress (or liberate) people. This is not a social blob. They are real people. Many informants operate in the realm of anonymity (pseudonyms). I was not. No one in *Sidewalk* was anonymous. The place (Sixth Avenue) was not anonymous either."

Alibi echoes Hasan's sentiment: "I want the world to know what has happened to me." The act of telling or of moving one's life beyond the realm of the personal is a repudiation of silence and an act of participation in the larger con of the academic world: academic ethnographers need subjects in order to advance their careers, and the subjects, if they are sophisticated, will use the cultural apparatus in order to canonize their thoughts, ideas, and feelings about the world in which they live.

This insight came to us from hearing Hasan's story about his dismissal from the law firm for no apparent reason other than his being a brilliantly outspoken black man in a world that accepted only those who conform to a set of white, male rules. His work as an autodidactic intellect (and now a Yale Fellow scholar) is what Duneier came to know and respect. We are not saying this is a universal sentiment among subjects, but, to some, revenge is a powerful motivator. Alibi's decision to partake in the con game is a repudiation of the forces that have worked against him his whole life, yet his desire to tell his story and share his diary notes is his attempt at immortality. He is leaving a record, an accounting. This, too, is an act of revenge as far as we are concerned, and this, we think, is why ethnographers need to understand why subjects talk to them. What's in it for them? What is the quid pro quo in the enterprise, and what is the psychological motivation?

ALIBI'S STORY

There might actually occur a case where we should say, "This man believes he is pretending."
—Ludwig Wittgenstein, *Philosophical Investigations*

I (Terry Williams) worry that Alibi's narrative voice is too decentralized and dispersed throughout the text. Perhaps the reader will not appreciate the power of what he has to say. Alibi lays out his life, memoir-like, which is part of the collage. It is virtually impossible to keep up with people in the con-game world. It is impossible to follow them and keep abreast of what they do. It is extremely difficult to get their real names, addresses, family names, and associates. Thus it is often hard to confirm the tales they tell. A con artist is someone who lies for a living, and Alibi told many stories, some true and some perhaps not so true, but these reports are the nature of the ethnographic enterprise.

The point of the following excerpt from his journal is to see what the reader believes. Can a con man ever tell the truth? My take on this excerpt is that here Alibi wanted to impress. Alibi's journal was a memoir that he had been writing for some time, starting before he met me, because he felt his life story was worth publishing. He often asked if I could get it published if we wrote it together. I felt that some of what he wrote was true and not embellished for my benefit, but I had doubts about some of the other stories. The pages he gave me, all handwritten, were rolled up and on lined paper, reminding me of a high-school term paper. When he handed it to me, he said, "This is part of my story." I kept it and occasionally asked questions about its contents. I did not change or alter any of his text, but every so often over the years he would tell me about an adventure he had in the city and ask if I was still writing about his life.

Take the following account from what he called his marijuana days:

> I smiled to myself as I recalled flying into Houston five weekends in a row to buy marijuana. This was back in 1976 and I could b[u]y gold reefer so called because of its color. I would purchase it for fifty to seventy five bucks a pound and resell it in New York for $50 to $60 an ounce. I would fly into town and take a bus from the airport to the Ramada Inn at Cross timber's [in Houston, Texas] and get a beautiful room at a great price around $56 a day. I would get seventy-five or a hundred pounds, stay a few days and fly back to New York. Sometimes I would fly in on a Saturday night and fly back on a Sunday night. Business was great. I remember one morning I was standing near 125th Street about twenty or thirty feet from the subway station on St. Nicholas Avenue talking to a fellow hustler. I had at my side a garbage bag containing twenty-five or thirty pounds of marijuana, which was part of the hundred pounds I had, flew in with from Texas the night before. All of a sudden four detectives jumped out of a gray unmarked Plymouth and rushed towards us, I just stood there not knowing who they were after. They quickly handcuffed my friend and whisked him away, as I breathed a sigh of relief. I picked the bag up and walked away never looking back.

This may be a true story; it may not. You cannot know exactly. I need not vouch for the authenticity of every con Alibi and his crew pulled off nor furnish a guarantee for every story I was told, but, over time, much of what he told me was eventually verified.

One example of both these matters is a story relating to his returning to Louisiana to be a jailer in the prison system. I had no reason not to believe him when he told me, and I wrote down whatever he said as part of his story, grist for the ethnographic mill, regardless of whether it proved credible. But this does not mean I always took his word for it; I have every right to check out, triangulate, and investigate what he says and see whether it is true. But the stories themselves are part of, and a significant aspect of, who he is and what the larger story is all about. When I questioned how he could become a jailer with a criminal record, he informed me that his connections would help. He said he was about to "attend a correctional academy. And it will be a great experience." The academy is located in Angola, Louisiana. "The Louisiana State Penitentiary is one of the largest in the country, over 18,000 acres, with seven different camps; including the infamous Camp J one of the toughest in the country with arguably the meanest prisoners in the country. That's where I will be training to be a jailer."

Examining self-reports is problematic on many levels, but the ethnographer has to trust his informants and on occasion dig around to verify the stories he's being told. After a bit of digging I found the Angola Correctional Academy and discovered a certificate Alibi received from there. Of course, this does not mean all of his stories were genuine, but he *was* telling the truth in this case.

In a past study I interviewed homeless people living in underground spaces in the city.[21] I had met one fellow several months earlier who told me he was married with five kids and had two brothers (one a cop, the other a priest) who lived in Chicago. A few months later I interviewed him again, and he said he was never married and had no kids. He still insisted his brothers were what he said they were. A half-year later, his stories changed once again. I realized that he wasn't lying for the sake of lying but rather that he had lied at first because he didn't trust me. Later, he was simply reinventing himself. The stories he told were a way he made himself more than what he was, which was a homeless person in a big city with no relations to speak of. This is in some ways how I see Alibi and his stories.

Self-reports have always been problematic for ethnographers in the field, particularly with certain transient populations: vagabonds, former offenders, people on the run. People are not believable and lie and bullshit and tell tall tales of one variety or another, but these are fodder for the ethnographer. One way the ethnographer counters such claims or self-reports is to triangulate, that is, to check out the story from other sources, friends, family, colleagues, probation officers, social workers, and the like. There are always two sides to a story and a third one to tell it. Self-reports may be many things to many people, but to dismiss them is to lose out on the colorful way human beings make decisions about who they are and what they would like to be. We hope that, in that spirit, readers will enjoy and learn from Alibi and the others in this text who wanted their stories to be heard.

ONE

ALIBI: PORTRAIT OF A CON MAN

We wear the mask that grins and lies / it hides our cheeks / and shades our eyes.

—Paul Laurence Dunbar

Though you will meet many con men and women before our narrative is finished, Alibi Jones is our main character, and in many ways he speaks for all the others. Alibi in particular personifies the con man, one who makes a living off of con games. By sharing his life story, he gives us a peek into the inner world of a con man and helps us understand something about his personality and about his actions and those of his confederates. His is a dynamic account; he and his crew find themselves in constantly changing situations. Ethnography is one of the few methods capable of capturing an individual in this way, and throughout this and the following two chapters, we will try to understand something more about Alibi the con man, the thief, the manipulator, and about the language he uses to persuade.

THE MAKING OF A CON MAN

Alibi said he was taught the art of the con by an Irish guy from York-ville that he met in jail. "He taught me about misdirection. And he said I was smart but that it takes more than smarts to be a good con man. 'You have to have balls,' he said, 'you got to pay close attention to every-thing and everybody as if you're looking for the first time. As if your eyes were opening up for the first time.' But I wasn't in there [jail] for that long a time, but I never forgot what he told me."

Most con artists learn tricks of the trade from other con artists, like Alibi did. As far as I (Terry Williams) can discern, unlike in Dickens, there is no Fagin-run school for con artistry—though gypsies are said to teach their pickpocketing methods to their children, and supposedly, though this may just be myth, there is a pickpocket academy, the School of the Seven Bells, in Bogota, Columbia. According to legend, the schoolmaster wears seven bells attached to his clothing; each new stu-dent must extract whatever is in his pockets without making a bell ring.

Alibi learned how to hustle from a woman who "turned him out." She first tried to make him into a pimp, but because so much of the pimp game is about hustling, she inadvertently taught him the "hustle game," which included all the ways young men who want to hustle earn money by their wits. I wanted to know more about this woman, but he told me little about her or her influence on him.

He did explain how she introduced him to the world of hustling: "She taught me, for instance, about making money from hos because she said the first thing a ho will want to do is go back to her old friends, and you gotta stop her from doing that. Her life, once she turns that trick, is to be a ho and live in a ho's world, which is your world, the pimp's world. There ain't no turning back. What I learned from that is once you find a sucker, thump her head. Don't let her turn around. Don't let her go back; keep her looking at the prize, keep her occupied. As long you got her looking ahead, you got her in the game.

"Let's get to the peanut butter and the jelly of the sandwich. That's when she told me something that really applies to my whole framework for the con game, and that is this: she said a player can teach a ho to turn a trick, just like that." Alibi snapped his fingers. "But, if you trying to teach a ho or anyone how to hustle it takes a much longer period of time because you gotta pay close attention. You got to be aware of nuances, the little things. You gotta pay attention because the voice is important. I should say the tone of the voice is important. That tonality. Little things. You gots to pay attention to little things. What the person is wearing is important. Conning is the same; you gotta pay close attention to everything. Well, I learned all of this from her. But she had friends in the con-game world, you might say, and they started to pull my coat on a number of other things. All these worlds, pimping, ho'ing, hustling, gambling, overlap anyway, you know. All these individuals in the life have codes of behavior, language, understandings in common."

From Alibi's memoir:

I had started out writing numbers in East Harlem. I soon became a pimp, crap hustler, con man, fence, slum jewelry seller, fake liquor seller. I dealt in counterfeit money. I sold drugs in some of the after hours joints I ran. I was called the Master because of my shoplifting abilities, I could take someone in the store with me and get a coat or sometimes two coats and take it to the cash register and the sales people would staple the bag up for me and I would walk out the store. The person with me would ask me why didn't you take something and I would inform them that I had. They would always be baffled. But I was never arrested for any of those things. I also laundered money for a Latino gang, participated in credit card scams and many other activities but I never signed anyone's name on a purchase. I would get the cards from a dipper (pickpocket) or another source. But I was never greedy enough to sign any document, I preferred to take a fifty-fifty split, and there were plenty short story writers (forgers) around that would work on a fifty-fifty split.

Alibi is not typically a pickpocket, though he admits to having been in what he calls "pickpocket situations" and has used the "touch" to take advantage of a loose wallet or bag here and there. He learned that the key to being a good pickpocket is practicing the moves and knowing how to misdirect the attention of the victim at a critical moment. He also pays close attention, like his teacher taught him, and as a result he has a tremendous knowledge of how people behave in the city. He knows how to catch a stranger's eye in a city of millions; he knows that if you bump into a victim or "stall" him in the street, his hands will move to that part of his body where his wallet or money are concealed. (Police officers know this too. If a person flinches during a patdown, usually that's where the contraband is located.) Alibi tells of a guy named "Fast Eddie" who could "steal the crack outta yo ass and stink from shit. He could tell if the guy [mark] grabs his right pocket he knows that's where the money is. The right or left front pocket is the most difficult to pull off and the only ones who can do that are cannons." (Cannon is the con-artist term for master pickpocket.)

Alibi is not a "popcorn pimp" either, though he has had over his career more than one woman in a pimping situation. A popcorn pimp is one who uses any and all means to acquire cash, jewelry, drugs, counterfeit money, boosted clothing, anything to make a living, but rarely just prostitution. They are also referred to in the life as "simps" or simpletons, or simple pimps, hustlers who need to rely on brawn, not brains, and have no "game."

Alibi has not always wanted to be a hustler, but he feels he had little choice. He revealed his misgivings in a moment of reflection I noted in a journal entry:

I made no bones about the hustling world I had lived in but I stressed the fact that it was a mistake to have wasted many years in a somewhat negative way when I could have done things quite differently. I let them [people, friends, hustlers, cops, anyone he talked with] know quite honestly that I only entered the hustling world to survive and support my family. I told them that a majority of the brothers in prisons throughout the country was in prison because they were forced there by being unable to get a job. Malcolm X once remarked when someone made a snide comment about his being in prison, that the person shouldn't laugh at him for being in prison because in America all Black and poor people are in prison, they just didn't know it yet. I explained to them that I had been sworn in at the Post Office near Christmas time.

The post office he refers to here is on 125th Street between Morningside Avenue and St. Nicholas Avenue. He used to shoot dice on the side street at 126th Street, directly behind this facility. Alibi had applied for a job there, and he had apparently passed the exam to be a postal clerk when it was discovered a month later that he had previously been arrested for gambling. He was quite irate about this turn of events; the reference to "them" is those supervisors who took his job away. This anger would propel him to "get all of them back," meaning all of society—and conning was the method of his "revenge."

He went on to explain that point in his life:

So they told me that I couldn't be hired because I had been arrested for gambling. My wife was pregnant at the time, and after being sent to the United Parcel Service to start work there, I was given the same reason for not being hired by a supervisor from another facility. I couldn't at that time understand what that [gambling arrest] had to do with my ability to do the job. As I know now, it was just a stumbling block that was used . . . to keep Blacks in low paying jobs or no job at all. At one time in this country you could be turned down on virtually any job if you had an arrest record. It didn't matter if it was a misdemeanor or felony charge. Now you can't be turned down in most places for a misdemeanor arrest.

This experience of losing his job with the post office left Alibi with a lasting sense of disgust and hatred for everyone in authority. He used that seething resentment, along with his innate intelligence, to craft con games and hustles to seek his revenge.

CON MAN AS GHOST

Alibi is unlike the Invisible Man that Ralph Ellison described in his classic 1952 novel. Ellison's man was not only forced to wear a mask; he also lacked the ability to recognize that he was doing so. Alibi is cognizant of his mask and chooses to wear it because he knows that the mask is an indispensable part of his life as a con man and that it gives him the ability to fool or hoodwink others, to lie and cheat to get what he wants—usually money or something else valuable.

Even to his friends, Alibi remains invisible; even people who knew him for years do not really know him. "You won't believe this, but you know more about me than people I've known all my life." I (Terry Williams) was unsure of the truth of this, but I took it for what it was worth. Perhaps he was just blowing smoke about knowing more about him than anyone else. The other people I talked with about him over the years admitted to knowing little about his background. I knew he had a daughter and two brothers, both of whom are deceased, but I knew little else about his other family, his past, his values, his aspirations, or his dreams. The only "straight" jobs Alibi ever had was when he first came to New York and worked as a stock clerk or delivery boy at one of the dailies. I never knew him to do anything except hustle.

I know very little about his other crew members (see chapter 3), and what I did learn, I promised not to reveal. They, too, were largely ghosts to me. But how long could he or they stay in the shadows without the need to feel they belong?

The psychologist William James argues that most of us want to be noticed:

> No more fiendish punishment could be devised were such a thing possible than that one could be turned loose in society and remain absolutely unnoticed by all the members thereof. If no one turned round when we entered, answered when we spoke, or minded what we did, but if every person we met "cut us dead," and acted as if we were non-existing

things, a kind of rage and impotent despair would ere long well up in us, from which the cruelest bodily tortures would be a relief.[1]

Like Rinehart in Ellison's *Invisible Man*, Alibi does not see himself as another street-smart petty hustler but as a modern man who seeks invisibility because if he does not he will be caught and sent to jail, or some other fate worse than death, so he hides and creeps and finds solace in his ability to remain hidden, invisible not only to his victims (which is crucial to his survival) but to friends as well. Alibi never felt others could actually see him as himself. He felt that he was whole—in his mind he was—but he could not convince others of that basic fact. "I feel like that way sometimes," he tells me. "Just like an itch that I can't quite get to scratch." He compared it to a friend of his who lost a leg yet can still feel it via phantom pain.

Con artists must be ghostlike because they must be able to disappear in order to continue to survive in the city. Hakim Hasan, a contact of mine who worked on Sixth Avenue for many years as a street bookseller, entrepreneur, bibliophile extraordinaire, street intellectual, and card-carrying member of the subintelligentsia, describes it: "During the 1990s when I sold books on the street, I saw the three-card monte hustlers work on Sixth Avenue mainly near the corner of Eighth Street. They would literally appear out of nowhere. There would be a lookout man or woman. They would assemble a makeshift card table made up of boxes. These people were dressed like any pedestrian. They would appear like ghosts and in a matter of minutes set up the table and go to work. When the lookout person signaled that the police were coming (or something was not right), they would kick down the table and slowly walk (blend) into the crowd like ghosts."

Richard Wright considered the issue of being unrecognized and rejected by society when he wrote the introduction to *Black Metropolis: A Study of Negro Life in a Northern City*, by the sociologists St. Clair Drake and Horace Cayton. This pioneering work depicts an iconic "ghetto" and is an exhaustive survey of black life in Chicago. Some see it not just as a study of the ghetto but of the entire black community. It has been the sociological "bible" for several generations of social scientists, scholars, writers, and those interested in black life since it was published in 1945. Wright says in the introduction:

> There can be, of course, no such thing as a complete rejection of anybody by society; for, even in rejecting him, society must notice him. But the American Negro has come as near being the victim of a complete rejection as our society has been able to work out, for the dehumanized image of the Negro which white Americans carry in their mind, the anti-Negro epithets continuously on their lips, exclude the contemporary Negro as truly as though he were kept in a steel prison, and doom even those negroes who are as yet unborn.[2]

While Wright was speaking of blacks, his commentary also perfectly applies to the con artist: a dehumanized, nearly completely rejected and unnoticed member of society who wishes to be unseen so as to remain undetected when he hides in plain sight. The exception to this rejection, Alibi once said, is when black men, or con artists, are needed to "feed the system," as he called it. "The black man is invisible until there is a need to feed the system. If no blacks are wanted in a white neighborhood the police come around to harass him out. Whether he is driving a new car or wearing a new suit. If the jails need filling up they find every reason, no matter how silly, ludicrous, or inane the reason, they stop, frisk, and question."

CON MAN AS WANTED MAN

In other words, in Alibi's opinion, it does not really matter if he is a con or not when it comes to corrupt police; black men can be picked up, as Alibi was many times, just for being black. There are all too many examples of this. Consider the case of Louis Scarcella, a New York homicide detective who, back in the 1980s and 1990s, used deceptive tactics to convict at least seventy black and Latino men (one of whom died in prison) of crimes they did not commit. Many of those cases are now coming to light, and multi-million-dollar settlements are being paid to those wrongly convicted and their families.

As a black man, Alibi is as vulnerable as all minority men to policies such as stop, question, and frisk and the haunting legacy of vagrancy laws, Jim Crow laws, and other racially based law-enforcement strategies designed seemingly to incarcerate or emasculate members of minority groups, especially black men, overwhelmingly. And Alibi, like many others disenfranchised by arrest and incarceration, has been stripped of the most basic rights and privileges: the right to vote, the right to be considered for public housing, and access to student loans and to jobs.

Alibi and his consorts live in a "weird state" of "nowhereness," as he calls it, because he is a convicted felon. He was arrested several times for gambling, but he never spent that much time in jail and was always quickly released. He says being a felon is "just like being an unregistered alien, man. Don't you see that?" He said he had warrants for his arrest, although it was not likely he'd be caught if he played his cards right or kept cool, as he had these many years. But he lives with the possibility that he might be caught one day, and that weighs on his mind. He knew healthcare was out of the question. "Listen man, Obama talks about healthcare for all, but even if he did that I would still be out in the cold. Right? Am I right? I can't register or sign up for healthcare because if I would then I'd be in the system and they (the authorities) would find me."

He said he couldn't get licenses of any kind either, and that meant he could not even get a low-paying job if he wanted to. "So what am I supposed to do, starve? No, I ain't gonna starve. I'm gonna make me some money the best way I know how."

In part this kind of philosophy helps Alibi convince himself of his need to hustle. At one point he wrote in his memoir: "I took note not to glamorize the hustling world. But I also wanted to let them [his employers] know that it was nothing to be ashamed of. Whenever someone asks me even to this day what did you do in New York? My instant answer is I was a hustler." Hustlers and con artists often speak of their profession in the past tense, as if to say "I no longer do that" or to disassociate themselves from the acts of villainy they are accused of being part of. Or they point to the misdeeds of others as a defense mechanism, to draw attention away from themselves. In Alibi's words: "Many legitimate, or pseudolegitimate businessmen are some of the world's greatest hustlers. Some of America's wealthiest and best-known families owe their riches to a member of the family that was a notorious hustler. Yet today they look at hustlers with total disdain, forgetting or pretending not to know where their life of luxury had its beginnings. I assume some of them give away money to many charitable organizations as a way of feeding their guilt feelings."

CON MAN AS PUBLIC CHARACTER

Jane Jacobs was a social activist, urban scholar, and journalist who organized West Villagers in New York City to oppose an expressway that would run through—and potentially destroy—their neighborhood. Her work on urban life and culture was groundbreaking in that she highlighted previously overlooked parts of the city, such as the sidewalk, and analyzed them to a degree few urban theorists had previously done. In her classic *The Death and Life of Great American Cities*, Jacobs explains her theory of a public character and his or her impact on the city streets:

> The social structure of sidewalk life hangs partly on what can be called self-appointed public characters. A public character is anyone who is in frequent contact with a wide circle of people and who is sufficiently interested to make himself a public character. A public character need to have no special talent of wisdom to fulfill his function, although he often does. He just needs to be present, and there need to be enough of his counterparts. His main qualification is that he is public, that he talks to lots of different people.[3]

But the public character has other roles as well. In *Sidewalk*, the sociologist Mitch Duneier portrays a group of men on the margins in New York City's Greenwich Village. Duneier writes about public characters in *Sidewalk*: "The social context of the sidewalk is patterned in a particular way because of the presence of the public character; his or her actions have the effect of making street life safer, stabler, and more predictable."[4]

A public character's presence on the street can be a benefit to the neighborhood (for example, Jane Jacobs saw herself as a public character). But in other cases it is not. The con man's presence on the sidewalk may not be considered safe, stable, or predictable, especially for the unsuspecting resident or gullible tourist—in fact, it may seem quite the opposite. Jacobs had a keen appreciation for street life and saw a dense, diverse, action-packed street as crucial to a viable city culture. In her view the neighborhood was a great deal more vibrant and safe when people were engaged on the street. All this is true, but the con artists, pickpockets, and other hustlers who add to the action can deprive the street of its innocence. (We do not say this of all the con artists profiled in this book. As you will see in chapter 5, Otis is well known in his neighborhood and in our opinion qualifies as a public character of the good kind.)

Jacobs described sidewalk and street life in the city:

A city sidewalk by itself is nothing. It is an abstraction. It means something only in conjunction with the buildings and other uses that borders it, or border other sidewalks very near it. The same might be said of streets, in the sense that they serve other purposes besides carrying wheeled traffic in their middles. Streets and their sidewalks, the main public places of a city, are its most vital organs. Think of a city and what comes to mind? Its streets. If a city's streets look interesting, the city looks interesting; if they look dull, the city looks dull.[5]

The sidewalk is the street hustler's living room, parlor floor, and kitchen, the place where intimate acts occur and where he invites friends and foes alike; it is the space where the action happens, where misunderstandings become understandings, and vice versa.

Alibi uses the sidewalk as a place to observe—and then pounce when the opportunity presents itself. "I know when I was gambling in the street I would look at the guy winning the bets, and I would notice a lot of things he would be doing with his hands, with his body, with his talking; like I would notice if the guy is holding money in his hands and didn't count it. So what you do if once the guy has the money in [my] hand . . . So what you do if once the guy is trying to make his point you maybe fold up ten or twenty dollars and if the other guy wins you give it to him but if this motherfucker wins you keep the money in your hand, that's all." This was not the first time I was confused by Alibi's explanation and did not understand him, but I said nothing, just listened.

As contradictory as it sounds, Alibi is a both a ghost and a public character because his true identity is actually no identity at all. He sometimes must seem like an apparition in order to be a successful con artist, yet at the same time he has to be known, and is known, in the hustling world. Many con men and hustlers grapple with this duality.

Alibi maintains his distance from a world whose ways he finds exciting and frightening. His reasoning: "Because you can die, man. You can die in a minute. If a motherfucker catch you in his pocket you can die. If a cat find you in his bank account you can die. There are a thousand ways to be frightened, unnerved, and lost in this megamotherfucker and you better believe it."

If things got rough for Alibi, he would probably not fight or even argue. He was not the arguing type, maybe because he'd rather not fight. He is not the kind of man who hated others or carried out spontaneous acts of violence (at least not physical violence). This is was true of most of the con artists I knew. None was inclined to violence, and I tend to believe Alibi is typical in this regard. (Of course, there are some con artists who do not conform to the normal rules of the game, such as Sante Kimes and her son Kenneth, mentioned in the introduction. Or Christian Karl Gerhartsreiter, aka Clark Rockefeller, who took on a series of aliases, then married a wealthy woman and was able to live off her income. All of these con artists murdered their victims. I would consider them exceptions to the rule.)

As the sociologist Edwin Sutherland, who coined the term "white-collar crime" and wrote about professional thieves, noted: "The con man is a hustler . . . but usually stops short of violent aspects of the hustling trade; he [*sic*] is in fact an elusive and slippery character as he must be in order to avoid detection and stay one step ahead not only of the authorities but the street criminal who preys on such hustlers as himself."[6]

Alibi's penchant would be white-collar violence, the kind of violence that steals an old lady's life savings with a ballpoint pen, or an embezzling scam that swindles millions from a pension fund. He would con those same people if given the chance—indeed, he would say they deserved to be conned because of the larceny in their hearts.

ON FRONTING AND FLASH: AN EXTENDED FIELD NOTE, JULY 26

Alibi sits in a grey Cadillac with grayish leather seats, smoking a huge cigar, "fronting" in a cool way and showing off in a flashy way. In conversation, he mentions the number forty and I gather that's his age, though I'm not sure. Up until now he hasn't wanted to reveal his age, and he rarely makes a slip. He doesn't normally smoke, either. Tonight he's got his hands on a bag of counterfeit bills he says are altogether worth "forty grand." Perhaps that's what he meant by forty. I ask how he's able to drive without a license, but he says his license is fake. (I should have known. I admit that trying to catch him in a lie or a contradiction has proven difficult thus far.) He wants me to take some of this money and get drugs for him. I look at him incredulously as if to say, "Are you crazy or what?" And before I can actually utter the words, he laughs. "Just joking." He just wants me to contact Leo and see if he'll sell him some blow (cocaine) for a thousand dollars. Leo is my brother-in-law. He says he will buy smoke too from a guy called "Big Time," another of Leo's street-hustling buddies. He tells me to get in the car.

Alibi's desire for "revenge" against those who denied him his job took the form of living large—by any means necessary. The desire for "flash" inherent in modern American life encourages many people, especially the black and Latino poor, to seek material gain above all else.

This "flash" element is imbued in everything from advertising to media to fashion to music and beyond. The Cadillac, like the one Alibi shows up "fronting," for example, was once the car of choice for hustlers of all stripes—from mobsters to street pimps—but it has now been replaced by the Rolls Royce, Lexus, Bentley, Maserati, and Lamborghini. These are the new cars of choice of folks at the absolute top of American and international high society.

Or consider the extreme attention to fashion and style, a very important aspect of black and Latino cultures, especially for women. The special one-of-a-kind sneakers, Prada bags, and Hermes scarves all signify access to big money or indicate panache and exclusivity. In the 1960s, a common motto was "You are what you eat." Today, that motto might be "You are what you wear." Daniel, whom we will meet in chapter 6, makes his livelihood on Canal Street selling knockoffs to feed the designer-label addictions of those who cannot afford the real thing.

"Flash" is the main content of magazines such as *F.E.D.S* and *Diva*. These two magazines are so popular among the community that, a decade ago when they first appeared, they sold out as soon as they hit the newsstands. Today the street intelligentsia consider them the *Ebony* and *Jet* of the criminal underworld. These publications profile real legendary criminals from across the country—essentially, ghetto hustler superstars.

Flash is, especially, one of the major tropes in modern and commercialized hip-hop. You can't find a hip-hop music video that doesn't show all the "players" having fun, driving expensive cars, flashing gold, or bringing bling-bling to the mansion. The lyrics from Nikki Minaj's song, ironically called "Looking Ass Nigga," mocks this very trend: "Talkin' 'bout 'it's paid off' but it's financed, lyin' ass nigga / Bunch of nonmogul ass niggas / Frontin' like they got a plan, Boost Mobile ass nigga."

While the desire for "flash" is what drives most people to become victims of a con artist in the first place, the con artist him- or herself might or might not look flashy. The con man is a chameleon. At one point, con artists were as dapper as pimps, but these days they are just as likely to wear sneakers, or a business suit, or jogging pants, or a leather outfit. These fashion alterations are more often than not used as part of the ruse to attract or detract, to blend in more than stick out in the crowd. The sociologist Sutherland said: "The con, or confidence game . . . has many angles, but the central principle in all true con rackets is to show a sucker how he can make some money by dishonest methods and then beat him in his attempted dishonesty; for this it is necessary to be a good actor, a good salesman, and have good manners and a good appearance."[7] Alibi—and his compadres—are all good actors, good salesmen, with fine manners. That's what helps them melt back into a crowd when the con is done.

THE CON MAN'S PHILOSOPHY

Once I told Alibi about this guy Glaucon, who was dubbed the "Lord of the Tunnel." I originally met Glaucon in the underbelly of the city, in a tunnel, while I was doing a study on homelessness. I told Alibi I had learned a lot about life from Glaucon and that living underground had made him into a kind of existential poet-philosopher. "Well," Alibi said, "he's an existential con man, you know." I said Glaucon was as smart as can be, though a little nuts from hanging out in that dark hole so long.

I mentioned some of the things the Lord of the Tunnel told me, and Alibi appeared a bit put off, even annoyed that I was talking about some other guy who might be smarter than he was. I sensed that he was getting defensive, but I continued to talk about Glaucon. He had written this passage, which I read out loud to Alibi: "At no time perhaps than the present is it necessary for folks to strip away the illusions they live by and examine themselves and their motives realistically. When folks recognize the shakiness of human experience and the impossibility of finding support in traditional beliefs, the con man is inevitably thrown back upon himself." I was impressed by Glaucon's writing. I kept wondering, "Why is this guy down here? He's too smart to be down here."

Alibi responded, "Well, if he's so smart, why ain't he rich?"

I said, "I could say the same thing about a lot of people," but I then sensed Alibi was making a joke of sorts. I added, "because money isn't everything."

Alibi retorted, "No, but it's half of it."

Alibi said he sees the con man as similar to the underground man. Neither one is able to escape his self, and when either one tries to confront the self that they so often disguise, he might find solace in living underground or playing con games above ground. The "con man" he said, is in all of us, as he waxed philosophical about the tunnel man's exterior and interior world. For Alibi, interior and exterior are part of a larger spiritual reality.

"I see the world guided by certain principles," he offered, looking around, then straight at me. As he talked I observed his attire; his gold watch looked real, but I knew it was fake, bought on the street for twenty dollars. His suit was genuine but bought "hot" from a hustler friend who sold clothing on the street. His shoes were unpolished. His tanned complexion accentuated his dark eyes, and he had a slight mustache.

"Now, there's an inside and outside to everything. I mean to the game and to life. I read the eastern mystics, and I learned about these Hindu principles which is the key to all of their world. These mystics recognize that all insides have outsides. Because," he pointed at me, snapped his fingers, and pointed three fingers straight out, "check this, you don't know if insides have insides unless there's an outside and you don't know the outside is outside unless there's an inside. Right?" Looking for confirmation but getting none, he continued. "They dug this shit long time ago. They know the game is that we are all inside something larger than us and that's the universe. And that we all in the same big game as one no matter how we slice it. And guess what? I believe that shit. We all in it together. I cut my eye tooth on the big con," he revealed, rubbing his forefinger across his lips. Every so often he straightened his suit collar. "But the big con is a beautiful thing when you got a master artist working on it. The first thing you do is tie into the vic [set the person up by hooking them in the con], then you do the cake [money] trick [take the money]. After that, you cool out the vic [try to get the person who has lost money to accept the situation, not go the police, accept the fact that the money is lost and that nothing more can be done], then you put the vic on the bricks [send the person off].

"We are all the 'vic' for somebody or something. I know you have heard all this befo' but the thing is it's true. We are all vics in a big game of life. Bob Dylan has a song where he says we all have to serve somebody, and in the end it's true to that. I think it's true because everybody finds pleasure in playing games. We play the game of love. We play the game of death. We play the game of play. We play the game of confusion. It's theater really. Let me tell you a story. It's a short story but I wanna tell you this. One day I'm walking down Eighty-Fifth [Street] near Third [Avenue], and I see this long line of women, single women, young and old women, women couples, women with boyfriends, husbands, I guess too, but women with other women, a lot of young girls, and I say what the hell, is this lesbo-butch heaven or what? But when I get to the corner of Eighty-Sixth I see it's a movie line to see *Friday the 13th* or something like that, and I ask one of the women couples why they were going to see a movie that had blood and guts and probably about women being slashed and gored, you know.

"And they both say almost in giggling unison, 'it's fun to be scared.' And I thought about that for a while, and I said to myself, 'It's fun to be scared. What does that really mean? What are they really saying?' And it hit me. The world is drama. These movies are about drama. Them novels in the bookstore window over there is about drama. Life is about drama, and we all wanna be part of that drama. And we all in this drama whether we want to be or not. But me, I'm like the women. We both know the movie is a game. You know it and I know it. It's a game. It's play. It's fun. So sometimes life is fun and full of drama and sometime life is scary too. But its still life anyway you look at it. Take it or leave it. Most of us would rather take it than leave it.

"Con artists know that life is a game too. Politicians know life is a game because politicians know people don't really believe what they say. They hope people believe what they say even though they themselves don't even believe it. People are just now beginning to believe not what politicians say but what politicians do. I know that I have to be convincing in order for my game to work just as politicians do. This is also true of somebody like Quentin Tarantino who knows the game of movies. He knows the game and plays it like a master. That's what I'm trying to do. Play the game like a master."

Alibi said he knew more about life because he's been through everything. On the street he learned to manage impressions, rehearse his fictive talk. He cons black folk, white folk, Latinos, upper-class folk, middle-class folk, priests, soldiers, any and everybody. In the next chapter, we will see how.

TWO

CITY CONS AND HUSTLES

Keep yo' hands outta my pocket befo' I crack yo' head.
—Otis Spann, "Keep Your Hands Out of My Pocket" (1964)

There are many who think painters, actors, and musicians are the only professionals who deserve the title of "artist." We think differently about "artistic creations"; artistry comes in many shapes and styles. In our opinion, the con artist is just as much an artist as any other kind. Con artists are similar in terms of the way they work to master a craft. Consider the following encounter with Alibi, one of New York's master con men.

Early one fall morning I (Terry Williams) walked into a large department store with Alibi. Against all previous admonitions and advice from his crew not to, he had agreed to show me some of the tricks of the trade. His associates warned him it would be "bad luck," "against the code," and that no one had ever done what he was about to do. "It's like a magician revealing his tricks," they warned. Yet here I was walking into the store to observe him doing an actual con. It wasn't just any con. It was his "go to" con. When all else failed, when he had no money, was down on his luck, or nothing else worked, when the weather was bad, too cold to go out, too humid to move, this con always worked.

The problem is, he can only run this con every so often. It cannot be done every day, at least not in the same place, even in a city as large as New York. You can obviously move around town, but you must be careful not to "run the thing into the ground." We headed up to the men's floor and browsed. Then we separated, although I stayed close by to watch what he was doing.

After trying on several jackets and coats, Alibi took two coats and walked toward a cashier. For a moment he hesitated and looked around, as if to determine which salesperson to approach. He chose a young blond woman, perhaps in her early twenties. He had the two overcoats on his arm and handed them to her. As he did a clerk approached me to ask if I needed help. I was distracted for the moment but looked over and saw the cashier handing Alibi some money. He left one coat on the counter, placed the other one in a bag, and walked out. I did not see him give her any money or credit card—just the two coats. Out on the street a few blocks away, he showed me the receipts for the two coats. One was returned for cash, and the other one was in the bag. I'm astonished. How did he do that? What did he do?

Though we watch with careful eyes the magician performing the trick, we still can't quite see how it's done. This is the case with the con game. While I saw with my own eyes everything that Alibi did (except for that brief second when the clerk approached me), I missed a crucial moment when, he revealed later, he did something with the coat tags. He didn't reveal very much, at least not the crucial component of the con. He never broke the con-artist code, as it were, because though I asked him on more than one occasion, I still don't know what he actually did with those tags or what his actual words were. Perhaps this is because he intended to pass this game on to other con artists and didn't want it "out in public." The department store has since closed, the building is demolished, yet I still don't know how he did it. So although you can observe the con artist at work, and although he may take you along and share much of the trade, it does not mean you will always catch everything or understand everything said or not said.

In this chapter I will reveal some of the cons that Alibi and his crew allowed me to hear about and understand.

THE DICE CON

On a typical Friday afternoon, behind the 125th Street post office on 126th Street, I would see Alibi standing with several other men shooting crap in a game called Cilo (pronounced Cee-lo), which was Alibi's preferred dice-game hustle. I could see him and the other gamblers from my front window, rapping to the young girls as they passed, cursing at fellow players, drinking beer from paper bags.

Cilo is played with three six-sided dice and is said to have originated in China; Chinese immigrants brought the game to New York City. Derived from the Chinese wording *si-wu-liu* (four-five-six), the object of the game is to roll a certain combination, which earns points. The game typically involves high bets, and winning and losing happens at a furious pace. This sets the stage for bettors with a lot of money to go broke in a short period of time.

The game is similar to regular dice, except that the third die becomes the thrower's *point*, the number he has to throw continuously to win. The thrower can also throw 3, 4, 5 (which, like 7 and 11 in regular dice, wins automatically), or 18, in the form of three sixes, to win. The game is established with a banker and other players. Any player may assume the position of banker. The banker puts the money up to begin the game. There is no limit.

Let's say the banker starts with a hundred dollars in the bank. He holds the dice and will usually throw first. Before he throws, the players place their bets as to whether he will throw either 3, 4, 5, or 6, 6, 6, or crap out. If the banker throws 3, 4, 5 or 6, 6, 6, he picks up all the money from the table because those are instant winners. He may also place bets with the same players. A player may place a side bet on the banker for any amount. The house collects a 10 percent share of the money won in every particular game.

You may ask how this game is a con. It isn't—unless the dice are crooked (fake). On one occasion I went with Alibi to buy fake dice from an Italian man in Brooklyn. He acquired a box full of brand-new dice fixed to turn on the number three. Whenever a player called for new dice, Alibi would place his phony "three" dice into the game. (Players would typically call for new dice if they weren't winning for a long stretch of time or if they felt that their luck was bad.) Some players would bite the dice to see if they were hollow, but in Alibi's game, the new set of three dice felt just like the old set, since they were all rigged.

Alibi, at this time, was a hustler: cool, slick talking, dapper, charming, exuding confidence and street smarts. He made several hundred dollars from the game on a good day. I'm not sure if the other players ever caught on to the fake dice: that would lead to a serious ass-kicking at best and a shooting at worst. He defiantly and brashly broke the law by gambling in the street, and though the police would cruise by, they rarely tried to break up the game. (This was well after the 1964 Harlem riots, which were sparked when James Powell, a fifteen-year-old African American youth, was killed in front of his friends and bystanders by a white police officer. Prior to the riots, the cops would walk the beat swinging their nightsticks and strolling along with authority, but afterward, they were met with open defiance, most of all from the street-corner men.) He played until school let out and kids started walking home. Then he would stop the game until the kids left the block. He did not want the police to happen by and see him and his fellow players gambling, cursing, and getting up to their antics in front of children. This, he felt, might give the cops extra incentive to bust them.

THE MURPHY GAME

Alibi is late for our lunch date at Sylvia's on 126th Street in Harlem. He said the rain held him up because he had a "mark who just got wet."

I wondered what that meant; he wouldn't tell me, though I probed. After thinking on it, I realized that maybe his remark wasn't as mysterious as I thought; what he said was, in fact, exactly what he meant to say. He had a mark, it started raining, the mark got wet, and the game was called off.

At that time, Alibi started to tell me about the "Murphy game." The Murphy is similar to several other con games that go by different names but essentially involve a ruse to get someone to take money out of a bank account or retrieve cash from their home and pass it on to the con artist.

One method is to say that the money is evil and that the con artist will be able to cleanse it of all evilness. This is a classic gypsy con. Alibi was incredulous that anyone would fall for it. The gypsy tells the victim he (the victim) has an "evil aura" around him that is affecting his life and all those with whom he comes into contact: family, friends, lovers. All his possessions are also infected. The best way to rid himself of this evil aura is to get a special potion, which the gypsy knows how to make. The ingredients (typically a noxious combination of exotic and mundane items, such as John the Conqueror root, Oil of Olay, and an egg) cost a hundred dollars. The gypsy asks the victim to hand over the money; when he does, she immediately throws it on the floor as if it hurts her even to touch it. To a superstitious person, this sends the message that something is wrong with his money; it is bad, evil, not worth keeping. This is a way of priming the victim to turn over even more of his money.

The victim then must boil the ingredients with a teaspoon of salt. Once it cools, he takes the egg and holds it for ten minutes, then writes the names of all the people and things that have caused him pain on a piece of paper, which he then cuts into small pieces and puts under his pillow. The potion must be kept in a special locket, which only someone with cleansed hands can touch (meaning the gypsy). The locket costs two hundred dollars.

The next morning, the victim must take some of the paper, along with a piece of the egg, and put it into the locket. He must wear it for a week. When the locket starts to emit an odor from the egg, the victim must visit the gypsy to see if the spell has been lifted. At that point more money is requested. This is basically a "drag con," and it can go on for months—or until the victim's entire bank account is depleted. The gypsy tells the person not to reveal what she is doing to anyone because it will affect the power of the cure.

Another con involves a situation where the con artist walks by a potential mark and suddenly points out an envelope lying on the ground, which is found to contain money or a diamond ring. The con artist says that before he and the victim share the money, they should probably try to find the rightful owner. But before they do that, "trust" between them must be established. To establish trust, the con artist might ask to see the victim's identification, but more times than not the con artist tells the mark that some actual money must be put up.

The Spanish Prisoner con is one of the oldest, dating back to the sixteenth century. More modern-day versions, familiar to almost anyone with a computer and an e-mail account, involve a desperate, deposed Nigerian king who needs help accessing his fortune. In the original version the con artist tells the "vic" or mark that he is in touch with an aristocrat who has been locked up in Spain under a false name. The so-called prisoner cannot say who he really is without repercussions and is relying on the con artist to get the money necessary to release him from prison. The con artist asks the victim for some money, promising that he will be paid back fifty times what he put in when the prisoner is released. Once the victim has given some money, problems arise; more money is needed. By this time the vic is hooked financially and also, in most cases, emotionally because he doesn't want the prisoner to feel he's backing out at the last minute. So rather than lose the money he has already invested, and still fantasizing about the big payout at the end, he puts in more money. This continues until the vic is financially wiped out and the game is over.

Whatever variation it takes, the Murphy plays to the same elements as most con games: the victim's greed, larceny, desire to get something for nothing, trust, and gullibility.

THE HANDKERCHIEF-SWITCH CON

I got Alibi to tell me about other cons he'd perpetrated. "I learned this con from a woman I met with at an after-hours joint up on Forty-Fifth Street [145th] and we were getting high and I took her back to my place. I had a little spot I'd go when I was not downtown. It was right on Convent near City College. It was a studio decked out like a bachelor pad. You know, the shag rug, the blue lights. We went there and stayed all the next day and into the weekend. She started telling me she was married to a cop, and I freaked. I told her those guys are crazy and would kill both of us, but she assured me the guy was a fag and was not interested in her or any woman. After we stayed that weekend she began to tell me about these cons she knew and how she met her husband when he busted her and then let her go when she promised sex, but she found out later he wasn't really into women but didn't want his pals to know, so they had an arrangement. She said she knew many cons, and I didn't let on what I knew." She proceeded to describe one particular con to Alibi: the handkerchief-switch con, which involved wrapping real money in one handkerchief and fake money in another, then swapping the bundles so the victim is left with nothing. (Another variation on this type of con will be broken down in detail in chapter 4.)

Alibi continued: "She knew others she said her husband told her about that he and his cop friends did all the time to make money. She said they always kept drug money, and 'home base' was the term they used for the best drugs in the city. Home base was another word for the local precinct because all the confiscated drugs from a raid never got into the evidence room but back on the street to the cops' favorite dealers."

I later found this to be true. When writing my dissertation, one of my key contacts was the brother of my brother-in-law, Frenchy, who was a dealer. His supplier was none other than a New York City police officer named Piggy, whom Frenchy called "home base." Piggy would bring Frenchy drugs to sell, and he was not particularly concerned about my being around to witness these transactions. As far as I know, I don't think he cared. What could I do? Inform on him to other cops? This would have been suicidal on my part, and pointless too, because everyone in the precinct must have known about this kind of graft (as the Knapp Commission would later reveal). Captains, sergeants, and street cops all got something out of the deal, so my knowing about his participation would not have made him nervous in the least.

In addition, Frenchy got some of his drugs from a man in Nicky Barnes's Council crew. Nicky Barnes was one of Harlem's biggest drug-crime bosses at the time; he ran an outfit or crew known as the Council that controlled the heroin trade during the 1970s. Their main moneymaker was heroin, although the recreational drug of choice was cocaine, and most of the crew used coke and some sold as well. But it was Piggy's home-base connection that was the most consistent. I soon discovered that the best drugs on the street could be had from the precinct because they were uncut and high purity. (In chapter 10, you'll meet a retired NYPD officer who will reveal more about the police department's role in street cons.)

PULLING A CAT'S COAT

Alibi mentioned that sometimes he would "pull a cat's coat," that is, teach a person how to read a "mark" or run a small con like the money switch. A typical version of the "fast money change" game goes like this: A con artist walks into the bank with ten ten-dollar bills. He instructs the teller to exchange them for one hundred-dollar bill. Right after the exchange takes place, the con artist flashes a ten-dollar bill and says that the teller gave him the wrong denomination. At that point the teller reaches into the cash drawer and takes out another hundred and exchanges it for the ten. Thus the artist just made ninety dollars. To be quite honest, I do not know if this con really works these days.

THE SLUM-JEWELRY CON

I met Alibi at my sister's house one night; he had a box of fake watches to sell. Some were regular Rolexes, and others were diamond studded. They were surprisingly beautiful and certainly looked real to me, but they were completely fake. Alibi was sniffing cocaine with a woman friend he'd brought along, and they played music and danced. The conversation was about hustling and a con game he said was "sweet": the art of selling what he called "slum jewelry." In the slum-jewelry con, you convince a person to buy a piece of jewelry that they think is worth a lot more than what it actually is. Slum-jewelry cons work best in gambling situations where lots of money is floating around. Once, Alibi was gambling in the street and got word about some players coming into town. Alibi had gotten several fake Piagets and Rolexes. At the time, the genuine articles were quite popular, and any player on top of his game would want to wear one just for the "flash" value. But the slum-jewelry con could not be run or operated just anywhere or on anyone. "You had to be careful not to do that shit close to home or someone might find out and fuck you up. It was a 'fleeing con,' which is to say you had to do the con and flee." Alibi laughs when he tells this story.

"I had bought a bunch of watches from my Providence connect and had them in my crib. I knew some cats had come up from Baltimore to gamble at a spot you probably been to, off Convent and Forty-Seventh [147th Street] at the Yacht Club [an after-hours club], and I went there and sure enough you had a bunch of cats with lots of cash. Well, I just waited until they had won, or I had lost, and would offer the watch at a discount and ask them if they wanted the watch for a steal. This was a fake Piaget with a diamond crystal worth two grand and this cat bought it for eight hundred bucks that I paid fifty dollars for. Of course I never saw him again, and that was the way it was supposed to be."

The selling of fake jewelry was "sweet" because it embodied elements of the con-game strategy, but more importantly, it brought in "easy money." "In slum-jewelry conning, the person might know that it's fake. That's the thing: they know its fake, but they buy it anyway," he said.

He went on: "Think for a minute when a woman buys a Gucci bag on Canal Street. They know its fake, but they buy it anyway, right? Why do they do that? I'll tell you why in a minute. Let me explain something to you first. You know, selling slum jewelry is a great game, that slum jewelry. I'll tell you how it works because it's part of what I'm trying to tell you. I'll tell you almost all the slum jewelry I get comes from Rhode Island, and it comes from a mob boss, up there from Providence. That's where all the fake stuff come from because all the knockoffs come from there. All the fake jewelry, fake liquor, [fake] soap. They have all of these stores downtown, and they usually run by Italian dudes. And they make a lot of money. But they put them together—the watches I mean—they put them together up there. Whether it's Piaget or whatever, they do them in Providence.

"Usually they only let one guy in at a time to get the merchandise. And these are guys they been doing business with for a long time. So let's say you want to get some liquor, right? Well, the best place to sell liquor is at a bar because ain't nobody going to check it out in a bar. You might go into a bar and see what someone is ordering and you see what they drinking and then you go over and whisper to the bartender that you got a bag full of this or that liquor. You tell them that you selling it for like $2.50 a quart, and you can make a lot of money on it, especially if a guy is buying ten to fifteen bottles a night. Friday and Saturday nights, you make enough money to last you the rest of the week. Let's say the liquor is twenty-five dollars a bottle in the store, and one of the favorites is eighteen- or twenty-year-old Scotch. Let's say, Johnny Walker Red or Johnny Walker Black and you would probably be asking for 40 percent less than what they want in the store and they be trying to knock off a few dollars anyway. So you might get five dollars extra out the deal, but what the fuck you can always get rid of extra bottles because somebody's going to buy it, you know?"

Alibi went on like this, making no sense in terms of sticking with the original story about the slum-jewelry con game. Although I wanted to know more about it, and about how he manipulated people into buy-ing the fake items, I didn't interrupt him or try to steer him one way or another; I just wanted to hear him out. What exactly is he talking about? Where is he going with this story? Why is he so incoherent or, rather, inconsistent in his talk? Maybe it was the drugs he was doing. He finally stopped for a moment and went to the bathroom with the woman. I chalked it up to what is known in cocaine lore as "coke talk." (I should admit I often found Alibi's language baffling, confusing, and just plain unclear. I sometimes asked him to repeat himself, and that got in the way of my being able to record him accurately. I'm not sure if he did this intentionally or not.)

Alibi's slum-jewelry con could be classified as one that does minimal damage to the victims—that is to say, minimal damage beyond financial considerations.

THE CURRENT-EVENTS CON

The con artist reads the newspapers, is aware of the latest news, and will use those events to construct a reasonable, reliable story that people will sympathize with while the "topic is hot." Political issues can give a con artist an opportunity to milk the mood of the people, to take advan-tage of the heated emotions around an issue. Hakim Hasan, the street bookseller we met in chapter 1, told me about one con he witnessed back in the day: "There was a white lady who hung around the same time as the three-card monte players, and she would set up this stand with a famous magazine cover of a woman being fed into a meat grinder [*Hustler*, June 1978]. The photo of the woman in the meat grinder was graphic and provocative, and many women put money in the box with-out asking questions. She would scream, 'Fight back, women! Fight back!' She claimed that she represented some feminist cause. Yet we all knew that she was running a hustle, and people gave her money. I'd say that she certainly was a public character too in the sense that people saw this lady over and over again on the corner."

Hakim continues: "This woman was known as a con artist using the most important new theme to emerge in the city: feminism. There was a real organization called Woman Against Pornography, and pornography at the time was considered a precursor to rape. This woman took advantage of the political climate for her own gain. By the time Women Against Pornography released a statement saying the woman did not represent their organization, she had already disappeared."

What was her con? What was her ruse? It was pretending to be part of a respected organization and playing on a popular perception that women were being used and abused by men. Alibi used a similar strategy when he would pretend to be from the deep South during the civil rights movement or have one of his crew pretend to be part of South Africa's apartheid struggle. Alibi explained: "Well, in the 1960s you had people very upset about the civil rights movement and what was going in Mississippi, Alabama, the white supremacy stuff. So I would dress up like a country bumpkin, use my southern drawl, and pretend to be from the southern civil rights struggle, and that worked well."

This is a pretender's game or a performance con where the artist acts out a role. You tell people you are from Mississippi or South Africa and convince them that you represent the poor people there. Could they help with a donation for a worthy cause? The con artist has to look and sound the part. The southern drawl or the South African accent are all part of the ploy to convince the gullible that you are who you say you are. I once heard this ploy used much more bluntly by a beggar: "Can you spare a quarter for my disorder?"

Alibi continued: "In the 1970s it was South Africa in the news, and we used the apartheid issue to get people to pay attention." They would use the accent of a person supposedly from South Africa because at the time many New Yorkers felt sorry about the way blacks were being treated in South Africa and thus were more sympathetic and vulnerable to various games, such as the Murphy con, or they would pretend to represent a charity that would help the struggle in South Africa or a relief organization. "When the 1980s came around I was not too interested in women's issues but we brought a woman into the crew just to make it politically correct. But having a woman made it easier to get people to talk, especially if she was pregnant. The computer cons came later." More recently, Alibi considered using a Russian immigrant character in one of his "games" but felt New Yorkers had no sympathy for Russian newcomers and so decided against it.

New Yorkers, by and large, are a sympathetic lot, and many believe in human rights and freedom. A con who pretends to be a political victim from a repressive regime or a woman who claims to have been abused in the pornography industry can count on the average New Yorker's liberal sensibilities. The savvy con knows this and plays on it.

While the con artist will do most anything to extract cash from a mark, there are some activities he will not do, and one is begging for loose change or other forms of mendicancy. For the serious con artist who wants to maintain some degree of integrity and dignity, street panhandling and using violence are to be avoided. Alibi is quick to point out how panhandling is beneath him; it is an "absolutely undignified" behavior. "I'd rather starve than beg," he said. He knew guys who just "came off vacation" (got out of prison) who begged because they couldn't get a job. "And they made hundreds of dollars per day running down the 'beg game,' but for me this is absolutely undignified." He spoke of one guy he intended for me to meet but never got around to it. He said the guy would tell me about the many spots in the city for getting a buck. "But nobody begged in the places where they might be seen by people they know. Some guys have gone down south to panhandle but not in the city." Begging or mendicancy is not a con game, per se, and not against the law (unless a person is aggressively panhandling).

There is no pretense on our part to have exhausted all the various cons out there in this chapter, as that would be impossible to do, nor can we boast of verifying that each con presented here could still work on a mark in today's world. We simply want the reader to see the outlines of the life of a con artist, whose tricks and exquisite villainy must always change with the times.

THREE

THE CON CREW

Most con artists have a retinue of associates, friends, contacts, and partners, and as a unit they are referred to by various names: crew, mob, outfit, shill, slide, troupes, tools, buddies, snitch, ace, and main men, all of whom assist in one way or another to ensure the success of a job. They share codes of behavior and a common language.

A con crew (outfit or mob) is a collection of people with various skills who come together to perform a specific con and then disperse. They come together for simple reasons. They are old friends, or they met in prison, or they are recommended to one another because they have similar interests or skills. Occasionally people come together based on kinship or family ties. Trust among con crews is not as rare or compromised as you might think: cons live in a small world, and to break trust (i.e., steal all the money) not only will get you hurt; it will also damage your reputation so that no one will work with you. Few grifters make enough from a single con to retire. They must work in order to survive. Trustworthiness is crucial to a con artist's enterprise and health.

Crew members always maintain some contact with one another. In some situations, a peer group will develop into a crew (the contemporary

descendent of the teenage fighting gangs of the 1950s and 1960s). Yet
a crew is different from a peer group, in the sense that it has a distinct
identity attached to it: a name, a code of behavior, rules of engagement,
words of honor. There are street buddies and peer groups everywhere,
not just in poor areas of the city. Crews have a fairly formal structure
and generally coalesce around a turf system in urban areas. Crews
are usually established to make money, to avoid jail time, and to protect one another or "watch one another's backs," as folk say in the
street. Crew members may also rely on one another for positive support, participation in informal sports competition, sharing of material
resources, and the like.[1]

Some con artists have innate abilities linked to natural gifts (such
as good looks, quick wits, and persuasive tongues). These gifts are
essential to make the con game work. Cons who are recruited into
crews through word of mouth usually are well known for certain traits:
being the best boosters (shoplifters), having the quickest hands, talking the fastest or smoothest (i.e., having the "gift of gab"), or having the biggest butts. "Big-butt women" are often recruited because
they can use their assets to distract a mark by bumping or rubbing up
against him. This kind of enticement is a ruse to get a mark's guard
down or soften him up for the con. Big-butt women are also used in
pickpocketing games. Employing well-endowed women or attractive
women with large behinds to distract the mark is something Alibi said
his con friends used to great effect.

Con games are also about street social capital, and one purpose of
the con crew itself is to increase this capital by widening the acquaintances you do business with. The sociologist Alejandro Portes wrote
in "Social Capital: Its Origins and Applications in Modern Sociology"
that "social capital is discomposable into two elements: first, the social
relationships itself that allow individuals to claim access to resources
possessed by their associates, and second, the amount and quality of
those resources."[2] In other words, social capital lies in the social net-
works Alibi possesses: the con artist's "little black book." It also refers
to what the criminologist Edwin Sutherland calls common links, i.e.,

acquaintances. Alibi has friends, and he calls on those friends to get the things he needs to perpetuate his acts of rascality. Unlike others in the underground, he has some social capital but little money. Friends provide him with information about where easy marks might be found (Javits Center, Times Square, or Atlantic City, for example) or with ideas about cons that have worked in other cities; he is just as likely to provide them with new knowledge he picks up in the street.

Alibi introduces us to some of the roles within the con crew: "The people in the con are called the outside and inside men. They used to call the outside man the 'hooker,' the 'roper,' or the 'steerer.' In the drug business you heard of the 'steerer,' right? Well, the roper is like a steerer, the one who brings the buyer to the drug dealer. You know what I mean? Well, in the flim-flam the roper brings in the mark. He sets up the mark. Now the 'vic' is called the mark. The 'inside man' is the person who takes the vic and runs the con down."

Before going any further, we would like the reader to get to know the others in Alibi's crew. Interestingly, it included both women and men. In our experience, there are women who work in the game, but only as side players or bit players. We have no idea of the actual number of women who are master con artists.

ALIBI'S CREW: FIELD NOTE, FRIDAY, JUNE 10

The first member of Alibi's crew I (Terry Williams) met was Ace, who speaks a patois he uses while performing certain con games. I have been in contact with him ever since I first met him.

I met Skip, a quiet, intelligent, reserved, middle-aged man, while I was filming interviews in a crack-house location. The con crew used to meet at McDonalds on Lenox Avenue right down the street from this raggedy crack house. I met Skip at this house, unaware at the time he was connected to Alibi or anyone else. He introduced himself, saying he was trying to "rehab," and he asked if I needed any assistance with the filming. After a few weeks, he mentioned the con games he was into, and I told him I knew people too. Skip said he met Alibi in an after-hours spot.

Herlene wears a crisp nurse's uniform and is used in the game as what Alibi calls the "shade" (to block a vic's view), and she is able to "stick" (hold the vic in place) in part because she has a big protruding ass. Skip told me about her while we sat at a midtown bar. An hour into the conversation and four drinks down, he told me how Herlene and Alibi were once lovers; she wanted him to pimp her, but they never got it together.

Alibi denied this conversation. "What really happened is that I couldn't take her personality and the kind of person she was. I was no fucking sponge nor did I want to be. My heart was somewhere else at the time."

For Alibi, love is conquest through total surrender. Surrender, he said, is freeing himself from the feeling of being alone and dominating "his" women until they surrender. "I like women who can take instruction. But she never really wanted to surrender to me totally. She never wanted to lose herself or her personality. Do you know what I mean? If she can't do that she can't be pimped. Or I should say she can't be pimped by me. In other words, she never wanted to be pimped."

My take on all this is that he really didn't want to be a pimp himself. He says he never beat a woman, but in this instance, he said, that's what she wanted him to do. I did not see this as a weakness but as a strength, something to be proud of, not ashamed. My feelings about pimping were known to him: I found it disgusting and vulgar, though I never said this out loud, and he never said anything about my feelings to those he knew. I could certainly write about it and talk to pimps, and have done both those things; I am a recorder, not a priest. I'm not out to change anybody or anything, just record the facts and some of the flavor, not preach but appreciate those trusting me to tell their stories.

Mrs. Wilson, a big, chain-smoking woman in a blond wig, was a master booster (shoplifter) Alibi knew back in the day; she was also a friend of Herlene. She insisted on being called Mrs. Wilson and would get upset if anyone referred to her any other way. As a master shoplifter she would steal or rob establishments without the use of violence or weapons. She employed special coats with hidden interior hooks and often verbal ruses to confuse clerks; she also used smoke, fake fires, or physical disturbances to hide her actions. She would usually get to work around closing time or during busy holiday seasons. Skip tells me that Mrs. Wilson had a reputation for using the "gypsy approach," which is to cause as much mayhem as possible to distract those who might otherwise catch on to her actions.

Edge, an apprentice of sorts, is tall, slim, and quiet. He had been a pickpocket, and Alibi said he has quick hands. He was used by Alibi to obtain stolen goods.

Once I was introduced, most of the crew eventually warmed up to me, except Herlene and Mrs. Wilson, who did not seem pleased I was there, for reasons briefly discussed in the introduction.

I knew that the whole crew—in spite of their outward appearances—were nervous about my being around when they were involved in illegal activity, and it was important both to them and to me that I stay as cool as possible. On the other hand, they knew I did not know where they lived or even their real names; Alibi told me several times that they even changed their street names for my benefit, as well. I never used the tape recorder when all of them were present, only with Alibi, and I kept my note taking pretty low key. As a matter of fact, I never even wrote much of anything if Herlene and Mrs. Wilson were around.

The women complained about me writing about the con game. My guess was that both of them were ashamed of what they were doing; it was not something they felt proud of, and here I was recording all of it. I came to the conclusion that their dislike had something to do with privacy. I had overheard Alibi say something one day about how Herlene and Mrs. Wilson did not want their privacy violated. (I think they also felt that Alibi was just "ego tripping" by having his story recorded "for prosperity [sic]" and perhaps should not involve them.)

I was violating their privacy, a precious gift that comes with living in a big city and that is indispensable to a con artist. Jane Jacobs writes a beautiful paragraph about the importance of privacy in a city like New York:

Privacy is precious in cities. It is indispensable. Perhaps it is precious and indispensable everywhere, but most places you cannot get it. In small settlements everyone knows your affairs. In the city everyone does not—only those you chose to tell will know much about you. This is one of the attributes of cities that is precious to most city people, whether their incomes are high or their incomes are low, whether they are white or colored, whether they are old inhabitants or new, and it is a gift of great city life deeply cherished and jealously guarded.[3]

And in his classic volume about New York, the American writer E. B. White wrote:

On any person who desires such queer prizes, New York will bestow the gift of privacy. It is this largess that accounts for the presence within the city's walls of considerable segment of the population; for the residents of Manhattan are to a large extent strangers who have pulled up stakes somewhere and come to town, seeking sanctuary or fulfillment or some greater or lesser grail. The capacity to make such dubious gifts is the mysterious quality of New York. It can destroy an individual, or it can fulfill him, depending a good deal on luck. No one should come to New York to live unless he [sic] is willing to be lucky.[4]

Perhaps my violation of their privacy was the rub, and I totally missed it because I was only thinking about myself and my study. I forgot one of the fundamental sacraments of doing this kind of work: I must respect people's wishes and not interfere in their lives if they do not wish it to be so. I decided I would talk with Herlene and then Alibi about this and then ask her if I should continue to include her in the work.

THE DECISIVE MOMENT: FIELD NOTE, AUGUST 10

I think I have identified the source of distrust regarding Herlene—and perhaps the others as well. It started with a comment I made while

talking to Skip at the crack house where I was trying my hand at direct-
ing a film for BBC/HBO. Skip asked me how I was doing, and I said I
was "on the job," an expression I've used many years now, ever since I
was a rigger working in high steel. Skip said to me, "Hey, that's what
cops say." The others reacted as well, and although I mentioned how a
lot of people use this expression, I later realized this must have been the
source of the rumor that I was an undercover cop.

I believe Skip mentioned this to Herlene and Edge and probably
Alibi, who assured them that I was a sociology professor and had written books about drugs and other illicit things, but of course this kind of
thing sticks with people, and if they want to believe I'm an undercover
cop, then they will believe it no matter what Alibi or anyone else says.

Alibi knew I was doing work in sociology, and this fact intrigued him
because he'd once taken a psychology class at City College and liked
the idea of discipline and scholarship. He also liked the fact that I had
earned an advanced degree at the university during our time together.
He was proud of me and felt it was a good thing to be the subject of a
possible book. In addition he believed this association was good for him
since he trusted me more and more and felt I would never rat on him or
betray him.

He also felt the crew would follow his lead and be just as impressed,
but he was wrong. Certainly the two women were not. The men did
not object to my presence so much, but the women were superstitious
and felt I would bring bad luck by coming around when they were
performing the con or even at other times, when they were doing their
"thing." I admit I was trying to get at what the photographer Henri
Cartier-Bresson called the "decisive moment," which he described
as "the instant recognition and visual organization of an event at
the most intense moment of action and emotion."[5] Bresson recorded
the lives of pickpockets with his camera. The stories in this volume
are snapshots of grifters and flim-flam artists at work and play, and
though the con game is play, a kind of agitprop against society, a
resistance to the normal order of things, it is also pure performance I
am trying to capture.

Though I was not taking actual photographs, I was taking linguistic snapshots of what the actors were feeling and doing at a key time in their preparation for a con game. I admit I overstepped my bounds and misread what was expected of me; I'm referring not to one particular incident but to the women's negative reactions in general. I should have simply walked out after I saw the women frowning and reacting negatively to my presence, even though Alibi had allowed me to be there. As I mentioned in the introduction, "being there" is the key to the ethnographic effort. One of the last things the great sociologist Hylan Lewis said to me at a City University of New York Graduate Center event was the importance of "being there." (Lewis was a pioneer of community studies and the advisor to Elliot Liebow during his groundbreaking work on *Tally's Corner*, a classic study of black street-corner men in Washington, D.C. He was teaching at CUNY where I was doing graduate work.)

At any rate, that day with Alibi was awkward, and I told him it would be the last time I would show up when the women were there; I would prefer just to talk to the men.

As a matter of fact, I decided to talk to everyone separately after that time and did not always tell Alibi whom I was going to talk to next. I knew where all the members of his crew met, and I knew when to meet them. Now that I'm able to look back on the situation, it appears clear that my intentions were honorable and that none of them had anything to be concerned about. But the issue of privacy bothered me at the time. I had never really faced that while doing this type of research, and it posed a dilemma.

I also worried about Alibi losing his crew if they all felt I was somehow stressing them and jeopardizing their livelihood—or worse, putting them at risk of jail. I do not think any of them trusted me wholeheartedly, except perhaps Alibi; the women certainly did not, and the questions the men asked on occasion were surely inquiries to see if I had slipped up or said something different from the last time we talked. The issues of shame and privacy are difficult because I'm not sure how to address this, but I felt awkward and a bit embarrassed when I insisted on accompanying Alibi into situations that I felt would add a sense of authenticity to the ethnography. I felt I needed to see as much as possible to get the story right. I never considered the situation to be particularly private because Alibi had sponsored me, had introduced me to the con world. At the time I felt there were no privacy issues to speak of, and this attitude, right or wrong, emboldened me to pursue the research.

ONE WEEK LATER

Alibi called, said I should go to Lucky's on Sixth Avenue. He would meet us uptown around eight o'clock. By the time I got to Lucky's, Skip was already standing at the bar, and Herlene was on her way. Twenty minutes into the conversation she walked through the door. Skip, Herlene, and I left the bar at 7:40, to meet Alibi at a raunchy fleabag hotel on 111th Street to discuss the finer points of the con game.

In the cab Herlene and Skip were reticent. I complimented her dress, but she looked at me as if afraid of compliments; maybe she found them suspicious and untrustworthy. She said nothing until I paid the fare. Alibi had told me earlier that there isn't much conversation before a con. Everybody is reflective, toning up their mental muscle for the performance, getting ready, preparing their language, gestures, and nuance for the "game." "We're like politicians in that way," Skip said, sounding like something I'd heard from Alibi.

"In what way?" I asked.

"Well, we work the public."

I was still stuck on the "silence" angle. What does silence do? Help the con work? I did not realize that I was on my way to a con in progress. I thought they were just going to talk about how they do it. Alibi had previously told me how he would not listen to music, or a radio, or watch television, or talk for a whole day before a con; I was puzzled yet fascinated by this act of self-denial. I wondered then about it but didn't push the issue.

Alibi too, mentions politicians. He sees them as glorified con artists of the twentieth century because they create ruses out of the same elements: the gift of gab, saying what people want to hear, making promises without the slightest intention of fulfilling them, being capable of creating and maintaining strong impressions in people, and weaving fictions—all components of the classic con game.

"Newt Gingrich, for example," Alibi said, "is able to convince people like billionaire Murdoch or the Koch brothers that he's the man and that he can get the rich—who are the politicians—to help him flim-flam the public. People believe in certain politicians, and they flock to them. But," Alibi reminds me, "he's a con man pure and simple. When this guy had his contract on America [speaking of Gingrich], it was a fraud, and he knew it. But by the time the people got wind of it he was gone until he came back." The Contract with America was a document written by Newton Gingrich and Dick Armey in 1994 detailing the policies the Republican party promised to implement if they became the majority party in the U.S. House of Representatives. Ultimately the Republicans won fifty-four House and nine Senate seats. The contract was viewed as a success by many and as a clever ruse and political ploy by others. At the time, President Bill Clinton referred to it as "the contract on America."

The situation was more than awkward in the cab; neither Herlene nor Skip said anything, and I felt as if I was walking on eggshells. Alibi showed up, sensed something, pulled me aside, and explained that things were not working out. Would I be willing to talk with him in a day or two? I agreed and left for home. This was a weird situation, to say the least, but I understood how things got twisted in this business of trying to do work with people committing illegal acts. I never quite knew what they were going to do that night or why Alibi had initially invited me along.

A few days later Alibi, Skip, Herlene, and I were at the bar again on Sixth Avenue. When Alibi got there, he and Herlene went off to the bathroom. Skip asked me about sociology and why I was interested in writing about them. I had told him some of this before, but after a few drinks it became clear he'd forgotten the conversation.

I told him one of my professors was part of a group of scholars who helped launch something called ethnomethodology. I did not go too deep into detail; I only said it was a way to study how people use language in everyday life. The way con artists use language was fascinating to me. Alibi and Herlene came back to where we were sitting, sniffling, and she said she had to leave. Alibi too said he'd be back in an hour; could we just wait for him? After a few more drinks I left; Skip stayed, saying to me, "looks like everybody's in the mustard trying to ketchup." He laughed, adding that he had to "see a lady about a baby gorilla."

THE CON CREW IN ACTION

One unseasonably warm afternoon, Alibi and two women stand near a phone booth on the corner of Forty-Second Street and Seventh Avenue, Times Square. The two women, one light skinned and one with a darker complexion, are casually attired. The lighter-skinned woman holds a black briefcase and wears thick glasses. The darker woman, a few feet away, is wearing a tightly fitted brown dress, black wig, and short grey overcoat. She holds a newspaper under her arm. It is too hot for the coat, and she's perspiring. The light-colored woman walks away down the street and stands under a movie marquee.

I'm standing near a Florsheim shoe store across the street from the women. The crowd crisscrosses the sidewalk. Number One Times Square has a giant electronic ticker-tape running, and every so often our national debt spreads across the screen. Cars, mostly yellow cabs, move downtown in an endless stream of movement, hesitating only at red signals, blinking, honking, and swerving. At the curb, customers with outstretched hands, gesturing fingers, and nodding heads try to catch a ride.

The city is nothing without movement. It's an eerie cacophony of streaming, bumping, pushing people who manage remarkably well to avoid one another more times than not. How does one get a stranger to stop and talk to them? Under what pretense? Asking for help? Needing directions?

A white male walks down the street with a map of New York in his left hand. He stares up at the blinking SONY sign, hesitates, and looks around, appearing somehow not to be part of the crowd. As he walks by, Helene approaches, shows him a piece of paper, and asks a question. He pauses for a moment to look at the note. As he does, Mrs. Wilson walks up, pretending to be a stranger to both of them. Herlene shows her the note and repeats her question. She explains that she's lost her way, that she's from South Carolina and wants to get off welfare. She can't find a job but is lucky enough to have been the recipient of some insurance money from her brother, who lost his leg in an accident. The police mistook him for a mugger, chased him, and shot at him, causing him to fall on the subway tracks. He sued and after seven years was awarded $600,000, of which he gave her $25,000. The man is listening, looking sympathetic. Helene flashes some of the money, and his eyes light up. Mrs. Wilson tells her to put the money away. This is New York; she has to be careful. Herlene pretends she's lost but still wants to have a good time in New York before going back to South Carolina. But she says she's afraid of walking around with so much money and wants to find a lawyer to help her invest it.

Alibi has his back to them, pretending to use a payphone. He has explained to me what's going to happen next. I see him start walking ahead as Herlene, Mrs. Wilson, and the man make their way toward Forty-First Street. I'm still standing across the street and can't see much, but before long I see the two women leave and the man, standing, holding a bag.

Two hours later, I sit in a Times Square hotel room with Alibi, waiting for Herlene and Mrs. Wilson to show up. The hotel is typical commercial vice-area sleaze, the kind of place you'd use for a questionable assignation. The two beds, both of which sink in the middle, have a dingy, off-off-off-white look that is barely a color at all. The brown chair in the corner is met by a faded white wall. Two bugs crawl across a blackish dresser with mismatched knob handles. A tiny, thin, cracked mirror reflects the bugs as they head toward the bottom end of the crack. The dresser lamp is half lit by a dusty shade. The television set is old, with a scratched screen, and the bathroom sink leaks, causing a constant dripping sound and leaving a rusty circle around the porcelain sink.

Alibi is tired now and wants to get paid and leave, but before he can complain too much, Herlene and Mrs. Wilson arrive. Before they sit down, they tell me how I could have jinxed the con; they have never had anybody watch them before. "Telling you about the con is like a magician telling his tricks. I hope you know that," Herlene says, sounding pissed.

Alibi defends me by saying that I've written about all kinds of illegal things and that he's known me long enough to trust me. He then takes out a joint and a small package of cocaine and offers it to the women. They smoke and snort and before long are willing to talk about the con.

"First," Alibi says, changing the subject slightly, "You know this is all illusion—just like a magician. It's like working with mirrors. You got the big crowd, the tape running around that big building with the deficit popping up the numbers behind you. Hell, the deficit. The fucking deficit. What about the credits? Don't we got no credit in this big motherfucker called America? How is it we don' have no, ugh, any [he corrects himself] credits? But there are people all over you, all around you, in your sentences, catching your phrases, smelling your ass, spitting on your conversation, you got to find a way out. You know, you got to get the one vic who's caught up in all of this, and you got to find your spot, ask that one question that will make him stop and give you eye contact for one nan-o-second in all this walking madness. And then you find him. You got that moment, and now you have to play it.

"What you have to play is the art of misdirecting attention so that your particular magic will seem to appear. You got to get him into character like the novel guy does, like the movie master guy does, like the preacher man does, like the great actors do. You got to convince this man, this person, that your talk, your movement, your sentences, out of all the ones out there in and around him, all competing for his attention, yours is the one most important."

I asked Alibi what they said to the vic in the street, because Alibi knows the con ("I've done this con a hundred times"). But before he tells me, Herlene starts to act it out: "Hey mister, can you help me find this address?"

Alibi, as the white male: "I don't know, but I sure can try. Let me see what you have here." Helene shows him a piece of paper with an address on it, and before he can say where it is, Mrs. Wilson comes up. Then Herlene flashes what's called the "Chicago bank roll"—a wad of bills with a hundred-dollar bill on top and fifty single bills underneath, so that it looks like much more money than it actually is.

Herlene says, " 'Let me ask this woman, maybe she can help,' and I show her the paper."

I believe this is where the con must be deeply persuasive in order to hook the vic. If at this point he shows any suspicion, or if there is intrusion by the police, or if friends of either party show up, the game is broken, and the vic will leave.

Herlene says that when she flashes the cash, both she and Mrs. Wilson look to see if the vic "gets big eyes." "If he starts "buggin' " about the cash or shows any of these signs, he's our man." "Buggin" refers to the widening eyes of the victim when he sees the money.

"Now the cake [money] is to make the vic think Herlene is a fool," Alibi informs. "And when she drops the note, Mrs. Wilson winks at the vic to confirm that Herlene deserves to be beat." This is called the "hook," when the larcenous heart of the victim becomes the key part in the con-game sequence. I see Mrs. Wilson's role as crucial because she elicits the larceny in the heart of the mark.

Herlene then says: " 'I just gave a man two hundred dollars just to bring me here' [Times Square], and Mrs. Wilson tells him I was ripped off, you see, and we continuing to walk and talk."

Alibi: "What we do here is get the vic's sympathy and get him to come along because we know the money is still an incentive, or he may feel obligated to help now because he doesn't want to feel stupid."

They walk toward Forty-First Street between Seventh and Eighth Avenues. Herlene points a shop where she will "buy something special" before leaving New York. Mrs. Wilson looks at the guy and says, "We can't let her go in there with all that money. Well, look, why don't you [meaning the vic] hold the money until she comes back." She takes out a bag to hold the money in. Then she hesitates. "No, on second thought, how do we know you can be trusted? We know she can be trusted [pointing to Herlene]. I know I can be trusted [here, she takes money from her bra and places it in the bag], but what about you?"

At this point, to demonstrate his honesty, the vic follows suit, placing his wallet inside the bag as well, saying "I can be trusted too." The bag is handed over to the vic. He then goes to put it in his pocket. "Don't do it that way," Mrs. Wilson says. "Do it like this," she instructs, and demonstrates by taking the bag and placing it inside her coat. This move gives her the opportunity to switch bags inside her coat. The vic takes the bag and puts it inside his coat. Herlene steps off. In a few minutes Mrs. Wilson leaves the vic to get a pack of cigarettes, and he's left holding the bag, which is filled with useless paper.

As we will see in the next chapter, where we will dissect a con like this one in much more detail, the con game has to have certain structural features if it is going to be successful: an ability to recognize and play upon the vic's character (i.e., greed or larceny), fluidity, and a seductive quality that pulls the vic along. The trance of the con is predicated on believability. Without it, the con artists would not be able to hold the vic in suspended animation.

THE EMERGENCY-PHONE CON

It was three months before I heard from Alibi again. His call was surprising because he wanted to borrow money. He assured me he was going to hit it big soon and wanted to know if I wanted to see another con game.

On the following Friday, I met Alibi at a drug den in the west eighties. It was here I witnessed the emergency-telephone con and reunited with members of his crew. I entered the house at the ground-floor basement level through a rusty, creaking iron gate. The kitchen area was full of pots and pans, scattered over cupboards and open cabinets. The sink was leaking, and the refrigerator was padlocked. "Only my woman and me have keys to the fridge," Alibi informed me. "But let me show you the back room." We walked straight back to a room that featured a clean wooden table in sharp contrast to the old chairs with missing arms and legs discarded in the far corners. The ashtrays were full of broken cigarettes; the carpet was scored with black holes from burning butts. There were no windows in the room, and the chairs were well worn, with straight backs and sunken cushions. Near the door on a wooden tray sat food scraps, straws, paper wrappers, beer and soda cans. A new broom and dust pan stood in a corner.

"Look at these." He pointed to a wall full of broken musical instruments. The room was like an instrument graveyard: a hollow bass fiddle, a saxophone with no keys, a flute missing a bottom, a fiddle with no strings, an oboe with holes stuffed in the front opening lip, a guitar broken at the base, with a rusty clarinet protruding out the end. All of these instruments were now nothing more than gadgets, their souls plucked away because of some lost appendage, left mute and discarded in the back room of a music man's crack house.

Herlene, in her nurse's uniform, was seated in a rattan chair on the left side of the room. She started talking quickly about how a man she stopped and asked for a ride didn't blink when she said she needed help. "He just kept looking at my titties and my ass and I knew his dick was getting hard and his mind was soft. He checked under the hood and tells me my battery was weak, so I asked if he could fix it for me. I told him I'd give him something to remember me by."

The room was funky with lots of people smoking and drinking beer. Alibi didn't come in with me at first but waited at the door talking to Edge and Quick, two men in their late twenties. They were attentive and followed Alibi's every move. I sat next to Herlene. A roar went up when Alibi came in the room.

"Yo' money, what the fuck are you doing here?"

"Hey motherfucker where's my money?"

"Where you been?"

"On the lam," Alibi says with a big smile.

"On the lam, yeah I bet, on the scam."

Alibi tells them all that they have work to do.

A small tape recorder resting on a back table is manned by Herlene and Quick (one of the young men Alibi was speaking with), who sit down behind Alibi and to his left. Alibi has a list of phone numbers on a pad. He looks them over and randomly chooses one from the middle of the list. He checks it off with a number 2 pencil, then dials the phone.

Alibi: (On speakerphone, using a New York accent): "Hello, this is an emergency."

Herlene and Quick come over and play a cassette tape with background noise, cars honking, people talking, music playing, to provide familiar street noises. They move the player back and forth to simulate the sound going in and out. The phone operator asks if the party will pay for the call.

Alibi: "Hello, my name is Officer Gelson. We, we have an accident here, and do you have any family in New York?"

Vic: "Yes."

Alibi: "What's the name of your relative?"

Vic: "I have two brothers and a sister. What's the problem? Who is this?"

Alibi: "Wait a minute, let me see? What—OKAY." (In the background, Quick mumbled something).

Alibi: "Sir, what is the name of your relative?"

Vic: "Charles. He's my brother."

Alibi: "Okay—we're verifying that his name is Charles—and you're his brother. Well, your brother says he was who he says he was and he's not hurt or anything, but he's upset and he better calm the fuck down or we'll run his ass in. Now he's got another asshole with him. This other guy has, ahh, warrants, and I don't know what your brother is doing with this scumbag but I'm gonna put him on so you can talk to him. Look, he's okay. But you gotta hold on a minute."

Alibi puts the phone down, waits a minute or two, then comes back: "Okay. We've confirmed what he said but the guy wid' 'em is such a loser—okay, and when he gets there you should make sure he picks his friends better . . . Listen, I got another guy on the line who does towing but you gots to pay the tow guy or he ain't coming up here. Your brother don't want you to tell anybody else about this until he gets there. Do you have call waiting? If not stay off the phone. We're not gonna take him in but this accident—he's been in an accident, and the guy he's riding with has stolen license plates. Also, this scumbag he's with told us the car was owned by the both of them. You see what I'm saying? Hold on, let me get the towing guy on and switch back to me. Do you have a pen? Get a pen and write down the address of the tow guy."

Quick comes on the line, pretending to be the towing man. He asks the party where they live, if they have a car, and how fast they can get to Seventh Avenue and 137th. Quick says, "I'll pick your brother up for forty bucks—but you gotta come up here right away and pay me before I go out there. What kind of car you driving?"

Vic: "I'll take a cab. Be there in ten minutes."

Quick: "I'll meet you at the corner of Seventh and 135th—about 7:20 p.m. You don't have to come to the building. If you come now I'll come out and meet you . . . listen, I'm gonna put you back with the officer, okay?"

Vic: "Okay. Switch me back to the cop."

Alibi: "Listen pal, let me give you my badge number. My number is 34789. My name is Officer Gelson, okay, Officer Gelson—what's your name?"

Vic: "Mr. Swain."

Alibi: "Okay, Mr. Swain. I wanna give you my lieutenant's name and number too, okay pal? It's Lieutenant Scarfo. S-c-a-r-f-o. Number 56890. Got that? Okay . . . you go and pay this guy and go right back home and the lieutenant will call you there."

Vic: "Okay."

Alibi stayed on the phone while Edge and/or Quick took turns meeting traumatized men and women, returning with cash. I followed Edge downstairs to see if the con really worked. Sure enough, a man got out of a cab, passed money to him, and jumped back into the cab. In between calls, we sat and waited.

Alibi, sweating, talked about life in his usual philosophical tone: "You know, there's something that is unpredictable about the con. Something that is so unsafe about it. Something that is more unsafe than sex. You know what I mean? You don't know what's gonna happen at any given time. You don't know if you gonna live or die in some of these cons."

Alibi is right: there is unpredictability, an existential quality where one does not know the outcome of an action. The con artist isn't sure if the vic is an undercover cop or a deranged person, wise to their deeds and waiting for the right moment to stab or shoot. At any moment a slip in language or gesture could give them away.

Of course, it is this unpredictable element that makes for an exciting thrill ride, combined with the possibility of reward at the end, that drives Alibi and the others to continue doing what they do. I think for Alibi the con game offered no easy solutions, just a little way to get money and a means of living dishonestly in a dishonest world.

After watching Alibi's crew in action I started thinking about how important verbal communication is in the game. I also saw the significance of motion, being able to move around and do things physically, and the ability to sense things, what has been called the "grift's sense." The "gift of gab" is a cliché so often used by people to describe the virtuosity of the master con artist, but what exactly does it mean to them? Is it just about being able to persuade a person to do this or that or move in one direction or another? Or is it more about charm and poise and grace, to extricate yourself from a difficult situation under pressure? And the same is true of this kinetic sense. When con artists move about, do they rehearse and choreograph their movements in a practiced ritual, or is it mainly improvisation? I did not have answers to all these questions but intended to pose them to Alibi and the crew the next chance I got.

FOUR

THE CON GAME AS STREET THEATER

The con is said to be a good racket in the United States only because most Americans are willing, nay eager to make easy money and will engage in action that is less than legal to do so.
—Erving Goffman, "On Cooling the Mark Out"

The con game can best be elucidated as a dramaturgical event, with the con artist as actor, the street as the stage, and the game itself as a practiced, well-plotted ritual. In well-established con games, the con men rehearse their "talk" and use it with great skill to direct the action, particularly that of the unwitting "street citizen" who becomes the mark (or victim). The con game has many of the same elements as a play: props, a stage, a director, actors, an audience, a plot, and, finally, curtains. The con game seduces an ordinary citizen into a staged situation played out on the street:

1. The prop (such as money, a note, or some other item) is used to pique the curiosity of a street citizen and launch the action.

2. The actors (con men) define the situation for the street citizen, who is turned into a mark.

3. The mark is involved in the action via verbal suggestion, subjective suggestion, and/or gestural suggestion.

4. The mark's ability to see clearly what is happening is clouded by a "temporary loss of self-consciousness."[1] That is, the mark is lulled to sleep, in a manner of speaking, in part because he is thinking about the money he will gain at the conclusion of the con. This state of mind only lasts as long the con game is in operation; afterward the mark returns to his senses.

5. The mark is at the heart of the play and shares the experience with the con artists. He concentrates on the ending and therefore cannot clearly see what is happening throughout the linear development of the con.

The con game, like a good play, must have certain features if it is to be successful: believability, universality, reflection of the human condition, fluidity, and a seductive quality that ensnares the audience. It must maintain a level of arousal that delays any suspicion of the plot while simultaneously enticing and inviting the audience to stay until curtains. Con artists, as individuals and in teams, must not only manage what they have planned, but they must carry off this presentation smoothly in the face of interruptions, intrusions, and prop failures.

Erving Goffman, a Canadian-born sociologist of immense importance who used a microsociological approach, often used the terminology of the theater when analyzing human and social action. He argued that people are actors on a stage, performing, and that, just like con artists, we only take off our "mask" (our role or identity in society) when we are "backstage," where and when no one else is looking. In the movie *Paid in Full*, one drug dealer tells another, "stay off the stage if you wanna get paid"—meaning, stay in the background and out of sight of authorities. That is classic Goffman.

Goffman recognized the importance of spatial dynamics in human interactions, and throughout his work we can find theories of relevance to the con game. "Teams perform in 'front regions'—spaces from which they are observable by their different publics. They rehearse in, relax in, and retreat to "back regions," where front-region performances are "knowingly contradicted as a matter of course." Front and back regions are connected through a "guarded passageway."[2] This element of teamwork is evident in the hotel con, which we will describe in this chapter, and indeed most cons.

THE HOTEL CON

In this chapter we will analyze the dramatic elements of one con game in particular, the "hotel con," which was told to us by a con artist who had completed it successfully. It resembles in some respects the con Alibi's crew performed in Times Square in chapter 3. It could begin anywhere, in any city: a Harlem street, Union Square in San Francisco, London's Piccadilly Circus, or the Shinjuku district of Tokyo. It includes several individuals, one of whom, in this particular example, must adopt a thick West Indian accent to make the con plausible. The second individual has been approached to help find an unknown address. The third appears, for all intents and purposes, to be a regular street citizen.

In the hotel con, props are used in the following order of appearance: First, there is the lost man with a West Indian accent. He appears to be a stranger from another country confused by the city he is in. He wears a cap, pea jacket, work boots, dungarees, and glasses. He is one of the two con artists in this drama, and he initiates the game by approaching the potential mark and requesting help in locating an ambiguous address that is written on a piece of paper.

The second actor (also a con artist) remains in the background. He only comes into the game after a mark has been chosen or after he receives a cue from the first con artist (usually, after the piece of paper has been handed to the mark). If the potential mark has already noticed the second con artist loitering near the scene, his suspicion may or not be aroused, but in a large, busy city, the con's lounging need not necessarily be construed as unusual and in fact might appear perfectly normal. The role of the second con artist is to act like a regular passerby.

Choosing the mark is obviously a key issue. Many residents of New York are uncompromising, but contrary to the stereotype, they are not necessarily rude and offensive, just hyperdefensive. Those born here—or those who have emigrated or migrated here—have learned early on to be suspicious of a warm hello from a stranger because being cordial can peg you as a mark. That smile might hide a devious agenda. New Yorkers know that amid the fast pace, (begrudging) mass cooperation, and fight for survival, there is always room to be scammed, ripped off, or outhustled. That smiling face might be about to ask you for something you can't give up or try to sell you something you don't want. This is just a part of life in the city.

The ideal mark is a person who looks like she can be conned, swindled, or fleeced. She is a regular street citizen who must be "made" or transformed into a mark. She becomes the mark at the moment when she physically accepts the paper note from the actors. Generally, the ideal mark would be a stranger in the neighborhood, someone of a particular ethnicity, gender, or outward appearance or who displays "tourist" behavior, such as looking up at tall buildings, holding maps, or carrying a camera. If the person projects a sense of gullibility, they may become a mark for the con artist. On the other hand, too much vulnerability could be problematic. A person who is suffering some kind of distress or is crying, hurt, or intoxicated might appear to be the perfect mark, but this is not necessarily the case. For one thing, the person might attract too much attention, and the con artist wants as little attention as possible.

Alibi once talked about how the eyes of the mark are important in the con game. Interestingly, Erving Goffman mentioned "eyes smiling" as a "tell," embedded in his notion of social recognition.[3] Goffman posits that smiling back "is a process of openly welcoming or at least accepting the initiation of engagement, as when a greeting or smile is returned."[4] Alibi says you can tell (no pun intended) if a person can be conned if they smile back; it is a tacit indicator that the person can be had. The con artist looks for people who are willing to reveal themselves, and the eyes of a victim tell you something about the person's vulnerability, or lack thereof.

In the hotel con, the most mysterious and intriguing of roles is played by this second con man, the anonymous onlooker. His job is to remain in the background until his cue—and assist in the getaway if things go wrong. As the con unfolds, he stands inconspicuously nearby, to be summoned when needed by some predetermined gesture—or if an altercation breaks out. He watches the whole situation at close range.

There are two universal aspects to this con. First, money is the key element used to seduce the mark. Second, the game relies upon the innately human urge to respond when others call for help.

Every con game is predicated on believability. Without it, the actors (con artists) would not be able to hold the mark in their grip. A single miscue or misphrasing can call into question the entire believability of the game. Like a theatrical stage performance, suspicion must be kept at minimum or eliminated entirely; in this case, that means that the lost person with the West Indian accent must dress like a West Indian, talk like a West Indian, and altogether appear believable as a lost West Indian person. If the first con artist suddenly loses the note with the address, or if the police happen by, or if a friend recognizes and greets them—all of these events would construe a kind of prop failure. It is also possible that the artist might start "bullshitting" (going off script), which might or might not work. Just as one can talk a "good game" on someone (also called "running the game down"), one can also bullshit for the same purpose, that is, attempt to work on someone's mind to get them to give up something.

If the scene, props, and actors all line up as they are supposed to, the hotel con should play out as follows.

Scene 1: The Con Begins

Con Artist 1 (the man with the West Indian accent) speaks to a man walking down the street (the mark). "Can you help me?" He presents a piece of paper to the stranger. The paper has an ambiguous address written on it: the address is not clearly written, and the sequence of numbers is off. Because the con is planned in advance, the artists have an address that is very close to a nearby address but not quite correct. Even the phony address has to be construed to be somewhat believable.

The hotel game, like all con games, is predicated on the notion of activating in the mark a particular trait or response in order to manipulate it toward a particular end. One of those traits is human goodness, or empathy—a willingness to offer help. This positive quality is exploited by the con artist and turned into larceny (as Alibi would call it) or greed, once the money prop is introduced. Remember Alibi's adage: if the mark does not have larceny in his heart, he cannot be conned. This is how many con artists justify their actions.

The paper with the address legitimizes the call for help; it helps establish the authenticity of the con game. The paper is evidence that the person needs assistance and is in distress: he is lost, he can't remember or find the address, thus making it necessary for it to be written on a piece of paper.

The paper also provides the mark with a physical item to hold. The physical gesture of making the mark hold something has many purposes. First, it distracts the mark's attention from the surroundings and from others on the scene who might indicate that what is happening is foul play, and second, it demonstrates to the con artist that the mark is interested in assisting.

The paper note also offers a chance for the con artist to link their physical dexterity to their cognitive abilities and create and maintain a kind of rhythm between the two. As you will see throughout this con, the successful con artist develops a holistic integration between what is said ("Can you help me?"), what is shown (gestures indicating either approval or rejection, such as a raised eyebrow or expression of skepticism), and the mark's verbal responses ("yes" or "no"). This rhythm must be smooth if the game is to be maintained. The con artist hands the note to the mark, who examines it and hands it back. That's a kind of rhythm, and it also starts the beginning of a connection (however slight at this point) between the con artist and the mark.

The mark is then supposed to say "What's the problem?" or something like that. This prompts the West Indian man to say, "I just came from the West Indies, and someone downtown at the Port Authority gave me an address to find a hotel on Forty-Third Street where I can get some pussy before I go back home. I have money I just got from a settlement, and I'll give you fifty dollars if you show me where this hotel is." He again shows the piece of paper with the handwritten address.

The West Indian man then reaches into his pocket and pulls out a roll of money that looks like a huge amount but is actually a "Chicago bankroll" (a fifty-dollar bill wrapped around several smaller bills). The money is the second prop; it introduces a larcenous, seductive element into the game to ensnare the mark. It also provides justification for the con artist to fleece the victim. Con artists may argue, in self-justification, that a person without larceny in his heart cannot be conned, but what they neglect to add is that this element of entrapment is part of the game.

The amount of fifty dollars is deliberate. It's not too small a price to pay for help nor too large an amount to arouse suspicion. The con artist must be sure that all props are neither doubted nor questioned but taken at face value. A fifty-dollar bill is small enough to be believable but large enough to be enticing. The other function of displaying money is to make the mark believe that the lost person is foolhardy and thus deserves to be trimmed of his cash. The larceny inherent in the mark's human nature is a key part of the sequence.

The mark is then likely to say something like, "No. I don't want your money. But I'll try to show you where the hotel is. I think it's around the corner."

Now another man walks past them. To the mark, he is another stranger—a street citizen. To Con Artist 1, he is a partner in crime. Con

Artist 2 is another actor in the production, trying to maintain a certain believability. Con Artist 1 then directs his attention to Con Artist 2. "Hey, excuse me. Can you help me? I don't think this guy [pointing to the mark] knows where this place is. I just came from Trinidad, and I paid some guy at Port Authority fifty dollars to give me an address for a place to stay."

At this point, the mildly insulting comment by Con Artist 1 would be reason for the mark to consider stepping off, but if he does not leave, it can only be for a few reasons: either the money is an incentive to stay, or he may feel obligated to help and does not want to appear stupid if he can't find the address.

Con Artist 2 says, with a pained expression, "Oh man, you were ripped off, that guy stole your money. You shouldn't show your money like that. Don't you know how people in New York City can be? Say, look man, I'll show you where the hotel is. Both of us [pointing to the mark] will show you."

Con Artist 2 defines the situation by exploring the behavioral possibilities and drawing the mark further into the situation. In this particular case, Con Artist 2 also immediately establishes a feeling of certainty in the mark by reinforcing how the lost person is indeed foolhardy and deserves to be fleeced. The incompetence and/or foolhardiness of the lost person is reinforced when Con Artist 2 notes that the man has already been taken for his money at Port Authority ("Oh man, you were ripped off"). He assists in eliciting the mark's "larceny" by nodding and winking to the mark, indicating that the lost person is indeed a fool and can be taken. He implies that they can, perhaps, not only get money for helping but maybe even more money.

He fronts (pretends) these gestures to pull the mark into the thick of the action. His role is crucial to the production. He must act as if he, a regular street citizen, is helpfully assisting two strangers. He establishes a "we" feeling by giving the mark the impression that the two of them are just regular citizens who happened along and are united in helping a stranger find an address. This puts the mark in the firm position of "us against them."

His actions are immediately decisive. Unlike the mark, who is unsure of where he is going, Con Artist 2 is not confused in the least by the ambiguous address. He immediately knows how to locate the hotel. He makes sure the mark does not leave by insisting that they both can find the address. Note that his behavior is "goal directed." It suggests that the mark is capable of responding in a predictable manner to the encounter. A particular goal can be reached.

By acting the part of the regular street citizen, he soothes the mark's feeling of aloneness or uneasiness in participating in the situation and also may eliminate any sense of doubt the mark may have toward the lost person. If the lost person has not seemed totally believable, or if there has been any prop failure in the game thus far, he attempts to make amends, to erase the error or neutralize it. This may happen if, for example, Con Artist 1 has made slips in his "West Indian" accent.

And once these ideas are planted, the mark begins to get drawn in and lose his sense of self-consciousness. People are not always aware of themselves as distinct units; indeed, the extent to which we are self-conscious at any given time varies remarkably. There are times when self-consciousness is acute. A person unaccustomed to public speaking who is called upon to address a large group may become so preoccupied with herself that she forgets what she had planned to say. On the other hand, there are circumstances in which self-consciousness disappears almost completely. When someone is absorbed in an exciting movie or novel and unaware of anything but the development of the plot, her vicarious participation is so complete she becomes aware of herself only when the drama is over or when something unusual happens to disrupt her concentration.

If the game is working correctly, the team of con artists has articulated the drama and has made the mark completely unselfconscious. The mark's concentration is now solely on how the money will be spent. In other words, the mark's eye is on the finish line. The mark has become a thief, and his greed has overtaken common sense. The talk of the con team is "co-doable activity"; it is an instrument to get that mark to give up something (eventually) or carry out an activity to the end.

The act of the two con artists is performed in such a way that the mark does not see (or is not supposed to see) that he is in fact the "chump" or "sucker" in the game.

At this point the importance of teamwork in the hotel con should be obvious. Goffman described a team:

> A team then may be defined as a set of individuals whose intimate cooperation is required if a given projected definition of the situation is to be maintained. A team is a grouping but it is a grouping not in relations to a social structure or social organization but rather in relation to an interaction or series of interactions in which the relevant definition of the situation is maintained.
>
> In suggesting that teammates tend to be related to one another through a bond of reciprocal dependence and reciprocal familiarity, we must not confuse the type of group or clique. A teammate is someone whose dramaturgical cooperation one is dependent upon in fostering a given definition of the situation.[5]

Goffman also writes: "Successful performances are staged not by individuals but by teams, who share both risk and discreditable information in a manner comparable to that of a secret society."[6] Thanks to effective props, well-coordinated teamwork, and his own desires, both greedy and helpful, the former innocent citizen, now a fully ensnared mark, is caught in the web of the hotel con.

Scene 2: The Trap Is Sprung

Con Artist 2 continues the dialogue, looking at the mark: "You know this guy shouldn't be holding his money like that. He could get ripped off." He looks at Con Artist 1 and says, "I don't want your money either. I'll just show you where the hotel is."

Note that in this speech, Con Artist 2 is both appealing to the mark's sense of larceny ("he could get ripped off") but also appearing charitable ("I don't want your money") and offering to help out of sheer altruism.

Con Artist 2 then looks at the mark. "Okay, man, let's take him over to the hotel." The three proceed toward the "hotel"—a predetermined building that the con artists have chosen in advance. The mark walks between the two con artists. Con Artist 1 walks slightly ahead. Con Artist 2 whispers to the mark. "Listen bro, this dude doesn't know what he's doing. We can take his money and split it."

The mark will typically say something like: *"No, I don't wanna do that."*

Con Artist 2 attempts to elicit feelings of larceny in the mark by getting him to admit, or at least gesturally approve, the possible transaction. Even if the mark does not verbally agree, he is still following the rules of the game by physically coming along. His "no" doesn't prevent the game from continuing. Since he is still walking with the con artists, he is continuing to help. Con Artist 2 continues, "Don't worry about it. We can take this guy to the joint (hotel) and then rip him off."

They arrive at the "hotel," which is in fact the back of a building. Con Artist 2 looks at Con Artist 1. "Look, here's the place. Go inside and see if you can get a room. You know I'm honest, and you know he's honest [pointing to the mark]. We won't walk away with your money like the guy at Port Authority did. But you know these guys in the hotel, well, they have prostitutes, pimps, and hustlers, and they gonna try and steal your money. So why don't you let him [the mark] hold your bread [money] until you come out and tell us whether or not you have a room?"

This part of the action is intended to demonstrate "honesty." If the mark sees the two con artists displaying their money in an open, honest way, then when he is asked to display his in the same way, later on, he will be more likely to oblige. Thus the money is used here to set up the mark later on. If the mark is asked to show his money, he may feel obligated to do so in order to maintain his self-image; in other words, if the mark is not dishonest, he will prove himself honest by showing his money or other items. Or he may unconsciously show his money before he actually realizes he is among thieves. He might also display his money out of fear. A combination of all those elements might account for his display of his money. This part of the game will only work if the team has been believable in conveying an honest impression. In some other con games, the artists might do this by showing their working papers, credit cards, IDs, and the like.

Con Artist 2 continues, "Everybody is honest here. Why don't we all put our money in this bag and then you [the mark] can hold it." Each person puts their money in the bag and hands it to the mark, who puts it inside his jacket. But then Con Artist 2 tells him he did it wrong. "No, no, don't do it like that. Let me show you . . . put it in your coat like this." He places the bag inside his coat, then gives it back to the mark, who does it the same way. Con Artist 1 leaves to go into the "hotel." After a few minutes Con Artist 2 tells the mark he has to pee and leaves. After a few minutes of waiting, the mark decides to check the bag—and finds out it is filled with Monopoly money. He has been successfully "slammed" (conned).

Final Act: Curtains

While the mark senses, feels, and believes that he and Con Artist 2 will take the money from the "West Indian," his actions, expectations, and motives in the game are very different from those of the con team. They, of course, hold the secret of the game between them. If the process is successful, the mark will be robbed of his money.

In a Goffmanian analysis,[7] the ability to influence the mark's definition of the situation is based largely on the con artist's presentation of himself. If the con artist is taken seriously (if he is able to lie successfully or present himself falsely by his impersonation of someone else), then the response of the mark to him will be in accord with what the artist would normally expect. He is an actor by virtue of his believable performance.

This suggests more fully how the mark is cast into a role (situation) in which he is involved with the con artist. The mark is compelled to respond to the con artist's call for assistance. The mark projects himself into the role and responds affirmatively by offering his help. The reverse response is also a possibility, i.e., to reject the request for aid and thereby thwart the con game. That the mark projects his own emotions and experiences onto the con artist ("I was lost at one time and needed help") suggests the symbolic nature of community as represented in a culture of shared identity. As Alibi once said: "When I have felt and revealed my innermost feelings to the mark/vic he can't help but give me his support (money) because I know when I have expressed these feelings, when my talk really works, the mark/vic will feel that I have touched his own feelings."

The philosopher George Herbert Mead further describes this interaction:

There are what I have termed "generalized social attitudes" which make an organized self possible. In the community there are certain ways of acting under situations which are essentially identical, and these ways of acting on the part of anyone are those which we excite in others when we take certain steps. When we assert our rights, we are calling for a definite response. Just because there are rights that are universal—a response which everyone should, and perhaps will give. Now, that response is present in our own nature in some degree. We are ready to take that same attitude toward somebody else when he makes the appeal. When we call out that response in others, we take the attitude of the other and adjust our own conduct to it.[8]

We argue, however, that the transaction may be much simpler: many victims go along with the con not only because of larceny but because they are overwhelmed, confused, and/or may be afraid of what happens if they do not comply with the con. This may account for why the mark continues to go along with the con artists even though he or she may know better.

FIVE

PETTY STREET HUSTLES

Some rhyme, some throw shows, some sew clothes / some hobo at the junction in between cars / some enter in functions in between stars / some teach, some preach saying they seen God / some put their money up, against mean odds / flipping real estate, stocks and bonds / dreams of rolling El Dorado's bumping El DeBarge / whatever the dreams, stay on ya deem the world is ours, it's the hustle.

—Common, "The Hustle"

n *London Labour and London Poor*,[1] written in the mid-nineteenth century, Henry Mayhew describes the costermongers or street people who sell a variety of wares on sidewalks, street corners, alleyways, highways, and byways. "Highway" robbery denotes thievery on the roads away from the city center. "The costermongers moreover, diversify their labours by occasionally going on a country round, traveling on these excursions, in all directions, from thirty to ninety and even a hundred miles from the metropolis."[2] The reference to the costermongers is striking because even now it is impossible to walk around New York and not see "street people" selling things either as they walk along on foot or from a fixed location (i.e., street vendors).

These street folks are extremely inventive; they find a specialized niche in the busy metropolis in order to eke out a living. These are the unemployed poor folks, children of struggling families, crafty youth with little education, homeless men and women, mendicants with limited means of support. Like Mayhew's London of the nineteenth century, the markets of New York City today are laced with street performers and entrepreneurs, artists, peddlers, sellers, buyers, pickpockets, and assorted hustlers. Common today are the bootleggers of bottled water, pirated DVDs, and loose counterfeit cigarettes, or "loosies."

PITCHING DVDS

Often in the most deprived neighborhoods—where police tend to focus their attention on violent crimes and controlled substances—petty hustles tend to thrive. Along the busy sidewalks of Fulton Street in Brooklyn, Roosevelt Avenue in Queens, Fordham Plaza in the Bronx, or 125th Street in Manhattan, hustlers make their sales and exploit the heavy foot traffic. I (Trevor Milton) lived off of one of these hustler highways in Brooklyn and would be greeted with hundreds of offers per day; once, a hustler even penetrated into the comfort of my home.

One Sunday morning, after having a shower and breakfast, I heard a knock on my basement apartment's window. Slowly drawing aside the shades, I peeked and saw a familiar face. Flashing a big toothy smile— eyes squinting underneath his Yankees baseball cap—was Otis, a local street hustler I've known for many years. Otis was older—likely in his mid-fifties—but he dressed young: large sagging jeans on top of black Nikes, XXL plain white t-shirt to cover his waistline, hanging from his 140-pound frame like a curtain.

Before I could greet him, he jumped into salesman mode. "What's up, fam!" I don't think Otis knew my first name, so he instead chose to

call me "family." I'm coming through to see if you need any movies."
Glancing down at a satchel hanging from his hip, he continued, "I got
that *Troy*. I got that *Spiderman 2*. I got some copies of *I, Robot*."

Laughing to myself, I made my way to my front door. "Hold on. I'm
coming out."

When I got outside, he smiled and offered a "pound" with one hand.
He held several pirated DVDs in his other hand, spread out like a fan,
wrapped in cheap cellophane plastic with photocopied covers inside.
He clasped his hand in mine and pulled me into a partial hug. "Wassup,
fam? You my man, so I figured I'd come here first."

Still holding my hand, Otis raised his other arm to show me the
movie titles. I could sense his desperation. His eyelids were swollen
as if he had been up all night. Otis generally had a worn-out look to
him. His hands were dry and chafed, fingers curved from advanced
arthritis, cheeks sunk from malnourishment. He walked with a limp
after being hit by a car years back, but he never sought proper medical attention. Otis always spoke about living with his mother, but I
never saw where he lived; in fact, he could have been homeless. On
this particular morning, Otis looked exhausted. I put my hand on his
shoulder and freed my right hand to look through the DVDs. "Let me
see what you got."

Otis continued his speech. "These are top quality. No heads in the
shots. I got these ones, some kid's movies . . . " He lowered his voice.
"And I got some adult films, know what I'm saying? If you're looking
for that!"

I laughed. "No, I'm good!" I picked out a few videos. As a customer
of pirated DVDs, you know what you're getting into: most of them are
poor quality, cheap, and sometimes they won't play in your player, but
in most cases they are, at a minimum, watchable. "Otis, I got to be honest with you. I was trying to watch one of your movies last week, and it
wouldn't even play. Some of the movies have tall dudes with Afros in the
way . . . I'll be honest, I'm hesitant."

Otis's smile disappeared as he let out a sigh. He glanced at a couple
of passing cars on the street behind him before continuing, "Look, man.

I know some of these movies is messed up. But I got some good-quality movies too."

"Well, let me get the good ones. I'll pay."

He glanced at the street again. "You know what?" He started walking away and motioned for me to follow him, "I'm gonna take you to the source. I mean, you're cool. They shouldn't beef with me at all."

As we made our way onto Fulton Street, he zigzagged through street vendors, shoppers, and other summertime foot traffic. Handshakes were liberal as Otis passed neighborhood residents, and though I had known him for years, I did not realize he was such a valued public character. In *Sidewalk*, the sociologist Mitch Duneier portrays a group of men who make their living working off of the streets of New York City. He renders their lives human by bringing the "subjects" into the heart of the book and making at least one of them (Hakim Hasan, who appears elsewhere in this volume) coauthor of the book's afterword.

Duneier writes:

[Jane] Jacobs had modeled her idea of public character after the local shopkeepers with whom she and her Greenwich Village neighbors would leave their spare keys. These figures could be counted on to let her know if her children were getting out of hand on the street, or to call the police if a strange-looking person was hanging around for too long. . . . What Jacobs means is that the social context of the sidewalk is patterned in a particular way because of the presence of the public character; his or her actions have the effect of making street life safer, stabler, and more predictable. As she goes on to explain, this occurs because the public character has "eyes upon the street."[3]

Although it may seem contradictory to think of a hustler as a public character who makes street life safer, Otis is a public character, and a kind of "anti-alms" man in the sense that he provides goods for the poor by reducing the prices on goods they cannot normally afford. The streets and sidewalks of Fulton Street buzz with informal street vendors like Otis: teenagers lay out bedsheets to sell pirated CDs, middle-aged

Caribbean men sell incense and oils from propped-up tables, and older gentlemen buy cigarettes for $4.50 a pack at the local bodega and sell "loosies" for fifty cents each. It's difficult to avoid the continual open-air salesmanship.

Four blocks and roughly twenty handshakes later, Otis stopped in front of an unassuming health-food store owned by a Trinidadian couple. Familiar with the store because they sold organic vegetables and freshly squeezed juices, I joked with Otis about buying raw cashews and plantain chips.

Otis waved his hand dismissively, "*Come on, man.*" Once inside, the young owner emerged from between two racks of handbags and baseball caps displayed outside the store. He approached with a big smile and a handshake.

After exchanging pleasantries, I told him I was there with Otis. Otis continued his hurried speech, "Hey man, can I take him upstairs? I need to re-up."

The owner glanced at me. "Sure, man. He's good people."

The owner walked behind the register and unlocked the upstairs door. Before he opened it, he asked Otis, "Hey. You looking for that?"

Otis stopped and stroked his chin. "Ye . . . Yeah. Yes, I am. Can you spot me though? When I come back with the cash you can take it out of that."

"No problem." The owner reached under the register and placed two dime bags of marijuana into a small paper bag and handed it to Otis. He opened the upstairs door, then quickly smiled as another customer wandered into the store.

Otis and I walked upstairs into a two-bedroom apartment. Several people were walking around, counting money and sorting through 8.5 × 11 sheets of photo paper. The living room, devoid of furniture, held a few men seated on the floor stuffing plastic sleeves with pirated DVDs and photocopies of movie covers. The right wall was lined with five desktop computers ferociously burning away new copies. In the middle of the floor, in front of the window, lay dozens of unorganized, knee-high stacks of ready-to-sell DVDs. Against the left wall sat a lone man at a card table counting money and talking on his cell phone. When he had hung up, Otis approached him. "Hey, fam."

The man offered a handshake. "Wassup, O?"

"Yeah, I'm looking to get some HQs today."

The man pointed to the piles on the floor. "Yeah, man. Go and pick out what you want." He then turned his attention back to counting money.

"No, I mean screeners."

The man looked up from the table. "Screeners?"

Otis pointed back to me. "Yeah, I got my man here. He doesn't want cams. He wants the high-quality burns."

In the pirated DVD world, there are two types of product sold on the street: "cams" (movies filmed in a mostly empty movie theater with a handheld camera) and "screeners" (high-quality promotional copies of movies yet to be released on DVD). Cams can be made by anyone with a movie ticket and a digital camera; many are mass produced by sec-ondhand filmers in countries such as Croatia and China. Screeners are illegally copied by movie-studio employees and production assistants; they are rarer and more expensive.

The man at the table put his money into a box. "And who is this?"

Otis stuttered for a moment. "This is my neighbor, uh . . . uh . . ."

I chimed in, "Trevor."

The man smiled and shook my hand. "Trevor? That's my cousin's name. Yes, sir. I'm Idris." He opened a large cardboard box next to the table and pulled out handful of neatly packaged DVDs. "Here's your screeners, man. But they go for eight dollars a piece."

Otis was quick to say, "I thought it was ten?"

Idris glanced up. "Yeah, you sell them for ten, but he's buying them from me." Idris laughed. "That's right, this is the real deal . . . well, a copy of the real deal."

I pointed to piles of DVDs on the floor. "And those?"

"Those are cams. Its low quality, but you're not paying twelve or thirteen dollars to watch it downtown next to a screaming baby, ya know?" His laughter caused Otis to laugh, but suddenly his tone turned serious. "I'll throw in two for free if you buy two screeners."

I began reaching for my wallet. "That sounds fair." I picked two movies from his hand and then walked over to browse the piles on the floor. As I looked, the ethnographer in me began to emerge. "So how many can you burn in one day?"

"Hundreds."

"Wow. You must make out pretty well in a week."

"Indeed, man."

I picked two more films from the piles on the floor and paid the negotiated price. I thanked Idris for his time, then Otis motioned to the piles on the floor. "Idris, can I re-up?"

"Re-up? You haven't even finished selling the movies I gave you yesterday."

Otis rubbed the back of his neck. "I know, man. I'll have that for you tonight."

Idris pointed at him. "Yeah, you do that. And you still owe me from Thursday. I'll give you a fresh stack when you bring that back."

Otis and I walked back to Fulton Street before going in different directions. "You need anything else?" he asked.

I shook my head. In my head I was calculating that he only made a dollar profit per DVD. Otis had dabbled in the drug world in years past, but he had chosen to settle on this hustle. I understood his urgency and the speed at which he moved. He had to keep pushing this if he was to stay afloat.

He offered me one more handshake and a pat on the back. "Alright, fam. I got to stay on the grind." He then disappeared into the crowd, and as soon as he did another man appeared in front of me half-whispering, "I got loosies. You looking for loosies?"

Pirated goods go well beyond movies. Loosies are single cigarettes sold from packs that sometimes are believed to be counterfeit. New York City's penal code does not allow for the sale of untaxed cigarettes. Pirating also goes well beyond the streets of New York. The same cam-recorded movies are sold in triplicate on the busy streets of China, counterfeit cars in India, fake perfumes and colognes in the markets of West Africa, and cell phones with "unlocked" sim cards and video games in bazaars in Colombia.

This business of copying yields millions of dollars every year. Pirating and stealing technology and trade secrets is something all countries have done for centuries. America stole manufacturing technology from the British, and the British stole tea-manufacturing techniques from India. The Koreans stole computer technology from Microsoft, and recently Chinese techies were arrested for hacking into American defense systems, and on and on. This is the way that businesses get ahead in the informal world while simultaneously fueling the formal economy. Even though many legit businesses push governments to punish counterfeiting, legitimate sales would lag without it.

THE STREET HUSTLE

New residents and tourists alike must be mindful of the endless hustles when walking down any busy street in the city because salespeople are everywhere, selling everything from clothing and books to illicit drugs and libations. Seasoned New York residents often have phrases like "sorry I don't have any money" or "no thank you, I'm not interested" ready to fire from the hip.

Hustling can provide a steady stream of capital because the New York City market is saturated with potential buyers. A satisfied customer might just walk home with a bootleg movie, batch of incense, or a stack of calling cards thanks to a quick transaction conducted on the street during the commute between work and home. Some hustlers are abrasive, like the men who sit outside train stations and violently shake cups full of change. I guess this is a matter of opinion, but some people may not see shaking a cup as abrasive; verbally abusing people who refuse to give money is much more so. But this is a matter of perception; it depends on who is shaking the cup, whether they are white or black, young or old, standing or sitting, grimacing menacingly or smiling.

All these factors play into how the public sees or interprets aggressive behavior.

What many label as "beggars" are in fact members of the mendicant class in the city and are actually hustlers, sometimes selling nothing but pity to gain a dollar. Others are more creative, like the teenagers who buy candy wholesale and sell it for profit on the subway in order to "raise money for basketball uniforms." Seasoned New Yorkers know there are no uniforms to be purchased, but they might play along because these are struggling teenagers—and also for the convenience of buying candy on the train. Some kid hustlers don't mask their real intentions; one sixteen-year-old selling candy on my evening commute announced: "M&Ms and Peanut M&Ms. One dollar. I'm not raising money for school. I'm not trying to buy a uniform. I could be robbing you right now, but instead I'm selling candy. You've got to respect that." Many passengers appreciated the sobering honesty; others seemed to find the remark distasteful. A few nodded in agreement and purchased candy.

Even though these hustles are a part of the social fabric of the city, they are illegal. Yet because police are more concerned with hard crimes, petty hustlers tend to be tolerated by law enforcement. Someone might sell cheap toys (with flashing pink and blue lights, loud bells and whistles dangling from their bodies) right in front of a police officer, and the act will likely be overlooked even though it violates New York's unlicensed vendor laws.[4] Most of these unlicensed vendors buy cheap goods from wholesale toy stores near Thirty-Third Street and Madison Avenue and then descend into the subway system to make sales; most of the time, cops turn a blind eye.

Much like remoras (fish that cling to sharks and feed off of their parasites, thus helping the shark)—or freegans, who dumpster dive outside of posh restaurants and supermarkets (and make sure good food does not go to waste)—illegal street vendors may seem like a nuisance from a distance, but in actuality they serve an intrinsic function in the city's ecosystem. They allow for greater consumer convenience: moving and purchasing cheap goods without breaking one's stride. They are fully aware of the petty needs of the average New Yorker, and they appear along commuter pathways and well-worn tourist and weekend walking routes to accommodate vice, habit, and curiosity alike. Maybe you've never tried a shawarma, but walk enough sidewalks, and the option will appear; maybe you've decided to quit smoking, but a local man selling loosies in front of a bodega has decided otherwise; if it starts raining during your daily commute, someone will reliably be there to sell you a five-dollar umbrella as you exit your train stop.

Petty hustlers are the creators and maintainers of "place" on urban streets. Their choice of physical space used often determines the desired and undesired places of commerce. The distinction between "space" and "place" are debated sociological concepts. In the geographers John Agnew and David Livingston's *Handbook of Geographic Knowledge*, space is defined "largely as a dimension within which matter is located or a grid within which substantive items are contained."[5] This is a very literal scientific definition that can be applied to particular city sidewalks, corners, stairwells, train platforms, etc.

Place, on the other hand, is composed of the geographic units created through human interaction and crystallized through memory and reputation. Agnew claims that "place is a meta-concept that allows for particular stories [to be] associated with specific places. . . . Place is therefore nostalgic, regressive, or even reactionary." Place is where prescribed activities are found; space is just where the activities happen to be held. For example, a famous restaurant is a place. If it changes its address, its space changes but its place does not. As the saying goes, "there's no place like home."

It is the duty of petty hustlers to make a home on the city streets, whether that's a card table on a sidewalk or a predetermined route up and down certain city blocks. Every time I stepped out of the train station onto Fulton Avenue, for example, I was aware that I was stepping into a "kitchen" where Otis and a few other known hustlers were cooking up schemes. Cigarette vendors occupy certain landings on the subway steps. Drug dealers hold down entire bodegas. For their customers, their whereabouts needed to be predictable.

THE BOTTLED-WATER HUSTLE

One type of street hustle that requires a large degree of predictability—for both vendor and customer—is the sale of bottled water. On a hot summer day, sellers of bottles of water can be spotted all over the city, from Concourse Avenue in the Bronx, to 125th Street in Manhattan, to the Brooklyn-Queens Expressway's onramps. Along the ten-mile stretch of Atlantic Avenue in Brooklyn, water vendors can be found at almost every third traffic light. When cars stop at a red light, young men use the average two minutes of stoppage to walk between cars, holding dripping bottles into the air, to make a quick sale to thirsty drivers. One day while driving along Atlantic, I (Trevor Milton) decided spontaneously to investigate this trend as one young man approached my car. "Water, one dollar."

I held up my hand to confirm a purchase. I handed him five dollars, and he had four ready to give back to me along with a twelve-ounce bottle. Before we finished the purchase, I shot him a quick question. "Hey, how many bottles can you sell in one hour?"

He glanced up at the traffic light, making sure it was still red. "I don't know, probably twenty or so."

"How about I offer you twenty bucks for thirty minutes of your time?"

"What do you mean? To talk?"

"Yup."

"Twenty?"

"Yup."

"Done." He walked over to a nearby fence and put a few bottles back inside a large cooler, then jogged over to my car, which I had parked at the curb. He shook my hand through the passenger-side window. "My name's Lee, like Bruce Lee." A handsome young man with a freshly trimmed mustache and goatee, Lee wore a white t-shirt, shorts, white socks, and shower shoes; a large straw hat shaded his face from the sun.

As I told him the premise of the book I was writing, I noticed police cars patrolling up and down Atlantic Avenue. "What happens if a police officer pulls up right now?"

Lee smirked. "Nothing. You know it's crazy, I started selling water when I was twelve years old. When I was younger they used to bother me. A couple of times I actually had to run. But I don't know. This year, they just don't bother people anymore."

"I imagine anything that's not taxed is illegal."

"No, but you see, water cost more now, before they used to just charge you for the case. Now they charge you for the case and charge you five cents for each bottle. So for a case of twenty-four, that's an extra $1.20. For a case of thirty, that's an extra $1.70."

I stepped out of my car and leaned on a shaded spot on the adjacent fence, attempting to escape the oppressive heat. I pointed to his cooler. "How much do you pay per case? For a pack of twenty-four?"

"Like seven dollars. But I try to go for the pack of thirty-five . . . When I have a car available to me, I try to go find the sales. I can get a pack of thirty-five for like eight . . . That's a twenty-three dollar profit for every case I sell."

"And where do you go?"

Lee shifted his attention to the avenue. "Bay Parkway and Fifty-Ninth Street. Coney Island. Sometimes BJs."

I tried to take a sip from the bottle I had just purchased, but it was frozen solid. I could only get a drop or two. "How do you cool down the water?"

"Basically, when you are doing this over time, you um, you gain experience on what to do. Before when I first started I would buy multiple bags of ice and put them in the cooler. But then I started to notice it was like six to seven dollars for a case, so that's only a seventeen- to eighteen-dollar profit, so then I'd keep buying bags of ice, and that would take away from my profits. So I started to buy the water days before and leave it in my freezer. And then I would bring them out frozen solid, and they would melt in the sun as I sold them . . . People like them better that way, anyway."

"I see a lot of sellers out here today. Is it competitive?"

"Truth be told, this is a real competitive type of thing because I used to sell right here." He pointed to one part of the avenue. "Like this little strip right here . . . And I started like three weeks ago—last week. What's today? Saturday, they changed the light pattern. Now there's not traffic there, so it's hard for me to sell."

Vendors like Lee are heavily dependent on the timing of the traffic lights. Predictability allows them to walk in the middle of the avenue for as long as possible in order to make as many sales as they can before the light turns green. They are also dependent upon which lights clump cars up and which ones tend to produce empty lanes.

He pointed at the adjacent traffic light. "You see how there's traffic here? It's easier to sell with more cars. You see that corner there. There don't be too many cars. There be like one or two maybe; before, this thing would be packed with cars." He pointed to a street that empties onto Atlantic Avenue. "Now look. It's only one car at the red light. Or like two cars. And it's hard to sell. And when you're selling water, you need a lot of different people to see you. It's like advertising; you need a lot of different types of cars to see you. And people used to always try to go there. I used to let people know, this is my spot. You can't sell here. But now that they changed the light pattern, it's hard to sell. I used to sell like . . . I try to sell like 160 waters a day, so that way my profit is like a hundred and change. But since that happened, it's difficult. Now I can only sell like eighty to ninety waters a day."

Questioning further about the competitive nature of the business, I asked, "So no one else wants your spot?"

He puffed his chest up a little. "Nobody wants it now. I used to have to keep telling people to 'Move! Move! Move!'" He pointed across the avenue. "And the people that moved, went over there, which is a good spot. But since they changed the light pattern, it's better. And this spot is good too. Now I try to sell whenever I can, if they don't be here."

Betty Lou Valentine writes in her 1978 book *Hustling and Other Hard Work* about the conditions that make it possible for young men like Lee to hustle and what it means to have a job. Valentine did her study in a poor working-class community, and she illustrated how the twin forces of economics and politics play a major role in creating poverty in ghetto communities. Her intimate narrative allows for a fascinating look and a deep understanding of how the community residents cope with poverty and social and racial discrimination.[6] For Lee, poverty and the deprived opportunity structure pushed him not to rely on a volatile postindustrial job market but rather create something of his own.

Young men and women like Lee can be found selling water along the streets and highways of the city, near the expressways heading out to JFK Airport or along the bridges and tunnels, waiting for drivers to slow in order to make the sale. The big question is why they are not working in construction or in the many service jobs throughout New York. Where are the jobs that would keep them employed year round and able to make a decent living? Why would they stand outside in the oppressive heat and sell water? Why are they hustling to make money?

These are the questions that get at the heart of hustling and the hard work it takes to maintain and survive in the city for poor residents, teens, adults, and children. Along with the hard work, there is potential for danger. Even something as innocent as water vending can drag individuals into territorial disputes: an oversubscribed traffic light means less money for all.

I asked Lee about these disputes. "How competitive does it get with people trying to hold down certain areas?"

Lee leaned into the fence and smirked. "It's competitive because you don't want no one to come and take your spot. Because when it does, it just slows things down for you." He pointed to a shaded area under the raised Long Island Rail Road tracks in the middle of the avenue. "You see right there, that's my little cousin right there. He sells for me."

I spotted a small boy standing at the side of the road, holding four bottles of water. "Damn, he looks like he's ten! How old is he?"

"He's ten." We both laughed for a moment before Lee continued. "He actually sells for me. I don't know why he's standing there, I told him to go down some."

Considering the various amounts of hustles in action in this part of Brooklyn, I further questioned the potential for conflict. "How crazy does it get? Give me a story. Have you ever showed up and somebody was already there?"

Lee rubbed his head as if to stimulate memory. "It doesn't happen too much, but like . . . Okay, last week? I didn't sell . . . I sell Monday through Friday, and sometimes Saturday and Sunday. And if I sell on Saturday and Sunday, it's late in the day. I had a bad hangover on Saturday. So when you have a hangover, you don't feel like doing anything. So I didn't end up selling any water. And I ended up chilling with a girl that night." A big grin covered his face. "So, pardon my language, but I busted a nut off, and I was just relaxing, you know?" His grin disappeared. "So I go back out here on Monday, and I see some new guys out on my spot. So I come and I sat down and I'm like, 'Yo, don't y'all belong over there on that side?' So he looks at me and says, 'Well, I'm selling here now.' So I said, 'Naw, this is my spot. I'm out here every day.'" Lee clasped his hands together. "I mean, I'm not a gangster or nothing, I don't cause any trouble. But I'm a whole different person when it comes to my money. So now you're just trying to 'outman me' or 'outmuscle me' trying to take over my spot. And he said, 'This doesn't have your name on it.' So I said, 'You know, I feel you, but I've been living over here my whole life. And I've been selling right here.' So he said, 'Alright, let me go talk to my boss.' So he goes and talks to his boss and comes back and says, 'Oh, my boss told me not to move.' So I said, 'Where your boss at?' And he says, 'That guy over there.' So I went over to him and said, 'Look, I didn't come at your partner all disrespectful or anything. But like I said I sell out here. And this is my spot.' And he was like, 'Well, we didn't see you on no Saturday or Sunday.' And I was like, 'So, I'm out here Monday through Friday. I was hungover. I'm pretty sure y'all have seen me out here before.' And he was like, 'Yeah yeah. But that's a good spot.' And I was like, 'Look, man. Are you going to give me my spot or what?' And he was like, 'A'ight. A'ight. A'ight.'"

Unlike many territorial disputes around the sale of illicit drugs, this particular incident ended without violence, but Lee stressed there was continued tension. "So he moved, and then the next day he's in the spot again. So I come back and I'm like, 'Yo, what's up?' And he said, 'My boss said we can work this spot together.' I'm like, 'What part don't you understand? There is no together. You go on your side, I go on my side.

That's it.' So I had to go talk to him again, and he was like, 'Oh, you came out here late today, man.' I said, 'This is not a race. I'm not racing you to get to my place. This is my spot. This is my area where I sell. This is my premises.' He said, 'This is not a race, man. Understand? You came out here late.' I said, 'You're not my alarm clock, sir. So, I appreciate it if I can have my spot.' And he said, 'Alright.'"

Although many water vendors on Atlantic Avenue appeared to be disorganized and disunited, there are informal agreements and spontaneous treaties that lay the boundaries for each seller's vending space. Each seller is essentially able to create his own "place." Lee's was a small space—a half-block in each direction from the traffic light nearest to his apartment door—but it's his. Customers come to that traffic light seeking *his* water.

I wondered if it was more lucrative to work alone. "You make it sound like a lot of folks work in teams."

"A lot of people I do know work in teams. But me I'd rather work by myself. But like I said, I have my little cousin selling."

Because of the discomfort of being out under the sun, and the long hours, I questioned his choice of profession. "So, why water?"

Lee's face lit up. "Well, I'm actually a dance teacher. I used to go to Brooklyn College." Like many hustlers, Lee considered his water sales to be a side hustle. "Yeah, I'm twenty-three years old. Although I look young, I used to go to Brooklyn College. I was there for like three and a half years. And I'm not going to lie to you. When I was there I was BS'ing around."

I said, "Probably too many girls."

"Yeah, that too. So, I was BS'ing around, and I got kicked out. So I had to go to Kingsborough [Community College]. I've been going to Kingsborough for one semester. But I'm a dance teacher, and the studio is closed during the summertime. But I feel like it's something I'm good at."

Lee had his entire life ahead of him, which allowed him to dream and look at the water business as something temporary. "You have to have patience, and you've just got to know what you're doing and how you're doing it. And plus, people see me out here every day, so some people buy just because it's me. And I've been living around here my whole life, so people buy because it's me."

I thought out loud about this idea of trust. There are plenty of those who might try to sell unregulated and unsafe items, but the thought of brand-name water likely comforted many consumers. "I imagine, as long as this thing has the seal on it, water is water. So I imagine that people must trust that . . . "

Lee interjected, "You should be able to tell when you open it whether the seal is broken or cracked. And truth be told, if a person could find that many empty bottles and fill them up with water, and get paid, then they deserve it."

I mentioned how the past two summers had not been as hot as summers earlier in the decade, and I wondered if this affected his business. Lee agreed. "Well, last summer and the summer before that, I didn't sell water. Basically, I used to roll dice. Gambling." I perked up, curious about another potential hustler's topic. "I actually just stopped playing dice last week. Like I said, I started selling water again like two weeks ago. I had lost about $573, which is about a week's worth of money. And I had worked hard for it. And I had lost that money rolling dice."

This second side hustle piqued my curiosity. How lucrative could dollar bottles of water be? How much could Lee really walk away with in a week? Some say the average drug dealer can make up to five thousand dollars a week. I knew of a car thief that could make ten thousand per week. But water?

Lee explained the pros of his business. "I used to make like a hundred and change off of water per day. But I could make more than that if I had more freezer space and if that light pattern would go back to the way that it was. Now I could probably make like eighty or seventy."

"So let's say in a week you make about five hundred dollars?"

Lee smiled and nodded. "And I work about five hours, six hours a day."

I decided to ask about both hustles. "Let's say you want to inflate that money a little by rolling some dice. If you got a hot hand, what are you making in a night?"

Lee paced around on the sidewalk. "See that is something you can't really . . . you can't put a . . . you can't really predict. I can't give you an estimate. I can't give you an estimate because it depends on how much the person has on them."

Lee liked to engage in a common street dice game called Cilo, which we described in chapter 2. I asked about the risks of the game. "My understanding of rolling dice is that you don't want your hand to be too hot anyway."

"Well, actually you do."

"Oh, yeah? My understanding is that jealous ones . . . will envy that."

Lee rubbed his hands together. "Alright, let me tell you, see. If I don't know the person, I'm not playing dice with them. I only play dice with people I feel comfortable with. If this guy is a gangster, and I take all his money and he's going to try and do something to me, I'm not playing him in dice." I nodded my head in agreement as he continued. "Yeah, because I'm crazy over my money, so I can't imagine how a gangster is over his money."

"So what was a good night? Give me an example. Where you decided this is good enough, I'm going to walk away now."

Lee flashed a charming grin. "I'm a greedy person. The way I work is, either I'm going to take all your money, or you're going to take all my money."

"So it's all or nothing?"

"Yeah, well, the most I ever won in one night was five hundred dollars. But there's times—this is three years ago—this one kid took $2,300 from me."

"And you had that on you?"

"No, I went back and forth. No, he took it in two days. So, truth be told, he took $2,300 from me. And this was when I was at Brooklyn College. Now, I didn't go to school and I didn't go to sleep until I got my money back. I couldn't. That was too much money to lose. And basically, I won back from him $1,900 in that one night. But I don't count that as money that I won."

"That's still a four-hundred-dollar loss."

"No, no. Well, that too. But it was my money. If you want to be technical, then I won $1,900 in one night, but that was my money to begin with. Actually, I did win five and some change one time."

I asked further about water vending and inquired what he plans to do with the money.

Lee got more serious. "I'm saving up for school."

"Yeah?"

"You know, I buy the monthly metro cards and cell phone. And I'm usually a fashionable guy, but I'm saving up now. You know, I don't get no haircuts or nothing. I woof out. Then when school time comes back, that's when I get on my . . . handsome . . . handsomeness. You know, I go get some new clothes and sneakers. I got friends who steal clothes, and I buy the clothes off of them."

There were a myriad of street activities he appeared to be involved in. "Yet another hustle, of course."

"Of course!"

I began to wonder if the payout from these hustles could actually sustain a person's living expenses. "I'm wondering if there's anyone who pays rent off of dice."

"Truth be told, when I first started, I thought I would be able to. It wasn't too much but I was making minimum seven hundred a week. Just minimum, off of dice. So I thought I was going to be able to live off of dice for the rest of my life." Lee took a hand towel from the top of his cooler, removed his hat, then wiped his face. "You know, just live decently. I mean seven hundred a week is decent for someone not doing anything. And I had a whole bunch of extra free time on my hands. Then that went all down the drain, because all of that was beginner's luck."

Lee shook his head and put his straw hat back on. "I've played dice at six in the morning, ten o'clock at night. Three o'clock in the afternoon."

"Do you feel like you could pay your rent off of what you do now?"

Lee placed the hand towel around his neck. "Water? If . . . you know what's crazy? If New York was hot like this year round, then I could sell water all year."

"So summer, water. Fall and winter, you dance. Or you teach dance classes?"

Among all this discussion of water, dice, and dance classes, Lee unveiled yet another hustle. "But I'm actually looking into selling nutcrackers. Do you know what a nutcracker is?"

I was confused. "Are you talking about the dolls?"

"Its liquor. Its liquor and juice. You put them in these bottles and put the seal on them and sell them for like five dollars each one. You know, because a lot of people buy them." Lee explained that the requirement for a nutcracker is to buy any sort of alcoholic spirit, then mix it with a custom-made juice or iced tea. "I specialize in the Long Island ice tea type of thing. I get a bottle of lemons, I cut them up, I get the ice tea mix, and then I get a bunch of light liquor. I don't mess with dark liquor."

I began to think about the comforts of the legitimate job world: predictable paychecks, job security, incremental raises, fodder for one's resume—and in some instances health insurance—and I wondered aloud why he would choose this path. "So why not just some regular summer job?"

Lee slouched against the fence again. "I have this thing, I don't like to be told what to do. I have a problem. A problem with restriction and . . . authority." He wiped the sweat off of his face again and glanced up and down Atlantic Avenue. "Me, I'm not lazy, but if I want to lay down for another hour, I'm going to lay down for another hour. I've actually never had a regular job before. The only regular job I've had was a summer job in like 2005 . . . 2006. And then I did the part-time [2010] census [survey]. You know the census? I did that, but it was only for a couple of months. And then me and my cousin . . . Are you familiar with Coney Island?"

"Yes."

"Back in October they had that fight fest. To scare people on Halloween. And me and my cousin was dancing zombies. And three times a night we would perform, dressed as zombies."

I laughed. "Oh, because you can dance. That makes sense."

"Like, I've actually just never had a regular, regular job. It always had something to do with . . . you know, Census, you worked whenever you wanted to work."

HUSTLER GENERATION

Lee liked to work without restrictions, a seemingly impossible combination. He is a product of his generation: not lacking in work ethic but lacking the motivation to stick with anything long term. Many "millennials" (those born between 1985 and 2005) live in a world of fast information, with an expectation for continuous, instant gratification. Quite a few youth look at all money making—whether legitimate or illegitimate—as hustles that can be turned on and off at a moment's notice.

This is the second generation of youngsters who have been pushed into a postindustrial economy without any vocational compass, yet this is the first generation that completely expects to make it on their own. Fed on tales of fifteen-year-olds inventing multimillion-dollar phone apps or rugged rap gangsters designing expensive fashion lines, many expect that one day wealth will just pop into their lives (as opposed to building it in a slow, steady ascension).

The sociologists Williams and Kornblum wrote in *Growing Up Poor*—published at the onset of this generation:

> By 1990 the teenage and young adult cohort entering the labor force will be somewhat smaller—by perhaps three million—and the currently intense competition for entry level jobs may be somewhat diminished. But this is wishful projection, since this is based on no information about possible changes in the demand for young workers as opposed to the obvious supply. In any case, it is cold comfort for today's teenagers, who are experiencing unprecedented rates of unemployment, to know that their successors in the labor force may fare better than they. For this cohort, there is no salvation to be found in long-term changes in population size or age distribution.[7]

What Williams and Kornblum did not anticipate was the state's response to youthful unemployment, which was less focused on funding job programs or making jobs available through manufacturing and other means but rather involved the criminalization of poor youth, especially youth of color, who are now overrepresented in U.S. prisons. This encourages youth to become even more involved in the informal economy. As Milton wrote in "Class Status and the Construction of Black Masculinity," young black males still try to "fit themselves into the working class norms of old. The means of doing so [is] up for interpretation, and therefore could lead to illegal methods of obtaining wealth. The end goal is to gain wealth and display that wealth in order to garner respect and intrigue women."[8]

In the late 1970s, before the depression in manufacturing industries idled millions of additional adult workers, the "youth unemployment problem" was a subject of concerted federal policy and research initiatives. Plans to expand subsidized youth employment and training programs called for up to $5 billion a year for a wide range of approaches aimed at helping young people make a smoother transition from school to work.

Since the 1990s, these initiatives have been all but eliminated, and working-age youth have been left to invent miraculously their own careers. Not even a degree from a top-tier university guarantees job placement. Whether or not they are aware of the causes of the current job market, many millennials have accepted this and as a result have adopted a "fly high or crash hard" mentality toward income earning and an all-or-nothing, YOLO (you only live once) attitude toward life.

This has led to an abundance of young hustlers like Lee in New York City. The anthropologist Elliot Liebow wrote about this in *Tally's Corner*. This study of black street-corner men in Washington, D.C., written in an engaging novelistic style, is mainly about American culture, poverty, family relations, and friendship in a neighborhood where unemployment for the poor is endemic. The book in all of its essence transcends race, geography, and time and is widely considered a classic. Liebow wrote:

But the street corner man lives in a sea of want. He does not, as a rule, have a surplus of resources, either economic or psychological. Gratification of hunger and the desire for simple creature comforts cannot be long deferred. Neither can one's flagging self-esteem. Living on the edge of both economic and psychological subsistence, the street corner man is obliged to expend all his resources on maintaining himself from moment to moment.[9]

The work ethic expressed by youth on the street corner is in evidence here, as is the desire to better themselves at opportunities in which they can be their own bosses. As the author Betty Lou Valentine put it, "hustling is hard work."

Unsure of his future, Lee had many irons in the fire, hoping that one of them would pay off, waiting for one of them to send him skyward. "I'm actually into film. I create skits. I put them on YouTube. One skit I did, two summers ago when it was a hundred degrees outside, I recorded my friend. He had put on a snorkel jacket with sweatpants and Timberlands. And he just walked outside while it was a hundred degrees. I recorded random reactions to people while he did that. Complete strangers. So I cut it up, because I know how to edit it. With concepts and everything."

Lee is also an amateur filmmaker, but his production equipment was limited. "I don't have the MacBook and the Final Cut. If I had that, then the stuff that I'm using would be . . . Because everything I use is regular. Basic camera, basic regular editing program. And people tell me, 'Your stuff is really good. Especially because you don't have any effects or nothing.' If I had the effects and stuff, then—" He smiled as he looked at the sky. "Aw man."

Being a Generation Xer, I suggested the path of old, maybe an outdated and unrealistic option: "You should get back into college. Use their stuff."

"I am. I was supposed to go to the Art Institute, but they want thirty thousand a year. At first I was going to get the loan, because truth be told, if I get into school then I'm going to do something with my life. Because I know film. Sometimes I just know things, camera angles and everything. But my father told me that I should go back to Kingsborough for one more semester, and 'while you're in there you can apply for a bunch of scholarships,' so by the time next semester comes 'you can have some scholarships instead of taking out four loans.'"

I had exceeded my promised thirty minutes, so I ended the interview. I thanked him for his time, and he thanked me for the opportunity to share his story. I climbed back into my air-conditioned car, and he resumed his current hustle in the blazing heat. Between red lights, Lee would dream of ways to fly.

SIX

CANAL STREET AS VENUS FLYTRAP

Everyone's got a hustle. You just have to create the need.
—Daniel

Canal Street—located in lower Manhattan and stretching from the Manhattan Bridge on the East River to the Holland Tunnel on the Hudson River—was named after a canal that was dug in the early nineteenth century "to drain a contaminated and disease-ridden 'collect pond' into the Hudson River. The pond was filled in 1811 and Canal Street was completed in 1820 following the angled path the canal had."[1]

Today Canal Street is a bustling commercial strip. The neighborhoods of SoHo and Little Italy run along its northern edge, Chinatown and TriBeCa along its southern edge. It is a place of secondhand commerce and bartering and a space for unaccounted cash to be made. Canal Street is also famous for its counterfeit goods, which peaked in sales to enthusiastic travelers most recently in 2002.

Canal Street was the first home of the diamond district in New York City until it moved to Rockefeller Center in the 1920s. In the 1960s, Canal

Street was at its height as a commercial center for high-quality goods. Daniel—Trevor Milton's respondent who grew up working in specialty stores along Canal Street—explained that the neighborhood began selling cheap goods after the 1970s: "In the 1980s, you had surplus stores just selling junk. But people love that junk."

In the 1990s, the electronics stores really took off: cameras, cassette players, CD players, gadgets . . . you name it. The sidewalks are choked with throngs of tourists, visitors from upstate and the suburbs, native New Yorkers, and assorted travelers, all seeking one bargain or another.

THE SET-UP

Canal Street is a hotbed for hustlers and con men who work directly out of the storefronts. In this chapter, Daniel lays the groundwork for how the hustle is put over on an unsuspecting tourist. You will get a sense of the stark relationship between hustling and the aboveground (formal) and underground ("gray market") economy.

Daniel is a member of a longstanding family of store owners on Canal Street. He is also a close friend of one of my (Trevor Milton's) former students. When I explained the planned direction of this book to my student, he immediately thought of Daniel and his life spent hustling on Canal Street. Daniel and I planned to meet for the first time in a luxury hotel one block north of TriBeCa on a cool summer's day. Our scheduled time passed, and Daniel didn't show, nor did he call or send a text. As I waited, I sorted through old e-mail messages before the hotel concierge approached and suggested that the second-floor lounge might be a more comfortable place to sit. Surprised by his hospitality, I agreed. The lounge was well lit, with big windows and plush chairs. Moments later Daniel emerged from the elevator, wearing designer sunglasses and a disarming smile. We shook hands and sat for a moment.

Daniel's family had sold electronics, souvenirs, and other tourist goods on Canal Street for several generations. Though his family's dealings had always been honest and legitimate, Daniel and his peers, as they became imbued with the culture of Canal Street, began to see opportunity for conning, hard renegotiating, and what he would call "slamming." I had told him about the book, and he was eager yet cautious in his desire to talk about the family business. I often wonder why people tell me what they do, but after listening to Daniel it dawned on me that there is a human need not to be relegated to anonymity. I also realize there is a quid pro quo: in exchange for his time, he wants to be mentioned in the book (using the pseudonym he gave me).

I began to summarize the book again. "I'm interested in the world of hustling and conning. How people 'get over' on each other in New York City. Essentially something that has been a part of the fabric of New York City for more than a century."

He listened with a distracted look in his eyes, then motioned to the elevator. "Come on. Let's go upstairs." This hotel required guests to use an electronic key to reach the upper floors. As the elevator doors closed, Daniel reached in his pocket, pulled out a card, and inserted it into a slot next to the call buttons. Two young women behind us began to grin, and one of them said, "Oh, lucky us!"

We reached the top floor and walked past a long indoor bar to the outer deck, which offered a breathtaking view of the Lower East Side, downtown Manhattan, and the Hudson River. Elegantly dressed couples lounged near a clear pool, holding martini glasses, enjoying the scene. The balcony edge was sprinkled with scantily dressed pairs of young women, who were looking away from the skyline back toward the entranceway to gawk at those entering.

Daniel—who is tall and slightly overweight, with an unshaved face, wearing tattered cargo shorts, worn tennis shoes, a t-shirt, and a faded white baseball cap—was a puzzle. Most of the people who walked along the balcony had impeccably pressed clothing and expensive jewelry. Daniel dressed like a bar back but walked around like he owned the place. In spite of his attire, he exuded confidence.

Daniel provided me with what anthropologists call an "emic" perspective (a view from one within the group being studied rather than the view of the one studying). He guided me though the lore of his world while offering detail and motivations for exceptional behaviors. Much like "Chic Conwell"—the professional thief who is the subject of Edwin Sutherland's book *Professional Thief*—Daniel provided insight into Canal Street hustling as a vocation. Sutherland's book detailed the life and keen business sense of a professional criminal in Chicago in the 1930s. Even though cheating others and conning "marks" are seen wrongful acts, they still require an ample amount of entrepreneurialism. As Sutherland wrote, "Just as the salesman learns of fertile territory, new methods, new laws which affect the business, so does the thief."[2] To be a successful con artist, like a legitimate business owner, one has to be organized, have a detailed strategy of execution, and an understanding of risk and reward.

Daniel motioned to the southern edge of the balcony. "Right here. I want to show you a good view of Canal Street." Before I could ask any questions, he pointed to the street and launched into a practiced speech. "Canal Street is a world in and of itself. From the pickpockets, to the junk artists, to the bargain stores, to the whisperers[3] who sell handbags, everyone is just trying to make money. This location is begging to vacuum money out of people's pockets. And it's all about this street's proximity to downtown, to the train stations."

He pointed to a building below us. "Just look at this Maserati dealership. It's perfect. You got Wall Street guys driving up Sixth Avenue before they make this turn right here to get into the Holland Tunnel. And then they get stuck at this light. They look to their left and see these shiny new luxury cars that they know they shouldn't buy. They hear the wife's voice telling them 'no,' but they're stuck at that light. And those cars are on display twenty-four hours a day, lights and all."

Daniel held a lighter in his hand but gave no other indication that he was a smoker. He tapped it on the railing. "Everyone's got a hustle. You just have to create the need." He then took his cell phone out of his pocket. "Look at this," he said, tapping the protective silicon case around his phone. "I sell these things all the time for like fifty bucks each. But they're great! Have you ever seen the commercial with the guy who drops his phone from a ten-story building?"

Perplexed, I answered, "I haven't . . . No, I haven't seen that one."

"There's this commercial where this guy has an expensive smart-phone. He puts on this case and drops it from a ten-story building. He runs downstairs, turns it on, and then makes a call. It's hilarious!"

Daniel removed the silicon case from his phone, then snapped it back on. "I don't know if I'd do that, but these things are tough. Look." He smacked his phone against the railing a few times, creating a ringing sound. "Look, I've had so many of these smartphones. They're so fuck-ing fragile. Cracked screens. Dead buttons. I got one of these, and my phone has been mint for like a year." He glanced down at my pocket. "What kind of phone do you have?"

I removed my phone from my pocket. "HTC. It's been good to me."

Daniel grabbed my phone from my hand. "Bro, look at this. You got scratches all over this thing. You're going to crack your screen if you keep carrying it like that." He handed the phone back to me. "You want one of these? I usually sell it for like fifty, but I can get it to you for forty."

I put my phone back in my pocket, embarrassed by its condition. "Yeah, I guess." Looking to see if he had a handbag or backpack, I added, "Do you have some with you?"

Daniel paused to take in the look on my face and then smiled. "I got you."

"I'm sorry?"

"I just nailed you! These phone cases go for ten bucks retail, but I just bumped you 300 percent, and you thought you were getting a discount!"

I looked at the ground and shook my head.

Daniel had created that hustle out of thin air. That phone case was cheap silicone. He had even made up the television commercial. He grabbed my shoulder. "Bro, this is what I do. Everybody's got a hustle." He pointed back down to the street. "I knew this guy that worked for that Maserati dealership. He used to take people to this same deck, get a few drinks in them, and then start talking about the cars." He rubbed his hands together. "So he'd get guys saying, 'Oh man, I wish I could test drive one of those,' and he would be like, 'Let's go downstairs. I'll open it up for you.'" Daniel began to imitate the mark: "'What? It's three in the morning. You can do that?'" He waved his hand over his shoulder. "'Yeah, sure.' Then this guy opens the dealership, starts up a floor model, and lets the guy drive up and down the West Side Highway." Daniel clapped his hands together. "The guy gets slammed. He does the paperwork at four in the morning and is told to come back the next day to drive it off the lot. All you have to do is—"

I nodded. "—create the need."

"Right! Create the need. People don't know what they want until you tell them."

Daniel is animated and downright obsessive in his thoughts on "creating a need," but he is also a typical capitalist and a natural salesperson. Con artists and hustlers do not necessarily disagree with the ideals of capitalism. In fact, they are born out of capitalism and are the archetypal evangelists of its philosophy. Advertisers bank their careers on creating need where there is none. Sleight of hand, false promises, and preying on people's insecurities are all techniques used to sell something as simple as shower gel. Daniel is simply stepping into a role that has already been carved out for him.

THE FLYTRAP

Canal Street is world renowned for its discount shopping and the possibility of bartering for a good price; this is where Daniel learned the art of a more legitimate confidence game. The rental rate for storefronts along the busy thoroughfare is only slightly lower than that for businesses in midtown Manhattan, and wholesale items cost the same as anywhere. It is to the store owner's advantage to drive prices as high as possible in order to maximize profits.

The Venus flytrap—named after the Roman goddess of love—lies still in the swampy forests of the Carolinas. Its lush pink hues and sweet pheromone stench attracts unsuspecting flies, bees, and spiders who believe they have scored a pollen-filled flower, ripe for indulgence. As the insect advances into the plant in search of riches, the trap springs, and the plant drains the life out of the insect.

Canal Street is a commercial Venus flytrap, with hustlers trying to lure potential patrons into open-faced storefronts and sunglasses booths. Some women travel hundreds of miles by plane just to purchase knockoff handbags on Canal Street. Men grind through overcrowded sidewalks looking for discounts on smartphones, video games, and watches.

Canal Street attracts New Yorkers and tourists alike with bright lights, designer perfumes, and the most luxurious brand names—all with the promise of discounts. Vendors know who to look for and who to look past. I asked Daniel who are the best people to "slam."

He leaned against the rail. "Oh that's easy: tourists. Rich tourists, if you can find them."

"Can you describe to me the best-case scenario? The best mark?"

"Sure. That's the guy with his wife and his kids. They just got off a plane, and his wife wants some handbags, and the kids want all the junk toys that they see." Daniel laughed. "The husband? He just wants to get out of there, so he buys up a bunch of stuff quickly and leaves, but if he's rich? Then you can really slam him. Hey you can't buy your kid this remote-controlled car without this matching robot set and these custom batteries." He turned to his left. "You can't buy this handbag without this matching wallet. All the girls in New York have this set."

"But how is it a slam if you're just selling a product, and they're willing to buy it?"

"Easy. You switch them out."

"Switch them out?"

Daniel smirked. "A bait and switch."

"Do you sell them something that's broken?" I asked.

"No. No." He pointed to me. "Look. You're a New Yorker, right?"

I nodded. "Sure."

"So where would you buy a digital camera?"

I laughed. "Definitely not a secondhand store. Probably Best Buy."

"Right. Best Buy, because they have to guarantee a certain quality." He snapped his fingers. "Their con is the insurance. They know you don't need that eighty-dollar insurance, but that's a whole other story. Let me get back to you on that one."

He pulled his sagging shorts to a proper height and continued. "A bait and switch is when I advertise one price and then you end up paying another. So, I'm selling a Canon Digital SLR with an LCD screen worth $500, but I'm advertising it for $250. I got your attention, right?"

"Sure."

"You come into my store. I show you a sealed box. It's legit. So you're ready to pay $250."

"Sure."

"But."

"But?"

"The zoom lens is going to cost you another $150. The battery costs $150. I got this ten-gig memory that you absolutely need for $150. And I'll throw in this carrying case for $50."

I laughed out loud. "Okay, so now you got me for . . . $750."

Daniel snapped his fingers. "Right. So now I'm making $250 on top of retail, and if I really want to slam you, I'll switch the good SLR with a different Canon worth $150. Now, I really got you."

I understood. "So that's a real bait and switch. They think they have something, and you give them something completely different?"

Daniel rubbed his chin stubble. "Well, mostly not. Not really. The value is in what we can buy wholesale. My store used to have a deal with Sony. We'd get stuff from them and rehash it."

"Rehash it?"

"It means to make something brand-new again." He pointed across the Hudson River toward New Jersey. "Sony gets a lot of returned goods, damaged goods. They can fix it up, but they can't sell it again. That stuff sits on a shelf in their factories in New Jersey. Boom! We come in, buy up all the damaged goods, fix it up, shrink wrap it, and put it out for display."

"So the customer can't even test it if it's shrink wrapped."

"Precisely. I mean, it might work just fine, but something with a retail value of $500 has a $150 value after it's been rehashed."

I smirked at him. "But you sold it to me for $750."

His smile grew to the largest that I had yet seen. "Precisely."

It all sounded too easy. The naïve customer, the below-market products. Many come to Canal Street to bargain with the vendors, and if the price isn't right they tend to move on. Some customers are picky and are wary of scams. I asked, "So what if that doesn't sound right to me? What if I don't want to pay that?"

He snapped back, "Then you're cheap."

I was taken aback. It felt personal now. "I'm cheap? I *know* better."

He waved his hand dismissively. "Bro, if you want to come into my place with all that 'know it all,' then I'm more motivated to slam you. Listen, there's a difference between those who will pay and those who won't pay. Those who won't, get screwed. The cheap guy? I hit hard and fast. The more you argue the price, the more I keep adding items you don't need."

WORKING THE GIMME GUY

For Daniel and his peers along Canal Street, the slam is not just about seeking out easy prey; it's also about the challenge, the competition, the intangible trophy earned when getting over on the "know it all." Street credibility could be earned with the right high-priced target. Daniel tapped his lighter on the railing again, then put it into his shirt pocket. "What you really want is a rich tourist or a Wall Street guy. Businessmen get slammed the most. They pay whatever you tell them to pay. You know, in this business you have to learn people. Study people. Start up some conversation and find out what makes them feel pleasure, then treat him special. Boom! I got you."

"So the rich guy is the best target?"

"A rich tourist." Daniel cleared his throat and motioned to a small circular table with two seats. I sat but he remained standing. "I'm going to tell you a story about this guy named Mr. Badesh." Daniel looked to the street and rubbed his hands together. "Mr. Badesh was a 'Gimme Guy.' "

"A Gimme Guy?"

Daniel began pointing to imaginary shelves. "Gimme this. Gimme that. I'll take five of these. Gimme that over there." He shrugged and pointed his hands at me as if to suggest that I should know. "This guy was some hotshot European tourist. Flew into New York for like two nights, and he wanted to bring back some stuff for his wife and kids. He had just got done shopping on Fifth Avenue [one of the most expensive shopping areas in New York]. You know? Bags for his wife, clothes for his daughter. Now he wants some gadgets. And he's just picking randomly off the walls, 'Yeah, I'll take three cameras. That radio looks nice. Gimme that watch.' And racks up ten thousand dollars in merchandise quick."

Daniel and the workers in the store immediately recognized this man as a trophy. Daniel stepped in closer to me and lowered his voice. "So the owner is watching this from the back and decides to call in his guys." Daniel explained that there are workers whose sole purpose is to conspire to slam wealthy customers with free-flowing wallets. To get the right amount of money from a wealthy patron, the use of props, bait, and distraction has to be a well-orchestrated performance. For the purposes of this book, we'll call them a "slam team." Their job is to roam around on Canal Street until they are called.

Daniel continued, "The owner gets on his phone and calls them [the slam team] into the store. And just as Mr. Badesh is about to purchase his goods, the owner comes out and says, 'Mr. Badesh. It is an absolute pleasure doing business with you. But if you want to see the good stuff, I can invite you into my private room.' Mr. Badesh agrees, and they go to his office in the back. The owner's office is filled with designer furniture, expensive paintings, and really comfortable chairs.

"So the owner says, 'Mr. Badesh, please won't you have a glass of my best scotch.' Mr. Badesh agrees. Now he feels at home." Daniel pointed behind him. "Meanwhile his guys come into the room with the stuff he's already bought, already neatly boxed up, and neatly place it to the side. The owner points out that he has better cameras, better watches, and better gadgets. And while they sit and drink, his guys keep walking in and out of the room with different stuff to show Mr. Badesh, 'Oh Mr. Badesh, I have a son, too. He loves this video game system and all these games.' "

Daniel sat down in the chair opposite of me and leaned back. "So they're laughing. The owner has fed him four drinks at this point. They are talking about family, their wives, and Mr. Badesh is buying everything that's thrown in front of him—he ends up spending $350,000!" Daniel snapped his fingers. "The owner calls three cabs so he can get all of this stuff back to his hotel room. The guys box everything up and load it into the cabs, and then Mr. Badesh is gone."

I leaned back in my chair, too. "That sounds like a good slam."

"Sure, but that's not even the best part!" Daniel leaned toward me again. "So the owner knows that Mr. Badesh is flying out of New York the next afternoon. So before this guy can sober up and figure out what just happened, the owner shuts down the store for the rest of the day and then shuts it down the entire next day."

I was fascinated. "Wow."

"So when Mr. Badesh shows up the next morning, the gates are down, and he's stuck with that stuff. And what's he going to do, call the police? He has a receipt saying that he spent $350,000."

Daniel looked through the glass below the rooftop bar's railing. He looked somberly for a long moment, as if contemplating his past. "That was back in the day, though." He continued to stare and lightly laughed. "The sidewalk wasn't crowded, but there was a crowd." He pointed to my notebook. "Write that one down."

He snapped himself out of his nostalgic mood and became animated again. "We were busy and making money. I mean, there were racks filled with Oakley and Fendi sunglasses. Handbags were in piles inside and outside the stores. And girls were going crazy over them! Tourists would do a little shopping in SoHo and then walk down to Canal for the discounts."

With so many moving parts, I asked him how it all fit together.

"It's a complicated world, but there's a balance. You had the store-fronts selling the big items: bags, computers and what not. Then you had the whisperers."

"Whisperers?"

"These are the guys that walk around and sell stuff off their person, you know, 'Fendi! Louis Vuitton!' And the real hustlers were the guys with the watches, Rolexes. They would work Canal during the day and then move up to Times Square at night. So you had like twenty hustlers and 450 vendors working the sidewalks."

"Were these guys selling the same things as the vendors?"

Daniel pointed to me. "There's your balance. More recently, the whisperers are all Senegalese guys. If they were selling the same stuff as my store, I would chase them away with a bat." Daniel waved his hand dismissively. "And they're soft. All of them are illegal, so they know not to cross any lines." He laughed. "I chase them. Police chase them. I saw this guy hop over two cabs to get across the street only to get hit by a third cab. Crazy."

Daniel leaned forward in his seat. "So you had to deal with those guys, the pickpockets, and the ladies selling junk art on the edge of the sidewalk, all while trying to slam the tourists. So me and the guys that I worked with had to talk fast; work in teams." Daniel explained that there was a coded vocabulary that was necessary in order to communicate in the customer's presence. He explained a few. "'Rehash': that means to make something new. 'Jedge': that meant someone was a dick. 'T.O.' for turnover. 'I.N.D.' for the Indian guys. 'Che Che' for the Chinese vendors. 'I.T.' for Italians." Many of these terms reflect the multitude of ethnicities jockeying for power on Canal Street: from Italians, Chinese, Indians and Pakistanis to Arabs, Israelis, and West Africans.

Daniel smiled to himself again. "Oh, and when we talked prices? We had to make sure the tourists didn't know what we were saying, so we always used 'lat' for everything. 'Lat' just means half. So one of us would ask the other, 'How much is this?' 'Lat fifty.' Meaning twenty-five. 'Lat twenty-six.' Meaning $1,300. We would negotiate with each other over how low we wanted to lowball the customer without the customer having a clue what was happening." Daniel leaned back in his chair and inhaled the memory for a moment. "That was the heyday." He slapped his hands together and then crossed his arms. "And then the Internet ruined everything!"

"How so?"

"Because of eBay. All the electronics we sold could now be found on eBay. And with the customer being able to price check everything, they know they're being slammed. Plus, why would you make the trip to Canal Street for a camera when you can buy it on eBay for like twenty bucks after winning an auction?" Daniel shook his head. "It's ridiculous."

COUNTERFEIT CRACKDOWN

Daniel loathed Internet auctions with a passion, but also contributing to the downslide on Canal Street was the push to criminalize the sale of counterfeit goods. Since the mid-2000s, both federal and New York City governments have been cracking down on vendors of fake handbags, watches, and "rehashed" electronics. In a city where so many depend on knockoff goods in order to maintain the façade of being fashionable, New York officials are stepping up their efforts to curb the sale of these items. New York's trademark-counterfeiting laws[4] were largely ignored until recently. Even with the increased attention, many still consider New York's antipiracy legislation to be incomplete.

Daniel reiterated, "This stuff has always been illegal, but NYPD didn't consider it as serious as drugs, so they left it alone. Giuliani only cared about drugs and the prostitutes in Times Square. But then things changed under Bloomberg. All this guy cares about is money, and Canal wasn't producing enough for him. Plus, companies like Chanel and Louis Vuitton started complaining, 'We're getting burned by these guys.' So Bloomberg started taxing."

Under the Bloomberg mayoral administration (2002–2013), the NYPD began to enforce vendor laws that were already on the books but that had been largely ignored. Street vendors began to have their licenses checked. Food vendors—even those who pushed small ice-cream carts—were required to pay for a "food protection course" and then apply for a limited license. Street vendors struggled to maintain their livelihoods; many found it nearly impossible to obtain a general license legitimately. Licenses are in such high demand that food-vending licenses have been moved to the NYC Department of Health and Mental Hygiene under the current de Blasio administration. General vendor licenses are still available through the New York City Department of Consumer Affairs Licensing Center, but they only issue 853 licenses per year, and the waiting list is "currently closed."[5] Some say the average wait time for a license is five to seven years. And with police raids cracking down heavily on sales of unlicensed merchandise, this has created a new set of unintended consequences.

Whereas Canal Street vendors would openly display counterfeit goods on the sidewalks in the early 2000s, police raids have pushed these items into Canal Street's back rooms, or into the hands of whisperers carrying trash bags, or into two-bedroom apartments several blocks away from Canal. In 2008, Milton followed a friend who attempted to buy a set of knockoff bags in midtown Manhattan. We had to follow a young man in a hooded sweatshirt for several blocks before he entered a luxury apartment building, winked at the doorman, and led us fourteen flights up to a two-bedroom apartment, which required a spoken password to enter. The entire apartment was filled—wall to wall, floor to ceiling—with Gucci, Prada, and Louis Vuitton handbags; they must have been stolen because each bag had its original registration card inside.

The federal government will soon have its hand in the prosecution of counterfeit goods with the passing of the Design Piracy Prohibition Act (HR 2033, currently tabled).[6] This law would "extend copyright protection to fashion designs" and would make it a federal crime to distribute counterfeit goods, but not knockoff goods. The legal scholar Lynsey Blackman, in her article "The Devil Wears Prado [sic]," explained the difference between the two: "counterfeit merchandise actually attempts to pass off non-authentic merchandise as that of the original designer, often by illegally using a designer's trademark. . . . Knockoffs are simply less expensive copies of a design, frequently made from more affordable fabric and materials."[7] If you are not paying attention, you might not notice that a Prada bag actually says "Prado" or that a pair of Gucci sunglasses actually says "Cucci." Both categories are illegal, but only one would be punishable by the federal state attorney.

Like the Bloomberg administration, the current de Blasio administration is not only focused on the fashion industry but on bootleg items generally. The term bootlegging—originally used to describe tall and loose-fitting cowboy boots where illicit goods could be hidden—was officially adopted into American English during the Prohibition-era 1920s. It was a term used to describe the manufacturing, distribution, or sale of illegal alcohol. Today, this term is used to describe the sale of all counterfeit or knockoff goods. Bootlegging has historically been a huge part of the fabric of New York City, but now there are multiple campaigns to stop it. The NYPD often boasts about successful raids on bootleg DVD producers, such as one man who was found with over 44,000 DVDs and CDs in his small Brooklyn apartment: a bust worth over $550,000 in counterfeit goods.[8] Normally, headlines with numbers like these are associated with drug busts.

Even the Motion Picture Association of America has gotten in the act with their "see-something/say-something"-style ads, which encourage people to use their "eyes and ears . . . to help stop street vendor piracy!" From fashion to electronics, the original companies are concerned about lost sale revenue, and local governments are concerned about lost tax revenue.

When I asked Daniel about these lost revenues, he believed it was "all bullshit. The city is just trying to get its cut now." Daniel believed that counterfeits and knockoffs actually help the industry, not hurt it. "What? If it wasn't for Canal Street, no one would even know who Louis Vuitton is. They would not be popular. That company should be thanking Canal Street for the boost in sales."

This certainly might be true, as many New Yorkers—and tourists alike—have developed a keen eye for knockoff goods and therefore go out of their way to purchase the authentic brand names. Blackman's article was skeptical of the antipiracy laws. She asked, "In a fashion-obsessed world, [is it] even possible to control an industry that thrives on imitation[?]"[9]

This inevitable drive toward imitation—coupled with the keen awareness of consumers who buy the goods—has driven the market to produce fewer knockoff goods and *more* counterfeit goods, resulting in an uptick of more clandestine salesmanship.

HUSTLING AND THE LAW

The administrative code of New York as it relates to vendors offers an intriguing insight into the world of street selling by hand, cart, and table in the city; since general vendors (food and merchandise) are required to have a license (which is all but impossible to obtain), the "hustle" grows out of these restrictive circumstances inherent in the law. But how these laws are enforced is somewhat of a mystery. Crackdowns on street vendors are cyclical and depend on many factors. One is geographic (finding blind spots in surveillance), and the other is police arrests since vendors must deal with undercover police officers—and confiscation of vendor merchandise poses a real and consistent problem.

There is a great deal of stress in this regard, and it is important in terms of understanding the spatial dynamics of vending in New York City and to a large degree why it gave rise to folks selling goods by hand. This aspect of street selling (as far as we know) has not been studied in any depth. Vendors are not allowed to set up tables or carts beyond a certain proximity to phone booths, newsstands, intersections, and entrances to businesses and subway stations. They must be a certain amount of feet from the curb and from the property line of a business. They cannot set up over grates. If the city actually enforced these many regulations, then at least 80 percent of vendors in prime locations would be eliminated—both those who have a license to sell goods as well as those who do not. This means the law is enforced informally, sporadically, and selectively, and when it is enforced to the letter of the law it generally means business owners have complained to both the police and politicians.

The rise of Business Improvement Districts (BIDS) in New York and their political clout forced vendors to move off sidewalks, vendors such as the Senegalese whisperers, mobile vendors who also sell in prime locations along Fifth and Madison Avenues. Maneuvers by the police forced these African sellers to develop a street strategy of movement, and they became hypermobile salespeople. This trend began to evolve as far back as the 1980s. The anthropologist Paul Stoller argues in his book *Money Has No Smell: The Africanization of New York City* that the first Senegalese came to New York as street vendors in 1982 trying to sell their wares in midtown Manhattan.[10] They originally applied for and received vendor licenses but because of heavy fines decided to join the underground economy and stopped paying taxes to the city. The whisperers follow and adapt to migratory patterns in the city, keeping from the spots where police surveillance is currently at its strongest.

Though not seen as con men, the Senegalese whisperers adopt the "hit-and-move" style similar to the three-card monte hustlers. They sell merchandise from bags (not carts or tables) and set up their area with easy and quick escape routes in mind. This strategy is used in Europe as well. In Barcelona, Spain, and Florence, Italy, the same strategy is employed: a canvas pallet displaying the material is easily wrapped up and made portable if police arrive. You might even say the three-card monte players are the forerunners of the whisperers and that the whisperer status is part of a natural evolution of being underground by going above ground, so to speak.

The application of these counterfeit laws, untaxed good laws, and the city's administrative code (title 20, 465-20), which restricts the placement of vendors on city sidewalks, have reshaped streets where goods are sold all over New York, especially where there is a high concentration of minority residents.[11] As scholars, we believe it is important to understand this trend: we recognize that the city acknowledges its illegal street vending but makes sure to get its cut of the profits through fines and taxes.

A person like Lee (whom we met in chapter 5), who sells bottled water from a fixed location in Brooklyn, has to be "on the run" standing still. He is, as Alibi noted in his reference to drug addicts who shoot heroin and cocaine together, "running fast slow." Lee argues how he has a spot (informally considered his proprietary space to sell goods), but, if the police roll up on him and say: "Hey, by law you are not allowed to sell here," what is his counterargument? What does he do? In a matter of seconds, his lucrative selling spot—and his livelihood—is gone.

Still, people like Lee and Otis (who sells DVDs and is known in the community) are hustlers, but, hustling is entrepreneurial at the root. The example of the "nutcracker" (liquor and juice) provides insight into liquor sales generally. In formal establishments, for example, how do we actually know what we are drinking—which is to say: who guarantees the composition of what we are drinking? It seems that everyone is trying to make more money by "watering down" the product. The law attempts to chase away illegal vendors, but it often chases them into deeper layers of the same illegal activities.

A STROLL ALONG CANAL

I (Trevor Milton) decided to walk Canal Street from end to end as a tourist on a fall afternoon to witness with my own eyes what Daniel has told me about—even though Daniel had warned me that most storefronts had been "taken over by Indian guys selling souvenirs." This rang true; most of the outdoor racks were dominated by postcards, "I ❤ NY" pins, and cheap t-shirts depicting New York landmarks. Brand names had all but disappeared, replaced by unrecognizable flashing toys made in China and gaudy jewelry. This is not to say that the counterfeit industry has disappeared; it has only moved backstage.

As I walked the street, African men drinking beer from plastic cups—who appeared to be transient and seemed as if they might have been sleeping on the streets—began to whisper as I passed, "Louis Vuitton. Prada. Rolex. Burberry." The black trash bags, which I originally thought carried their possessions, turned out to be full of counterfeit merchandise.

I approached one man out of curiosity. "Let me see what you got." He opened a trash bag full of lady's handbags and began his sales pitch. "I got Coach, Prada, Marc Jacobs, all for a good price. Thirty a piece. I got the best price!" Other men started to descend as I shrugged my shoulders: "That's nice. Thank you."

I continued down the street and stopped at a jewelry store. The jumbled display of silver and gold in the window was overwhelming. At times I couldn't tell where one item ended and another began. I stepped inside to see what most customers were shopping for when I was approached by one of the workers. "How are you doing, sir. Can I help you find something?"

I continued to stare at the floor-to-ceiling racks. "Nope, just looking."

He glanced down at my empty wrists. "You need a watch? I got the best watches." He put his hand on my shoulder and led me to a glass display case. Sliding it open, he continued, "I have Fossil, Michael Kors, Swiss, all of the popular brands."

I smiled and decided to entertain his pitch a moment longer. "Okay, but is this the best you have? Where are the good watches?" I knew little to nothing about luxury watches, but I suspected he had a more exclusive collection.

He glanced out to the sidewalk for a second, then removed a key from his pocket and opened a small metal drawer below the glass case. He pulled out a small, hard-plastic box with about twelve watches resting on a blue velvet cloth. He gently picked up a couple of them. "This is where I keep my Bulovas, Versace, and Rolexes." He held one up. "Check out this Bulova. Very popular. This thing goes for seven hundred retail, but I can sell it to you for seventy."

I felt the slam coming. I elected to skip a few steps. "A 90 percent discount. How can you afford that?"

He furrowed his brow and smirked, also electing to skip several steps in the slam process. "Because it's a knockoff!"

I laughed.

He continued, "You know what you're here for."

Before I let it go any further, I initiated my exit. "Well, maybe not now. I might come back later."

He immediately put the watches back in the box and locked them back into the metal drawer. Before I could leave he handed me a card. "Come back anytime, or call me. I'll deliver jewelry to your home." He flashed a quick smile and moved on to his other customers. The name on the card was Amin (Arabic for "truthful" or "trustworthy"). He promised "custom jewelry and cell phone accessories."

I learned generally how the game had changed since the early 2000s, but the hustlers and con artists on Canal Street had not been eliminated; they had simply adapted. They had evolved. With every push to rid the city of counterfeit goods, the counterfeiters simply moved around to evade the watching eye. Players like Daniel and Amin could continue to slam people; they just had to change their technique.

SEVEN

THE NUMBERS GAME

If I ain't telling you the truth, a pig's pussy ain't pork.
—Alibi

Nellie McKay, a scholar and critic of African American literature, wrote of the numbers game and the promise it holds for
many black Americans:

How, we may ask, can a people in this neighborhood, who often evidence a remarkable astute political understanding of the difficulties
facing them and all blacks in white America, still maintain such an
implicit faith in the fantasy of individual and communal economic
revitalization through the numbers? The sheer futility of this collective dream belies the internal strength and sophistication of a people
who survived American slavery and beyond. On another level the numbers game, as metaphor of this particular human situation, constantly
reminds us of how tenuous the wellbeing of black American life has
always been, and to the extent to which the oppression of race, class

and gender influences the aspirations, hopes, and expectations of this entire group of people.[1]

Policy (lottery) is big business in the ghetto. In *Black Metropolis*, a panoramic view of black Chicago community life in the mid-1940s, the sociologists St. Clair Drake and Horace Cayton portray a typical "policy station":

> The station is located in the basement at . . . an apartment building. On entering the station, you notice, to the right, a pressing shop. Along the walls are three trough-like racks with signs reading A.M., P.M., M.N. These are the receptacles for the drawings for morning, afternoon and midnight. These troughs have a section for every wheel for which the station writes. There are small blackboards on each side of the wall where lucky or hot numbers are placed. Each week, or two or three days, as the case may be, advertisements of all the important wheels are placed in a conspicuous place. On a table is a large scrapbook with drawing pasted in for months past. These drawings are for reference and are often used by patrons to determine their daily plays. In the rear end of the station behind a barred cage resembling a teller's window, the writers are stationed. A tailor's sign camouflages the entire station—the only sign in evidence on the outside of the building.[2]

The "bancas" policy, or numbers racket, is as important and relevant to many immigrants today as it was almost four decades ago when Drake and Cayton wrote that description, and for the same reasons; many new arrivals cannot get jobs in the formal economy because of a lack of documentation, education, or qualifications. Many people in the black and Latino communities view the numbers game as one of the few ways to escape poverty; they have seen neighbors open businesses or buy cars and homes with money made from a "hit." Many argue the state lottery is nothing more than a state-controlled numbers game, and many believe it was instituted to compete with, challenge, and eventually replace the numbers racket.

THE NUMBERS OPERATION

Harlem's numbers operation has been an institution in the community since the 1920s. Once controlled by Italians, blacks, and Jews—though originally the brainchild of Casper Holstein, an African from St. Croix, who, while working as a janitor at a Wall Street brokerage house, came up with the idea for a "numbers game"—it has been taken over these days by blacks, Puerto Ricans, Cubans, and Dominicans. It is still one of the revenue sources for organized crime. Today, the numbers game is headed by "Spanish" Ramon Marquez, a New Yorker of Puerto Rican descent. "Spanish Ramon," in turn got his start from his father's bodega, which had a "Number's Hole" connected to it. He later made the acquaintance of the Pleasant Avenue mob boss Anthony "Fat Tony" Salerno, the underboss of the Genovese crime family, to whom he paid money in order to maintain his racket.

The business is carried on by a host of immigrants, old-timers, and young turks. In the Dominican Republic, numbers is very popular among the socially and economically marginalized.

Alibi explained how it works.

Field Note Entry: December 1

I mentioned to Alibi that I had met the writer Louise Meriwether at a party years ago and asked about her book *Daddy Was a Number Runner*, and she said it was all true. A tall, lanky woman with a warm smile, she told me, "My daddy was a numbers runner, and he used to tell us stories about the daily business. I wrote the book because my life was impacted by what my father did and how I grew up as a girl in the neighborhood."

Alibi told me he never met Meriwether but knew about her social activism. "I read that book back in the day and loved it, though it wasn't fiction to me but real life. Of course there was a lotta things that wasn't in that book about the numbers though, like shipping numbers, which is for regular bettors if they hit [guess the correct numbers], they take it to the spot [the location where players are paid]. Also a lot of guys can be runners, but not many get to be bankers, in part because bankers are usually tied to the mob."

The numbers are arranged from 000 to 999 and pay thousand-to-one odds. "The payoff is divided between the banker and the player. The banker takes 400 off the top and only pays out 600 to one, sometimes 500 to one. In certain instances some numbers are 'cut' to pay out 300 to one or 400 to one. One cut number, 796, comes out with regularity and is called the 'dead number' because it is the number listed for death in the family in the dream book."

The dream book is a compendium of everyday events and items—such as birthdays, colors, horses, cars—that are assigned numbers. If any of these items appear in the bettor's dreams, they are told to play that number, as it will bring them luck. The use of dreams to find a winning number is very common, and there are many resources available to interpret dreams, including specific people who are experts in dream interpretation, a series of dream books, and even consultations via phone available in English and Spanish. Among Latin American and Caribbean immigrants, the practice of reading the numbers behind the dreams is very common.

Writers, Runners, and Bankers

"The reason they are called runners," Alibi explained, "is because they do a lot of running around picking up numbers and cash from customers or bettors and do most of the footwork in the business. They travel the neighborhood and note down the numbers that people want to play. Runners have a 'book' of players they take numbers from every day. Depending on the size of their book (number of players), their take can be anywhere from four hundred to a thousand dollars a day."

As a runner, Alibi made about five hundred dollars a day, depending on the book. Since more people lose than win when they play, the profit is then split and given to the bank. The bankers are people who receive the daily receipts and pay out to the runners the money made by the players who hit the parimutuel number—based on the day's earnings at the New York, Philadelphia, or Florida racetracks. The parimutuel number is based on a system of betting on races whereby the winners divide the total amount bet, after deducting management expenses, in proportion to the sum they have wagered individually. This type of wagering is often referred to as "betting among ourselves."

Alibi pointed out that numbers operations still make lots of money on any given day. "The average is eight thousand to twenty-five thousand a day in business. Then sometimes the bank pulls in between five to seven grand a day and depending on a lot of factors. But there are others in this business that include writers in the spot, then you have the controllers. These individuals are the runners' bosses. They take the runners' receipts and deliver them to the banker. They usually make about a thousand a day. After the controllers, I guess you have the lookouts—no, I'm sorry, you have the writers."

The controllers/bankers are at the highest level in the policy operation; they get paid the most. They bankroll the operation and pay out to those who win. "Writers in the spot" are midlevel employees; they write numbers as customers come to the "number hole"—the location where bets are placed (barber shops, bars, restaurants, newspaper stands, and basements). Lookouts are at a lower level and are lower-paid employees. They are the young men who watch for police or other law-enforcement personnel in the street.

The "writers in the spot" take numbers from players who walk in to play rather than giving their number to a runner. They may or may not have a book, but they make about a "deuce and a quarter" ($250) a week. Some spot writers make a great deal more by keeping their own private book.

Alibi explained the lookout men: "These guys are the ones who look out for any trouble, robbers, street gangsters stupid enough to rob a spot, but also rough cops. I tend to think these boys are very street smart and valued for their ability to spot a cop in various disguises.

They make between $250 and three hundred a week. And then you got the pickup men, who are called that because, first of all they are all men and because I have never seen a woman do pickups, but they are like runners except they take the daily receipts from the spots and deliver them to the controllers. You might say they are a different type of runner. They rarely receive more than three hundred a week plus tips. Now the last on the totem pole are the office workers, who make about the same amount. And all I've seen doing this kind of work are women. And just like I never seen a woman as a pickup man in all the time I did this, I have never seen a man as a office worker or secretary. They are always broads, girlfriends, or friends of girlfriends who do the bookkeeping in the spots and make about $250 a week.

"As a runner I made my share of money, but I heard stories and saw stuff that was worth it just to be part of the scene. I remember seeing a guy staggering out of a spot one day bleeding like a pig. It turned out later he had hit for seventy grand, and the banker killed him and ran off with the money. Out of a thousand runners maybe, five would split with the cash, but I never heard of a banker doing that, in part because of what I told you before: it's the mob, and you can't run away from the mob. The mob guy back then, and maybe even now, is Spanish Ramon, who was given the power some say from Fat Tony, but the truth is Ramon's dad ran a spot and he (Ramon) was a runner who was very smart with the numbers and knew how to do business. He paid people on time. He paid people quick, and that got him a great rep because a lotta time a motherfucker would beat you and not pay you when you hit for a lotta money; that's why single action [betting on a single digit to win, rather than a combination of three] became so popular.

"You see the dude who was killed played with one banker, and people learned not to do that. And that's one of the reasons people play with different runners when they have large bets to place because bankers would tell people they got busted and so they stand a better chance of getting paid, and, plus, they don't get bumped off like that guy did with the seventy grand.

"We had cops 'on the pad,' or the 'nut,' as it was called back then, and they would come in and get two bucks a day from maybe twenty spots and take the money back to headquarters, for the division, the precinct, you know. The sector cars would get eight to ten bucks a day. Now you say, 'why pay these guys?' Well, they would let us know when the detectives would be coming to raid the spot by turning on their sirens in the block right before a raid would take place.

"But what you gotta understand is number running is a time-consuming business; you out there from around seven in the morning until five in the afternoon, seven days a week. But I got tired of it and started a con called 'phony preachers' where I'd mail out backdated numbers that had just hit. I got the addresses of people who played the numbers with me and a mailing list from the church where my woman was a member. She had no idea what I was doing.

"At first I'd ask the person to send the 'preacher' a few dollars when they hit, and I would send them six numbers. If someone hit a number I would send them a list of these winners and ask the person to bring me twenty dollars and nineteen cents. The nineteen cents was just to add mystery to it, because I knew most folks were superstitious. This was after I found a little storefront and set up shop there as a kinda jack-leg preacher. They knew I wasn't ordained as a minister, but since people was hitting these numbers people flocked to the front.

"I would give people candles and tell them to burn it on such-and-such a night and wait for the number to appear in the smoke when they put it out and people would swear they saw the number three or six or whatever. I would tell people to take a piece of crayon and draw a circle on the floor and if they had a problem with arthritis step into the circle and when they step out they will be cured.

"The amount I would charge for that was eight dollars, and that amount, the number eight they gave me, should be played the next day. These people were told to wear the Seal of Moses, which is basically a talisman people carry for luck, protection, to ward off evil spirits, and it's also called the Seals of Solomon from the sixth and seventh Book of Moses and is worn over their shoes, and I told them if they were having problems with husband or wives and/or if they had broken up, how they could get back together was by hitting the number, and I would tell them how to hit and what numbers to play. The funny thing is many of them did hit, and I had absolutely nothing to do with it. But they thought I did."

Just as the policeman, the fireman, the sanitation worker, or the shopkeeper rise early to get to their jobs, so does the con artist, the hustler, and the worker in the off-the-books underground economy. The following case is atypical of the people who run policy operations, and in this account a more detailed view is presented of how a Spanish numbers racket is run by a woman in what are called night numbers or *bolito*, at a location called the *banca*.

Maria: The Numbers Collector

Maria is a forty-five-year-old woman with a charming smile but a no-nonsense attitude; she's all business when she needs to be and quite personal and social when she has to be.[3] She has a handsome face with freckles around her nose and speaks with a low but firm feminine voice. Her attire is casual, not expensive looking, and although her dresses and pants are colorful, they are not provocative or seductive. The bettors and the people she works with respect her acumen and knowledge about the numbers, and they like the way she handles customer complaints and problems when they arise. She takes her job seriously as a collector, which is a person in charge of opening the banca, receiving the bets, passing the information to the owner of the banca, and paying off customers who "hit" or win by guessing the right numbers.

My first visit to Maria's banca was around eleven in the morning on a hot Monday in June. The banca is in a predominantly black neighborhood in Brooklyn with a small number of Latinos, all of whom are low-income citizens. I met her in her apartment, and then we walked to the banca, which is located in a three-story building. On our way, I asked her tell me the story of how she began this kind of work.

"During my first day in New York I could not find any job in the factories. Besides, I was a little lazy, and I did not like to wake up early." She smiled widely after using the word lazy to describe herself. "Next to my apartment there was a bodega that belonged to a man named Helito. They sold numbers there, and I saw how he earned his living so easily, just sitting and writing numbers, and so I said to myself, 'aquí es que voy' [that is my job]." She laughed. "Now, this Helito taught me how to sell numbers, and my opportunity arrived when his brother-in-law was leaving for vacation.

"I took the brother-in-law's place until his return. So I started learning the business until he got back. Around that same time a man who owned a bodega just five blocks from my home said he was looking for someone to sell numbers, and I told him I knew how to sell numbers, but that was false, I only knew a little bit. I began to work from the bodega, but it wasn't long after that the police took me to jail. When I got out of jail we moved to another place and opened a botanica [a store where people who practice Santeria and Catholic rituals buy religious objects, candles, and the like], and after that location we came to this place right here."

The personnel involved in the day-to-day operations of the banca were controllers, collectors, the banker, and pickups. The other subjects involved in a bank—besides the countless bettors—are persons located in a central office who receive the information from the collector of several bancas; the banker, who is the owner of the business; and the pickups, who take money from the collector to the banker or vice versa.[4]

As a collector, Maria is the face of the banca. It is not a job that requires high educational credentials, just relatively simple skills such as knowing how to write and doing basic arithmetic, sums, and multiplication. However, as the face of the business and as the person who receives the bets, the collector should have the ability to deal with different kinds of people and use those social skills and charisma to make people want to play the numbers at her location. In other words, both the owner and customers should have confidence in her abilities.

A Day in the Life of the Collector

Maria opened the door of the banca with a key and entered a small receiving area. From there we climbed a narrow staircase and stood in front of an apartment door. The guard stationed behind it unlocked and opened it for us. The statistics regarding the number of night number locations in New York City vary, but as many as 4,300 known spots have been suggested, all of which operate openly and with the sole purpose of serving numbers bettors. However, not all collectors have an apartment dedicated solely for this purpose. Other common fixed covered spots where numbers can be purchased are newspaper stands, candy stores, bars, hallways, basements, and street corners.

Jose, a short, balding Brooklynite in his fifties who worked as a collector, said, "Look, it is very rare to find one of those small commercial businesses [bodegas, restaurants, botanicas] that does not deal with numbers gambling. But not all collectors work in a fixed spot. Many of them are on a corner, waiting for people calling the bank from the public telephone. If you want we can visit some who work around here." In areas of dense working populations some collectors cover various routes during the day, collecting money and wagering information from a variety of locations. These collectors might also be serving in an office or a factory while they are selling the numbers.

We entered a small, three-room, air-conditioned apartment. The first room was furnished like a living room, with a table, couches, and a television set. Next to this room was a restroom. The second room used to be a kitchen and still retained a sink and fridge. Next to the fridge were three betting machines. The last room led to Maria's center of operations, which also had an air conditioner. The door to this room was half made of transparent glass, through which Maria received the bets, and the lower half was iron. Inside the room were five monitors that showed images of the street, the building's front door, the stairs, the apartment's front door, and the living room.

In the room were also several other devices: a telephone, a television to watch the lottery and for distraction when there were no customers, an electric stove where Maria sometimes cooked food, a hair dryer, an exercise device, and a bed chair. All this was used by Maria to take advantage of what she called "dead time."

Kneeling as she entered the gambling room, Maria started talking and getting information from another woman inside the room, Sandra. Sandra was a collector who took the first shift of the day, from nine to noon. Like Maria, she was a Dominican immigrant looking for a better future in New York. I stayed silent, looking around, while Maria talked with Sandra. As soon as Sandra left, Maria invited me to enter the little room and explained to me what she was doing.

"As soon as I arrive, I sum up all of what Sandra sold, count the money, check if everything is okay. When Sandra leaves, I take some sheets and take records of our sales, you know, just in case something happens. I like to have all my stuff clear." Then she asked me what more I wanted to know. I asked her to do what she normally does and let me watch her do it.

The Bettors

"Look! This is one of my clients," Maria said, pointing at a video screen that showed the street in front of the building. The cameras picked up people from the moment they entered and followed them up the stairs until they reached the apartment.

"But he is using a key to open the first door?" I said.

"Yes, I give a key to each one of my customers. With this key they can open the first door and enter the lobby. During the year I change this key, when some of the customers do not come anymore or when the police are getting too near to the place."

When the man was in the lobby, Maria pushed a button and he opened the next door. He walked into the building. From the screens, I could follow his movement as he climbed the stairs and arrived at the apartment where the banca is located. Once in front of the apartment, Maria pushed another button, the door opened, and he entered.

Security is an important aspect of the bancas because as an illegal business they cannot operate publicly, even though many citizens know of their existence, including the police.

The security is not only in place because of the police, however; another no less important reason was the threat of holdups. Maria has not been held up, unlike other bancas in the community. The fact that each customer has a key to the building signals a trustful link between her customers and the bank. All the bettors know Maria's name, and some of them like to converse with her when they come to gamble. The conversation is fluent if Maria allows it to continue; if she does not, she shortens her responses to "yes" and "no." She knows all her bettors by name and in most cases invents nicknames for them. I discovered this relationship between her and her bettors increased on the weekend. Looking for water in the refrigerator, I asked her, "What do you do with all the chicken you have packed in the fridge?"

"Oh! You know, every weekend the banker sends lunch and alcohol for the bettors. With this he encourages them to increase the amount of money they gamble. Sometime I also celebrate birthdays with some of them, but only those who give me good tips when they win."

On Saturdays and Sundays the bettors have a good time in the banca, playing cards and dominoes while waiting for the results of their bets to come in. The banca is transformed at this time into a secret and collective space for those who like to gamble but who cannot afford more expensive places. Maria's customers are low-level workers, factory workers, and a lot of retirees and seniors on welfare. Another collector from Brooklyn said to me, "A lot of those people do not have many things to do; their only entertainment is to gamble some numbers that make them happy."

I kept watching the first bettor when he went to the living room, thanks to the video camera and the monitor from which Maria watches everything that takes place around the banca. He sat down and took some papers from the table and began to read them and write numbers on the little piece of paper Maria gave to him.

"What are those pages that he is reading?" I asked.

"Ah! They check those pages in order to choose the number to which they are going to gamble on." Everyday Maria buys colored pages that appear daily and provide tips to the bettor. These pages contain the daily, monthly, and annual lottery reports, interpret dreams, analyze the horoscope, and advertise services like dream interpretations.

People choose their numbers in a dizzying variety of ways. The numbers can be related to a house number, car tags, a birthday, a social security number, personal ID, the interpretation of a dream, or the first number seen when the person wakes in the morning.

One bettor, whom Maria nicknamed Pájarito (Birdy), approached the collector's window and asked Maria the number of the building. She told him, "four, zero, two, five," and the bettor wrote that number down before giving to Maria several pieces of paper covered in numbers. These small papers are the betting slips in which the bettor prints the abbreviated name of the number game he is playing. Then he writes two columns of numbers; the first column contains the numbers he's betting on, and the second column designates the amount of money to

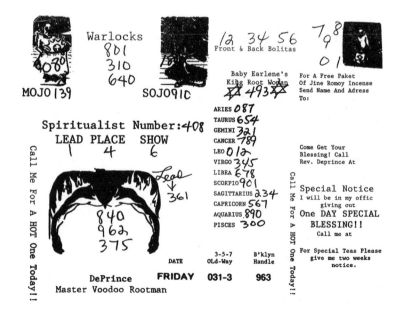

be gambled on each number. Maria takes the betting slips, each one of which has a yellow carbon paper behind it, then she sums and writes the amount of money wagered on each of the papers. She then signs and seals them with the logo of the banca and the date. Maria gives the copy to the bettor and keeps the original.

There is another way people bet: Some bettors call to wager their number by credit. Maria takes their calls, records the information on a betting slip, then places them in an envelope where she puts all the credit bets. These credit bettors come to pay later. If they get a winning number, they usually come the same day; if not, they may come the following day. But if they want to make more bets, they come later in the day.

The Winning Numbers

In Maria's banca a large blackboard next to the collector's window displays the different number games and lists the winning numbers of the last seven days. Some of the number games used the numbers drawn in the daily lotteries held in some states: Mid Day (MD) and State (ST, also called Venezuela), both of which use the numbers from the midday and evening lottery of New York, New Jersey (NJ), and Connecticut (CN). The other numbers games derive their winning numbers from designated horse and harness (chariot) races. These number games are called New York (NY), Brooklyn (BR), 357, and TH. The banca takes the numbers from the lotteries directly. However, the mechanism to compute NY, BR, 357, and TH is complicated. Maria became upset and lost patience with me on more than one occasion because I just could not understand all of what she was trying to explain to me. When she got upset, she would shake her head and fall silent for a minute or two; I would just sit and write things down or walk over to the fridge and wait until she wanted to talk again.

I should point out the method to compute those numbers is closely guarded, although Maria knew how to do it. Before the result of the winning number arrived from the controller, she had already computed it. She did it in secret because otherwise the banker might suspect she was colluding with the collector. It seemed that knowing this information, the collector could manage the bets independently.

Pointing at the TV screen (which was tuned to the off-track-betting channel), she taught me how to compute NY's wining number. "Look!" she told me excitedly. "The race ended, and now they are showing the result of the first race."

"What are those numbers?"

"I do not know, but we sum them, and that gives us a number."

She immediately summed up the numbers, which are the different payoff schedules of the horses that arrive in first, second, and third place. The result for this particular race was 22.80.

"And now what?" I asked.

"Well, we have to wait until the end of the second and third race to sum the three totals, and that gives us the first pulito of New York." Each digit of a centena is called single, or pulito.

"Wait! Wait! What is that?" I asked, impatient and confused.

"Forget it, let's wait until the end of the second and third race and I will explain you."

Half an hour later the third race was over. We summed the three totals (22.80 + 34.50 + 34.30), yielding the number 91.60. "You see one is the first number with which begins New York centena." I began to understand. "Ah! You take the digit before the period."

"Yes. And we will get the second number by adding the fourth and fifth race to this first total, and again take the number which is right before the period." At 3:30 p.m. the fifth race ended, and we were able to get the new digit. By adding both races (22.80 and 31.20) to the first total (91.60), we got our second number: 125.60. Maria continued, "Here you have five is the next number. Now, let's wait for the sixth and seventh race, and we will get the whole number." The sum of the sixth and seventh race gave us the number 188.40. Thus eight was the last digit. The winning number for NY that day was 158. With the eighth and ninth race we got another number to form what is called the fourth single of NY and the third bolita. (Bolitas are two-digit numbers.) This last number was four.

$R_1 + R_2 = R_3 = 91.60$	First single: 1
$R_4 + R_5 + 91.60 = 125.80$	Second single: 5; First bolita: 15
$R_6 + R_7 + 125.80 = 188.40$	Third single: 8; Second bolita: 58
$R_8 + R_9 = 188.40$	Fourth single: 4; Third bolita: 84

Here are numbers from the Belmont racetrack from July 21, 2003.

Race	Total
1st	22.8
2nd	34.5
3rd	34.3
4th	22.8
5th	31.2
6th	33.5
7th	29.3
8th	29.4
9th	56.7

I then asked how she computes BR.

Maria sighed. "I do not know how they do it. But that number appears every day in the *Daily News*." This number is derived from the total amount of money bet at the horse racetrack. The three last numbers of the amount of money bet (the track handle) is the BR winning number. "Track handle" refers to the total money wagered at the racetrack.

"People have a lot of confidence in this specific number because it appears in the *Daily News* every day, and if it does not, the bettors get their money back."

Maria then told me about another numbers game that people play at the banca: single, or pulito, and bolita. The winning number taken from the lottery or computed from the horse and harness races is called centena, because it has three digits. People gamble on those numbers too. For instance, there is the first single of NY, the second single of BR, and the third single of CN. If there are nine races in a track, there are four singles.

Bolitas are the two-digit numbers that result from the combination of the first digit with the second and the second with the third—and the third with the fourth in the case that there is a fourth single. For instance, in the winning number 1584, we have four singles of pulito (1, 5, 8, and 4) and three bolitas (15, 58, 84). The payoffs for the centena, single, and bolita are different. Per each dollar wagered the bettor gains $9 if it is single, $80 if it is bolita, and $700 if it is centena.

I observed that on the betting slip, the column indicating the amount of money bet was sometimes divided in two. Maria told me that there are two ways for betting on a centena and a bolita: straight and combo. When a number is betted as "straight," it is only read in one direction, but if it is "combo," it is read in both directions. For example, 53 straight is read as 53, but 53 combo is read as 53 and 35. A centena could have up to six combinations, as for instance 283: 283, 238, 328, 282, 823, and 832. The "combo" increases the probability of winning. That is why when people make bets on a number, they generally wager on both straight and combo. With a 20-cent

SINGLE ACTION CHART

	Front Days Out	Middle Days Out	Back Days
1 Has Not Hit	15	20	10
2 Has Not Hit	18	09	15
3 Has Not Hit	09	11	25
4 Has Not Hit	10	00	00
5 Has Not Hit	06	07	04
6 Has Not Hit	00	02	01
7 Has Not Hit	01	01	17
8 Has Not Hit	05	06	02
9 Has Not Hit	07	05	06
0 Has Not Hit	03	22	21

Best Front Bolitas	Back Bolitas
23, 12, 31, 40	17, 24, 00, 33

IF THE

SHOE FITS

582

PLAY IT !!!

583

108

369

745

BIG BLUE'S Nite Lite

NIGHTLY NUMBERS MON. THRU SAT.   60¢

NO. 2,409   FRIDAY JUNE 20, 2003

LET THE NITE LITE SHINE ON YOU

019 565 964
192 638 367

LAST NIGHTS RESULTS
3-5-7   YORKERS 644
HANDLE UNAVAILABLE
06/18/03 HANDLE 593
NYDAILY 475 WIN 4 7402

SIX NIGHT REPORT

	NIGHT 3-5-7	NIGHT HANDLE	NY LOTTERY	
MON	325	764	487	NITE LITE HITS
TUE	349	667	671	
WED	956	244	722	
THU	589	450	627	
FRI	896	979	852	
SAT	775	650	366	

24 HOUR HOT LINE
FOR DELIVERY CALL

straight bet the bettor could win $140 (one-fifth of $700), and with 30 cents they wager 5 cents on each combination, possibly winning $4 (one-twentieth of $80). The bettors also increase the probability to win by wagering on singles (remember that for each dollar bet on a single they get $9).

At first glance it seems easy to win at least a dollar if I bet on a single number. And I could wager a dollar on eight single numbers and certainly win a dollar. But Maria told me that it is not as easy as it sounds, plus people don't usually bet to win just a dollar. All these myriad possibilities of making bets at a low price makes this kind of gambling very popular among low-income residents. One man commenting on the lottery said this: "People try to get these millions, but I don't play the lottery. I don't think the lottery exists. I don't really believe people in fact ever win in it. I've been around for a long time, and I know of no one who has won millions of dollars from it. It's a perfect con. The banca is cheaper, and you can, and do, win all the time."

Time to Go Home

At five o'clock, when the winning number of NY appeared, Maria was ready to take a break for one hour, until the harness races started and people began to gamble for the 357 and TH number games. She went to her apartment to eat and rest a little. At six o'clock Maria was again in the banca, receiving visits and calls from the bettors who want to gamble mostly on 357 and TH. She also received calls from the main office five minutes before the end of each lottery or race. Throughout the day they called Maria to ask her to report what she had sold and to close the bets on the coming winning number. At 8:45 Maria was asked to give the last report, and her work was over. It was time to go home. That night on the way back to her apartment she told me, "I am tired of this boring work. Look! It is nine o'clock and now I have to prepare dinner. Here you can earn some money, but it is not worth it."

Maria's salary is $750 per week, but she gives $150 to the woman who takes care of the morning shift. In addition to her salary, she receives tips from bettors who win. However, she has to work every day, and there is no compensation for her work other than her salary: no vacation, no social security, no pension, etc. Besides, because of this job and her family problems, she had become a compulsive gambler.

The Gambling Blues

After several days of observation, I decided to interview Maria in a more formal setting, and I asked her if I could tape the interview. She felt this might be dangerous. Sometimes tape recording makes people suspicious because they fear the tape could be used as evidence to prove their guilt in a court of law. I explained to her that what I was doing was strictly confidential and that the taping would be extremely helpful in my ability to get all of what she said; if I tried to write it all down, I would never be able to do it accurately. She finally relented and allowed me to turn on the tape recorder.

I revisited the conversation about her decision to leave the banca. She was taking some courses to get a home-attendant license, so I asked her the reason for this change of heart. She responded: "I want to leave from here because here there is not any benefit. If you get sick you have to pay the day, if you have to solve some personal problems, you have to pay the day. These people think that you do not have the right to take a bath, clean your head, and go to a doctor. They want you to work for them long hours with the same salary. The banker wanted me to work from 9 a.m. to 9 p.m., but when I stopped working and I left the banca, it dropped the gains. So they called me again, and I came with the only requirement of having another collector to assist me. I have to go to the doctor. I am a woman who has to take care of her children, when I had them. My children left to school in the morning, and I did not see them because I was still sleeping, and when I get home at night they were already sleeping. So that is what my life was just like that. I need more money to pay my bills. Why does one want to make money to pay bills and have no time for her children and cannot tell them: let's have lunch together?

"Then it is not worth it. It is better to take care of the seniors, there you have benefits, because you fill your income tax, have social security, they give you Medicare service, and one has vacations. If they fire you and you already have six month working for them, you have right to collect. All of those are benefits. Here, this is an illegal business, it does not give you any benefit."

I asked, "But what have you got for the last nine years working for them?"

Maria shrugged. "Not much because sometimes I think I am stupid and I only think about the five-hundred-dollar salary. And I have been mother, father, and husband at the same time, for I have to take care of the children and my husband, and I never thought about me. I was thinking about the others, all the time. But now, I am thinking about me. I am getting old, I have to find something with which tomorrow I could help myself." She repeated, "I was always thinking about the others, and never about me. I thought that I was a machine for making money for the others. I also want to leave this job because I am gambling too much. You know, that is why I am taking therapy. I am talking to my psychologist once a week. Tomorrow at 9 a.m., I have appointment with my psychologist. I begin to visit her because I was a little nervous, but now I am bringing this problem to the table. But she only says to me 'you have to stop gambling, if not you are going to lose your house, and you will stay on the street.' That is the only advice that I receive from her. She has to give a solution, don't you think?"

Maria shared with me how she bet everyday—sometimes even more than her own salary—and felt that if she changed jobs she would not only have some benefits but some psychological relief too—and financial relief—because she would not be gambling so much. But for the time being she continued to gamble. Now that her kids were no longer at home and she did not have to care for them like she used to, she justified her compulsive gambling habit. "I know that it is bad to wager the whole salary," she told me, "but I am the one who is making the money in my family and instead of solving someone else's problem, I bet and wager. I am gambling more since I said that I won't give my money to my husband anymore because all he does is spend it and it's not on me that he does that. Instead, I am giving my money to the banker, but with the hope of winning one day. When I give money to my husband, I have no hope, it is like if I throw the money into the toilet."

When I asked Maria about the illegality of the numbers business, she explained how, though it is illegal, it is perhaps one of the few places where undocumented immigrants can earn a decent living. "This is a source of employment for many people that do not have any other possibility because of their lack of documents. The bancas do not ask for documents, they do not have any requirement. If they are legalized, they will ask for some requirements. They will need documents, and people have to be resident or citizen and have social security to get that. The majority of people who work here are illegal immigrants; they do not have documents. Almost all the women that I know who work in bancas do not have any documents. They arrived by illegal means, and they have not tried to solve their legal situation because they are making money. Maybe if they were working in a factory or if they have stayed unemployed, they would solve that situation. I can frankly tell you that from one side the bancas are good because they are a source of employment and one earns well, but in the other side one have no time to do anything."

A DREAM DEFERRED

Maria's story helps us understand that the banca is more than an illegal activity and a kind of organized crime. When one bettor was asked why he bets, he answered with a big smile, "I wager to leave this country. If I get something I leave this country. Do you know the problem that one suffers in this country? The hope of the poor is to get a winning number and solve all the problems or at least alleviate some of their problems. In any case, they [the United States] want all, they do not want to share. They say they want you to share in the American dream but they want it all for themselves."

The increase in number of bancas in New York is a manifestation of the recent economic crisis. In a society that cannot offer decent jobs and wages, the number of bancas increases. People look for alternatives in order to increase their income and survive. Maria explained, "Could you tell me how a person who works in a factory with six dollars per hour can live and raise a family in this city?" While working for a factory, Maria may earn no more than three hundred dollars a week; working for the banca she earns $550. It is clear that there are many people who gamble in the banca, people whose main and only objective is getting money. But pleasure is another reason, as Maria said. "People wager for pleasure. This is the only entertainment they have. There is an old man who gambles two dollars every day and wagers from ten to twenty cents on each number. He gambles for pleasure but not for money."

The banca is not only an employer but also a place of exploitation. Most of the benefits of the banca remain in the hand of the bankers; the employers earn their salary by working long shifts, without any fringe benefits. The only security enjoyed by the employers is that the bankers provide them with lawyers if they are caught by the police while doing their work. In addition to this exploitation, the probability of ending up as a compulsive gambler increases when one works in this kind of business.

This research has tried to broaden our understanding of one of the most common illegal—almost quasi-legal—activities in the city, one hidden in plain sight to most New Yorkers. The banca, a widespread business in the neighborhoods of New York, is one of our oldest illegal neighborhood institutions but one that has never been examined in any systematic way. It is part con, part hustle, part illegal, and part legal, but it also taps into that dream we all share of getting something for nothing and striking it big one day—sooner rather than later.

EIGHT

NEW YORK TENANT HUSTLES

We know the trouble and misery that landlords can cause New York-
ers. . . . But there are also plenty of bad tenants in New York City . . .
tenants who have caused serious misery for other tenants or house-
mates or building supers or the landlords who aren't slumlords.

— Elizabeth Dwoskin, *Village Voice*

New York City is a renter's town. Approximately 68 percent of New York's 3.2 million households are occupied by renting tenants, with 31 percent of rental units being rent stabilized.[1] Renting is a part of New York culture, so much so that many have fought for the rights of renters and voiced a growing discontent with New York landlords. This chapter focuses on New York City's laws governing tenant rights and their unintended consequences.

Renters in New York have taken years to shore up the right to be protected from the greed and guile of some of the city's landlords. This has also left the door open for tenants to take advantage of more honest landlords. Featured in this chapter is the story of Lorena (a pseudonym), a habitual hustler of landlords who has been living rent-free in New York City for more than twenty-five years. (Lorena is not the only con skilled in this art. A similar case in New Jersey involved a man named Mark Newton, nicknamed the "Teflon Tenant" because of his ability both to avoid being evicted and to force fed-up landlords to pay him to move out of their properties.)[2]

Starting in 2010, New York City's public advocate publishes a yearly list: "NYC's Worst Landlords." There were 6,712 buildings with violations listed in 2014, up drastically from 360 buildings in 2012 (the last previous year for which data was available).[3] The list included stories of owners cutting off electricity for months or leaving apartments rat infested for years. The "worst landlord" of 2014, Robin Shimoff, is the owner of 7,780 units in thirteen different buildings.

In a city with rental rates disproportionate to the national average, tenants have learned to band together in order to guarantee their basic living rights. This advocacy led to the creation of the New York Tenant Bill of Rights—last updated in 2008—to protect renters from the abuses of greedy landlords. Landlords are seen as the bad guys. No one has ever fought for the rights of landlords. There is no Landlord Bill of Rights. Tenants have all of the public-relations power in the struggle between owners and renters. And where there is an opportunity for the sympathetic struggling New Yorker to take advantage of the greedy feudal landlord, some are going to exploit it.

The criminologists Ronald Clarke and Donald Cornish claimed that crime and deviance are always preceded by opportunities made available by circumstance, neglect, and—most importantly—public policy. Accordingly, opportunities for crime "may tempt an otherwise law-abiding person into occasional transgressions. And the existence of easy opportunities in society might attract some people into a life of crime."[4] These authors argue that all persons are rational thinkers, so when an opportunity spontaneously opens a door to a criminal enterprise, the average person rationally walks through if they believe they won't be caught.

For example, if committing disability fraud only involved filling out a one-page online form in order to receive two thousand dollars a month, with no verification and no penalty, it would be rational to commit it. In the case of New York tenant rights, when tenants become aware of the loopholes in the laws, they certainly can find the rationale to take advantage.

LORENA: THE LANDLORD'S WORST NIGHTMARE

Lorena's modus operandi was to sign a lease, pay a couple of months rent, and then avoid paying any more by insisting on her rights as a tenant. After reporting code violations (such as unsafe living conditions, landlord harassment, and discrimination), tenants are immediately protected by the city until said violations are resolved. The city takes an average of twelve months to investigate these claims; tenants can live rent-free during the investigation. If a tenant plays his or her cards right, he or she can live rent-free for years, with full utilities, and sue the owner for civil damages without ever having to prove that their tenant rights had been violated.

I (Trevor Milton) sat down with Lorena's last landlord, Angelina. Lorena was a ghost and a legend that had since disappeared into the cityscape and therefore was unavailable for an interview. Angelina was a Human Services worker with a husband and two children. They lived in Long Island, but they owned a two-family house in the Bayside neighborhood of Queens. Angelina originally crossed paths with Lorena when Lorena was looking for a new place to stay.

Originally, there were no signs of trouble. Angelina put an ad on Craigslist, and Lorena promptly answered. She was the second to answer the ad, but Angelina had suspicions about the first respondent. "This girl came with this guy that was really familiar to me. And after we got talking, he said that 'we went to the Hamptons together. We hung out as kids.' And he kept saying, 'This is my brother's girlfriend. You know me. You should give her the apartment. I'm going to pay you six months in advance, cash. I don't want her on the lease.'" Angelina's suspicions overcame her. "You know, a little shady to me, right? So then I remembered, he didn't have a brother, he had a sister. So this is obviously his girlfriend and his kid. He has something to hide. So I said to my husband, 'We are going to have a wife behind this door. We are going to have problems.'"

Worried about the potential for an estranged wife chasing down her tenant, Angelina considered the unassuming couple that answered the ad a little later. "Now, this couple looks a little kooky, but they had no kids. This was a forty-eight-year-old woman of Puerto Rican descent and a thirty-six-year-old little Jewish man. So they were this mismatched couple. I mean, she looked like Rita Moreno! Her lipstick was really tacky, with big rhinestone earrings." Angelina smiled and laughed. "Kooky, but funny."

Shortly after their meeting, Lorena moved in with her boyfriend, Ezra, and they lived quietly in the apartment for two years. In 2010, Angelina began to notice some changes. "That woman was not the same woman that I saw at the beginning." She suspected that Lorena had begun engaging heavily in drug use, which eventually led to unemployment and the loss of her ability to pay rent. "What must have happened was that she must have been a drug addict, cleaned up her act, and was trying really hard to straighten out her life when she came to me. And as time went on, she went back to the drugs, and went back to her old ways. Because that is the only explanation for . . . in 2008 to 2010 she [Lorena] paid her rent every month!"

After December 15, 2010, the rent stopped. And eventually the upstairs tenant started to notice cockroaches. Angelina decided to inspect Lorena's first-floor unit. "I called her and told her it was no problem, that we just needed to get in there with the exterminator. Then she became adamant and accused me of saying she was dirty. I just told her that we just needed to take care of the situation and that I didn't know whether it was her or him who did it. But when I saw her, I noticed she looked different. I saw her declining."

From 2008 to 2010, Lorena worked full-time for a home-remodeling company. "And then the interactions that I was having with her started to get very short-tempered. She was slurring. By the time I came there to serve the thirty-day notice, she was falling down the stairs. She went from somebody who drank a Martini and smoked a joint to a heroin addict who couldn't even stand. And like, every time she came to [Housing] Court . . . she fell off the stand. *Fell off the stand*! Fell. Papers everywhere. She would be high in court. This is not the woman I rented to. The woman I rented to was kooky. This was a full-blown drug addict, slurring, falling! So, I think she did all of this, all of these years, met Ezra, and then whatever they did, they relapsed together, and she probably said, 'This is what I used to do. We don't have to pay rent.'"

The Con Begins

New York State Real Property Law §235b states: "Under the warranty of habitability, tenants have the right to a livable, safe and sanitary apartment."

At the beginning of 2011, Lorena began filing complaints with the New York Division of Housing and Community Renewal (DHCR), initially attacking Angelina for the roach infestation, which is considered a breach of the warranty of habitability. There is room for interpretation for what "habitability" means, but each complaint requires an investigation.

Lorena simultaneously began to file complaints with the New York City Department of Buildings, which enforces all of the city's building codes, electric codes, and zoning codes. For Angelina, the violations—such as "faulty wiring" or "loosened handrails"—began to build up; each required a day in court to prove false, and each violation came faster than it could be resolved. If the tenant's claims are ultimately proven to be false, then the landlord has the right to evict the tenant, but only for false accusations and not for any reason that can be interpreted as discriminatory. Executive Law §296(5), NYC Administrative Code §8-107 states: "Landlords may not refuse to rent to, renew the lease of, or otherwise discriminate against, any person or group of persons because of race, creed, color, national origin, sex, disability, age, marital status or familial status."

These false accusations had exasperated Angelina, and she initiated the eviction process, only to be met with more stalling tactics. "I had all of these violations. And they kept calling the inspectors to come in, and the violations are piling up, and if I don't fix the violations in a timely manner I have to pay civil penalties. So, I had violations and civil penalties piling up, while she's also renting the basement, but she's not allowed to be in the basement. There's a big heater in there. She's not allowed there." Angelina thought she had a solid case for eviction, as Lorena was renting the basement illegally, but Lorena had more tricks up her sleeve.

Real Property Actions and Proceedings Law (RPAPL) §711 states: "A tenant with a lease is protected from eviction during the lease period so long as the tenant does not violate any substantial provision of the lease or any local housing laws or codes." It was illegal for Lorena to rent the basement because of the heating equipment, and it would be a breach of her lease. Angelina explained, "She brought in her daughter and kids." But aware of the potential violation, Lorena preemptively complained to the Department of Buildings that Angelina was renting the basement illegally.

"So when the building inspector came she told him that a family was living downstairs. The inspector is so stupid not realizing that the kitchen door . . . there's no door there. If there was another family living in the basement, they would have access to her apartment. He never said, 'If there's another family, why do they have access to your kitchen and all of your possessions?' The inspector wasn't quick enough. He just took her word for it, that there's a family living in the basement."

In fact, Lorena's daughter and grandchildren were well accommodated. "She set up a little crib and a bed. And then they gave me a violation for renting the basement. And I'm showing them the lease, 'She's renting the basement. It's her! It's her!' They didn't care. We go to court. So I had to go to ECB [Environmental Control Board] court simultaneously with landlord/tenant court to tell them that this was a scam. She's doing this to get violations on the house, and she's renting the first floor and the basement."

Eventually, Angelina wised up and realized Lorena was too good at this hustle or con or scam not to have done it before, so began her own investigation to see if Lorena had any prior evictions. An eviction shows up on a person's credit report, and Angelina should have seen signs of it before she rented to Lorena. But if a tenant voluntarily vacates the premises up to twenty-four hours before the eviction date, it does not appear on the credit report. "So when you run someone's credit, you run the name, unless there was an actual eviction—where the marshal came and padlocked the door—there is no record. There's no record of the proceedings. The only way to get any kind of proceedings—which means they serve you with a thirty-day notice—is to go to [the Housing Court in] the actual borough and look it up."

There is no central New York City database for eviction proceedings. Angelina had to go to each of the five boroughs of New York City in order to sift through their individual files. "So I went to each of the boroughs to run her name after all of this started, to each of the borough's Housing Courts. So even if you went to Queens Housing and ran the name, the procedures from Brooklyn are not coming up." Angelina expressed some shock over the archaic system. "In this day and age, when you have a computer the size of a pinky nail, there's not one central database for eviction proceedings. Is that ridiculous or what?"

Angelina started to piece together a timeline not only to secure a clean eviction but also to generate a criminal case against Lorena. "So I went, because when I called the district attorney, he's saying, 'piece together this story for me.' And my attorney told me that there's not a central database, that I had to go to each borough. This I knew already."

Lorena also knew this, and she had manufactured multiple aliases. "One of her aliases was the real name that's on the [rent] check. She said that her nickname was different from the name on the check that she provided to me when she rented the apartment. Because it was a Spanish name, I thought it could have been. So it wasn't that farfetched that she had an English-sounding name because the name is very Spanish. When the district attorney cross-referenced all of the Social Security numbers, she had a Section 8 apartment in the Bronx that she was subletting. So she has an apartment in the Bronx that she is subletting while renting from me! There is a flaw in New York City that people are getting away with, so when I ran her name, a proceeding came up that happened in the 1990s. Then I went to the Bronx, back to 1985. She had twenty proceedings in the Bronx. I went to Brooklyn, same thing."

I asked for further clarification. "Do you mean that she went through eviction proceedings?"

Angelina became more animated. "Not evictions. She would leave before the eviction goes through. So when you run her credit: no eviction. But the eviction proceedings—which would tell you that this was happening—you would have to run their name in housing court." Angelina smacked the desk again. "Come on, you're not going to go to Brooklyn to run someone's name! You're not going to go to Bronx Housing to run someone's name! So this is how she gets away with it! There's no cross-reference of proceedings. So even though she's been in court a gazillion times since 1985, it's not located in one database. This is why she gets away with it. She went from Brooklyn, to Bronx, back to Brooklyn, to Queens, back to Brooklyn, to Queens. Since '85 she's been doing this."

With three decades of experience, Lorena had become a master of this con. File complaints, live rent-free for about a year during the investigations, move to another borough immediately before the eviction. She would put on a big show, then disappear backstage before curtains. Without any income, she could also apply for public housing, and then she could sublet that apartment for cash. I wondered out loud how Lorena had been getting away with subletting her other apartment. "She's not being chased by Housing and Urban Development? I mean, she has to go through them to get the Section 8."

Angelina laughed, "Section 8? That department's in a different name. We're not Section 8. So it's separate."

Section 8 is a voucher program designed to help low-income families pay rent. It is sponsored by the Federal Department of Housing and Urban Development (HUD) and managed in New York by the New York City Housing Authority (NYCHA). Eligible recipients of this program must pass an "income eligibility and asset test" to prove need. Once they qualify, they are only obligated to pay one-third of their rent total. Section 8 frauds—such as lying about one's assets or subletting the apartment—is equivalent to grand larceny theft and is punishable by up to ten years in prison.

Lorena had been walking the razor's edge by committing various acts of tenant fraud and Section 8 fraud but had figured out a system for avoiding detection. As explained by Angelina: "That apartment is under her name. So she's had that apartment, and she rents it out to people. So now the government is paying her, and she's collecting rent money. That's one issue. Simultaneously, she rents another apartment, and stays there for a little bit, she pays a little rent. She has two scams. One of them is: she 'can't afford to pay rent anymore,' another that she's 'mentally ill.' And this is all through my research of looking through the court documentation. So she went to Long Island Jewish [Medical Center] and got a doctor to say that 'she's mentally ill, she's applying for Section 8, and she can't pay rent anymore.' That procedure takes months and months and months, probably sometimes years. So while she's saying, 'I'm trying to get a Section 8 voucher. I'm on welfare right now. I lost my job. I can't pay you rent.' That's a stalling tactic. Then the landlord would start the court proceedings, she stays in the apartment for about a year while this is going on, and before the eviction goes through, she leaves."

Lorena figured out how to string together numerous twelve-month stints where she lived rent-free and only had to come up with two months' worth of rent at the end of each year. And if all else failed, she could fall back on her Section 8 apartment. Typically, when she has exhausted her Tenant's Rights hustle, she leaves voluntarily and moves on to the next. This happened at the end of twelve months with Angelina. "They [Lorena and Ezra] said they were going to leave. I said, 'okay.' They said, 'We paid the last month's rent.' I said, 'No, you didn't.' They said, 'Yes, we did. You said you weren't going to give us the apartment unless we paid two months up front.' I said, 'No, I didn't. Why would I say that?' They said, 'Well, can you give us a letter saying that we haven't paid this month's rent?'"

Lorena was already preparing for her next con by asking for the letter. "I said, 'No, I'm not going to do that.' They wanted a letter so they could go to Social Services to say, 'we can't pay the rent.' I didn't fall for it. Option 1, which she has done, is to file a claim against me. Option 2 is through the Buildings Department. When I didn't fall for 'Write me a letter saying that I didn't pay this month's rent,' I said, 'I'm not comfortable doing that. Just leave. Don't worry about last month's rent.' She started to call the Department of Buildings to get violations on the house. Her stalling tactic for not paying rent was, 'there are violations on the house. There's damage to the house.' She's doing a retaliation eviction because I called the Department of Buildings. They were leaving anyway. They said they were leaving January 31. She started to call the Buildings Department on January 18. How was I evicting them? They said they were leaving. I had a letter that said they were leaving, that they sent to my house. Didn't matter in court: they had the intention to leave, but they didn't have to leave." Although physically debilitated by drug use, Lorena was weaving a finely crafted web.

Trapped by a Con

RPAPL §749, Real Property Law §235 states "Landlords may not take the law into their own hands and evict a tenant by use of force or unlawful means. For example, a landlord cannot use threats of violence, remove a tenant's possessions, lock the tenant out of the apartment, or willfully discontinue essential services such as water or heat."

By January 2011, the situation had come to an impasse: Lorena and Ezra had stated they were voluntarily leaving, but they were not legally obligated to do so. Angelina started eviction procedures but was at risk of violating tenant-rights law on discriminatory grounds. But now that there was an illegal occupant in the basement, the Department of Buildings wanted the unit vacated altogether.

Angelina explained her legal quagmire. "Because there's a family living in the basement—and this is where it gets funny—the Department of Buildings is telling me, 'You must padlock the basement. You have an eviction order.' And I said, 'Help me get her out.' And they said, 'We're not in the business of evicting tenants. You need to evict her.' Okay, I'm already in court, but they say I need to padlock the basement. I called a locksmith. I called the New York City Department of Buildings at the locksmith's office, to tell the locksmith that he can put a lock on the door because he's refusing to do it. They said, 'If you do it, go there with the police and then padlock the door.' "

Angelina arrived at the house in Bayside with a locksmith and a police officer with the intent of fulfilling her obligations with the Department of Buildings. "I go and I padlock the basement. Then her attorney puts in an order, and in one day I had to go back to Housing Court. The court made me take the padlock off. I go to the judge, 'Tell him the New York City Department of Buildings told me to padlock the basement!' "

The Housing Court judge suspected that Angelina had "taken the law into her own hands" and told her that she had used a third party to evict Lorena; therefore the padlock had to be removed.

Angelina mimicked pulling out her own hair, "How can I follow the New York City Department of Buildings rules and follow the Civil Court at the same time?! You know what the judge's answer was? 'If she's in there when you padlock the door—God forbid.' "

The judge then asked, "Do you have all of the documentation? Because if something happens, it's on the court."

Angelina pled her case—explaining that the courts were being victimized by Lorena—but to no avail. "She was playing the system to get the violations so she didn't have to pay rent, simultaneously asking the court to take the lock off of the basement so she could have possession of it. And they know that I'm in such a bind now because the right hand doesn't know what the left hand is doing. If I was doing anything wrong, why would the police come with me to padlock the door? Why would the Buildings Department go and tell the locksmith to lock it?" Lorena had everyone where she wanted them.

Real Property Law §223b states: "Landlords are prohibited from harassing or retaliating against tenants who exercise their rights." As

Lorena was bombarding Angelina and the two separate court systems with complaints—all while remaining keenly aware of her rights as a tenant—she began to get creative, inventing new ways to retaliate against Angelina. "And I'm in the middle, so she doesn't have to pay rent. So there's a three-ring circus going on. I go there with the police again—and now she's pissed off because the police are coming—right? Because the police are on my side. So now she calls [NYPD] Internal Affairs and claims that the police had robbed her.

"So on Good Friday the Internal Affairs Bureau calls me up at my home and says, 'We need to come see you right away. Your tenant claims that she was robbed.' I said, 'What?! Nobody's helping me get these people out of the house, and this is ridiculous. You're taking this seriously?' They said, 'We're coming to your house.'

"So I went to the house—I kid you not—with my crazy Italian mother. And they put me in the police car with the recordings, and they said to me, 'Tell us what happened.'

"So I said, 'When I was following the New York City Department of Building's orders to padlock the door, and the Fire Department is there. You have to be kidding me. There's all of these New York City agencies there. Nobody's getting robbed. This is a scam, just to get you to not help me anymore. The only thing the cops did was stand outside. Nobody robbed her. Nobody was in there. Please help.' So, now we have Internal Affairs involved, so she had everybody running around, and she gets to stay there rent-free."

As Angelina was telling me this story, it appeared as though Lorena was beginning to flirt with danger. After twenty-five years—and eighteen different landlords hustled—Lorena now risked being countersued by the NYPD, who could seek economic damages for libel. But instead of backing off while she was ahead, she continued her reckless ways, continuing to try cons that worked in the past.

Penal Law §241.05 states: "No landlord, or any party acting on the landlord's behalf, may interfere with the tenant's privacy, comfort, or quiet enjoyment of the apartment." Angelina continued, "They really didn't live there anymore after May [2011]—so in May, they left their stuff there, but they didn't live there anymore. But what they did do was put video cameras everywhere. So the video camera—the door had a sensor on it—when I went in there, I had to go in there with the Buildings Department, Environmental Control, illegal asbestos test . . . I'm trying to get all these things done, and she just kept reporting all of these people. Because she could look on the Internet and she knew all the things I'm trying to do to fix all of these violations on my house, and all she kept doing was making phone calls to stall it.

"My poor architect, who's trying to help me, is now under investigation because this lunatic called and said 'he did a fake asbestos test.'" Angelina threw her hands in the air. "I mean, just craziness! So when I would open the door, and they don't need to live there—including the hurricane we had last year—I had to go in the basement to make sure there was no water. I opened the door, alarms go off, and it e-mails her wherever she is, and she calls the cops saying, 'My landlord is robbing me.' From a different location. She's not even there. The cops come . . . She's not even living there anymore, and they still had full possession of the house! They're not paying rent. I can't even get in my house. I can't check if there's water damage. They had full control of the house because according to Housing: 'as long as they don't relinquish possession it's theirs.' As long as they have one shoe on the floor, I can't gain back possession. This is craziness!"

By the summer of 2011, Lorena had created a new legal twist: Angelina was obligated to enter the unit in order to fix all of the problems listed in the violations, but Angelina—or anyone that she hired—could not enter the unit without Lorena's permission. "The only time I'm seeing them is in court, so I can't give them a heads up. I can knock on the door. I can slip something under the door. But they're not there. It's the biggest joke. So we're moving along, the whole summer passed, finally—because they were stalling—they weren't served. Housing Court begins to wonder, 'There's violations. What's that all about?'

"I said, 'I want to take back possession of the apartment, not back rent.' Because there's another law, an absentee landlord needs to register a three-or-more-family on owner-occupied land in order to collect back rent. However, this was a two-family house, but according to the Department of Buildings this is a three-family house because she said it was. So I can't even sue her for back rent because of this violation she had me on for having a three-family dwelling!"

I shifted in my seat—amazed at one person's ability to manipulate so many legal systems—and wondered out loud if she could be was aware of such a seemingly innocuous law. "So do you think she was aware of this two-family/three-family distinction?"

Angelina gasped, "She was aware of all of this because if you look back to 1985, every proceeding was the same thing. You couldn't sue for back rent. So either it was the Section 8/welfare excuse as plan A. And plan B is violations."

Through all of her publicly available searches, Angelina discovered that Lorena had used these tactics at least eighteen times. She would do everything in her power to stall, manipulating confusing and overlapping legal systems. All Angelina could do was keep track. "I couldn't really get in front of the judge until November 2011. So they stopped paying rent in court, they stalled, they wanted an attorney. We're back in April, and they hired an attorney.

"Now their attorney says, 'I was just hired, and I need extra time to get familiar with the case. But we won't move any further if my client receives moving expenses.' I asked him, 'Okay, how much is the moving expenses?' The attorney says, 'ten thousand dollars.' I screamed at him, 'That's not moving expenses. That's extortion!' He says with a smug look, 'No, it's not. It's moving expenses. It's going to cost them ten thousand dollars to move.'"

Angelina shifted in her seat. "So I didn't pay the ten thousand and exactly what I would have paid the attorney to get them out is exactly what they would have taken. It would have cost me ten thousand dollars to get her out in March or April, but it wasn't the right thing to do."

After six months of fighting, Angelina realized that she was becoming just another number.

Number nineteen.

How long could Lorena keep this con going? Who else would she victimize? "Everybody told me to pay her, including my first attorney, 'Just pay her! Just pay her. It's going to be a hollow victory. It's going to take a year to get her out.' And I said, 'I don't care.' My tolerance level for insanity is pretty high. I'm not doing this, because everyone else who has written her a check . . . and I'm thinking this before I researched all the cases . . . I'm thinking this is her M.O. She gets a check, and then she moves on to the next. She got away with $16,000 in rent. Right? She got a free place to live. She never paid her attorney. She only gave him the retainer. She never paid him. Do you know that you can't leave your client in the middle of a case?

"So she went to him and said, 'Oh, my landlord is kicking me out. Oooh!' Here's two thousand dollars. Here's the retainer. So then he says, 'Okay, we're up to four thousand or five thousand. And she says, 'I can't pay you.' She never paid him. So you know, God is so good, I told him, 'Why are you representing her? You are an educated man. Why are you representing this scum? He said, 'They're my clients; they have a right to an attorney.'"

Angelina laughed out loud to herself. "And he never got paid. It was the same thing with Con Ed[ison]. Her bill was up to five thousand dollars. So I asked, 'Why haven't you cut her power?' Con Ed says, 'Oh, we can't. She has medical equipment in the apartment.' I say, 'What?! Says who?' Con Ed says, 'Well, she filled out a form.' You mean to tell me all you have to do is fill out a form and Con Ed can't shut you off?!" This was a master at work.

Lorena had followed the same pattern before: avoiding rent by filing complaints, hiring attorneys without paying them, and then seeking a ten-thousand-dollar payout after a few months for "moving expenses." Angelina discussed her research findings. "The last time she did this in Brooklyn was in 2002. It was the same thing: the eviction never came through, and it was against her and this other man. There was a different boyfriend involved. So there was a little lapse. So from 2002 to 2008 I have the feeling she was cleaning herself up. And when I pulled that file—and you have to remember these files are old. They're not in the courthouse. So what they had to do is, I ordered the case numbers and it took six to eight weeks to get them. And then I would have to photocopy them and look through them. It was insane. Oh my God, even that one, she left right before the eviction. Very funny, she did the illegal lockout—exactly what she did to me with the padlock—to that woman in Brooklyn. So she knew, 'If I do this, I can still stall with the illegal lockout tactic.' And an illegal lockout is a $15,000 fine on my part."

Fortunately the Housing Court judge was able to see through Lorena's scheme and did not fine Angelina, and Angelina's persistent researching began to break the chain of hustles. "So every case she's brought against me has been thrown out. But she still stayed there for a year while it was happening. So the improper service [of the eviction notice] got thrown out. The illegal lockout got thrown out. She did the illegal lockout twice. April was the illegal lockout, but it didn't get thrown out until June."

The Curtain Falls

Lorena was relying heavily on the civil-court system to support her financially. Suing is a part of the fabric of New York, so much so that *Forbes* calls New York "Sue City": "New York City spends more money on lawsuits than the next five largest American cities—Los Angeles, Chicago, Houston, Phoenix and Philadelphia—combined."[5] Lorena was on pace with New York litigious legends such as Eleanor Capogrosso, who has filed as many as sixteen cases against landlords, hospitals, "and even a day spa."[6]

Lorena's litigious reach seemed to know no bounds; she would file new lawsuits if the first did not work out. Like a good con artist, Lorena has done her research and has a plan. If things do not work out, she has multiple escape routes. If the insurance con does not work, then she does not receive the payout, but she doesn't lose anything. If the lawsuit against Angelina does not work, she does not lose anything. If her complaint with Internal Affairs does not work out, then it goes away on its own. But by November 2011, she was spinning too many plates and began to lose track.

Lorena had filed a backup lawsuit—a failsafe—just in case her previous ones were unsuccessful. When the improper-service case was thrown out in Housing Court, Lorena claimed that she had fallen down the basement stairs and received an injury. She claimed that the railing was not fastened properly and that therefore her injury was the fault of her landlord. Angelina rolled her eyes. "Unbelievable, right?" Angelina knew that Lorena had vacated the apartment and could not have fallen. She could do nothing to investigate it herself, but she could circumvent this story through other channels.

After Angelina's attorney made an issue of it, the insurance company decided to hire an investigator, who discovered that Lorena had been living in New Jersey at the time of the alleged accident. The insurance company initially wanted to pay Lorena $15,000 to make the case go away but decided to throw out the claim once they realized that Lorena was outside of her jurisdiction.

Even though Lorena was admittedly good at what she did, Angelina figured that eventually she could outsmart her. "Now in April [2011], in open court, she mentioned on the record that she has not entered the basement since January. So now I have a sworn statement from the court. I gave it to the insurance company and asked, 'How did she fall down the back staircase in February if she claims in court that she hasn't been there since January?' The insurance company agreed and closed the case."

Like Icarus, Lorena flew too close to the sun and got burned. "So now she's lying so much that she doesn't remember what she's lying about. If everyone gives her $15,000 here, ten thousand there, she wins. This is tax-free money that she doesn't have to do a lot of work to get. She thinks, 'I'm going to put in this claim, and then the insurance company will pay me $15,000, and then they'll go away.' This lady is going to be too timid in court. She's going to pay me ten thousand, and then she'll go away. You follow?"

Having learned from the opportunist that had been conning her for a full year, Angelina in turn saw an opportunity to pounce. "So I call the district attorney and tell him 'This is premeditated. She's been doing this for years and years. Please don't tell me this is civil (court). This is not civil.' So I brought him everything, the patterns. I said, 'Look, this is her pattern. She did this here and here and here and here.' And I had the dates.

"He said, 'It's called a financial crime.' But he is going after her because he's more interested in her subletting a Section 8 apartment because that's a federal crime. Once he learned about that, he didn't care about me anymore, because that was a real crime to him." But even given all of the things Lorena did under Angelina's watch, Lorena's wings finally began to burn from something she had working on before they had met.

Angelina still sought justice for Lorena's other hustles. Eighteen different landlords had been conned. She began to call the other land-lords to see if they wanted to file suit. "One of them—who dealt with her from 2002 to 2003—was so scared, they refused to work with me because they just wanted to forget about her. They wanted nothing to do with it. They didn't want to acknowledge that they had anything to do with this case. Because they had gone through so much—same thing: illegal lockout. She did the same thing to them. Same thing I went through, and they did not want to talk to me."

Another landlord in Queens had since died. One in the Bronx could not be found because a different company now managed the building. The one couple that Angelina was able to track down wanted nothing to do with a lawsuit. "Please don't bother us. We finally got rid of her."

In the end, Angelina was disappointed she could not seek her own personal justice. Worried that Lorena would likely run this con again, she lamented, "So even for me, the next person that runs her credit, there will be no eviction. She was supposed to be evicted by Tuesday, but she left on Saturday. New Year's Eve was on a Sunday, which makes Monday a holiday. My eviction was going through on Tuesday."

On Friday, December 30, 2012, Lorena faxed a letter to Angelina's attorney stating, "I relinquish possession of the apartment." For her final performance, Lorena decided to exit in style. On December 29, after cleaning out the remainder of her things, Lorena called 911. Fire trucks surrounded the house, and she was eventually escorted away in an ambulance. Angelina later found the hospital records stating that Lorena had been inebriated from "too much Ajax inhalation." Lorena is still suing Angelina for her security deposit, but eventually Angelina won out.

Angelina is doing what she can to avoid this happening again. "We turned it back into a one-family, which is the quickest way to get all of the violations off. Now it's a legal one-family." The man who lived on the second floor—who has given her no trouble to this point—asked if he could move his family into the first-floor unit, and she agreed. Lorena, meanwhile, has slipped into the night, quietly targeting her next mark.

NINE

A DRUG HUSTLE: THE CRACK GAME

Why should these young men and women take the subway to work minimum-wage jobs—or even double-minimum-wage jobs—in downtown offices when they can usually earn more, at least in the short run, by selling drugs on the street corner in front of their apartment or school yard?

—Philippe Bourgois, *In Search of Respect: Selling Crack in El Barrio*

Of all the hustles of the informal economy of New York, the drug game is the most lucrative—and the most dangerous. Made popular in movie lore and gangsta-rap lyrics, the life of the drug dealer is attractive to many young men and women without formal job training and poor-quality education. Particularly for young people, legitimate opportunities are limited. As Trevor B. Milton wrote in *Overcoming the Magnetism of Street Life*,[1] "Current economic forces drive youth to two choices: (a) towards an extremely finite legitimate path to join the increasing army of working poor in the services economy; or (b) to the more attractive illegitimate path of street life."

Drug dealing captivates the interest of young entrepreneurs because of the fast riches that can be had. People hear stories, such as the one of "Lenny Starke," who *New York Magazine* reported was able to earn five thousand dollars per week selling cocaine around the five boroughs.[2] Starke is more legend than reality—an exception to the rule; research suggests that low-level drug dealers earn an average of $384 to $577 per week ($20,000–$30,000 annually).[3] Yet, the estimated value of the world drug trade is somewhere between $300 billion and $700 billion. $29.6 billion of profit is generated inside the United States off of cocaine alone.[4] In a nation with such a high demand, drug traffickers will never run out of consumers.

Toward the end of the 1960s, the United States began to confront the issue of illicit drug use. Politicians declared a "war on drugs," and President Nixon claimed that drugs represented a "national emergency" in July 1971. Governor Nelson Rockefeller of New York called for a mandatory fifteen-years-to-life sentences for drug dealers and drug addicts—even those caught with small amounts of marijuana—in January 1973.[5] He claimed to "have one goal and one objective, and that is to stop the pushing of drugs and to protect the innocent victim."

New York City was the first to adopt such draconian laws, but the city's drug problem only seemed to get worse. Heroin tore through the streets in the 1970s, and crack cocaine pushed the city to the brink the following decade. Hundreds of thousands were sent to prison under the Rockefeller drug laws, and rates of drug usage has dropped since the 1990s, but drugs still make their presence known.

It is estimated that there are one million drug users in New York City (16 percent of the population), with marijuana being the most popular drug of choice and pain relievers and tranquilizers coming in a close second. Although heroin and cocaine have waned in usage since the 1980s, they still comprise 93 percent of all emergency-room visits related to illicit drug use in New York.[6] The NYPD made 19,610 felony drug arrests and 57,255 misdemeanor drug arrests in 2013 alone.[7]

GETTING STARTED IN THE CRACK GAME

The late 1980s were among the heaviest drug-trafficking periods in New York City's history, and at that time, no drug had more of an effect than crack cocaine. "Crack"—a rock-shaped, more potent drug than cocaine in powder form—allowed more dealers to make their mark and more petty hustlers to up their game. As Terry Williams wrote in *Crackhouse*: "The major change brought about by the introduction of crack—a change that has played an important role in distributing the vastly larger amounts of cocaine available—has been the change in marketing methods. Crack offered a chance to expand sales in ways never before possible because it was packaged in small quantities that sold for as little as two to five dollars."[8]

I (Trevor Milton) met Ramon—a former dealer and user—to talk about his involvement in the crack game. He was eager to share his story. Ramon is Puerto Rican, in his late forties, with a warm smile and pleasant disposition. Despite his tale of heavy drug use, I was surprised to see a clean, fixed-up, healthy-looking gentleman in front of me.

I was interested in the underground economy and his account of the days on "the corner." As we sat for lunch in a deli in Harlem, he told me of how he was first introduced to crack cocaine. "I was working at a Herman's Sporting Goods store in the golfing department, and they had a store on Forty-Second Street. And back then cocaine was . . . you know, it was the drug. We're talking about maybe the early 1980s. This was what you would call the heyday. And, you know, I became the so-called [unofficial] manager of the golf department. And of course, I was sniffing cocaine. That was just the thing to do."

Forty-Second Street—and Times Square generally in the 1980s—was rife with drugs, hustlers, con artists, sex workers, and other highly tolerated illicit activities. "So, one day I go into the local peep show and people are smoking crack. I'm in a suit looking at everybody outside, and looking at all of these people moving. Next day I see this guy on the street with all of this money. I see this guy just like making money. Herman's Sporting Goods store was right down the street from

Bryant Park. I would go there and walk around on my lunch break. And noticed this one particular guy was making dough."

Ramon noticed people standing in a line long enough that it wrapped around the block. "I mean, I thought it was a welfare office or something. There was this line. And I was like 'whoa, this guy is making money. So, what is this dude doing?' I didn't know anything about crack . . . I knew cocaine. I heard about base, and heard somebody say the word 'crack.' So I see this line, and I'm like 'Really? I'm busting my chops, and this dude is clocking!'"

Ramon was making a livable wage as manager of the store, but his eyes lit up when he saw the amount of money the man on the corner was making. "So the guy at first—I'm in a suit—so he thinks I'm a cop. So we start talking. His name is Ramon, also. So he's from Santo Domingo [Dominican Republic], he can barely speak English. I speak Spanish. We start collaborating. So I say, 'Yo man, I want to invest. I want to get with this.' So, he's hesitant. And I'm like, 'Yo trabajo aqui. I'm the manager.' So he comes by the job and sees me working and he says, 'Ok. So instead of you giving me money, why don't I give you packages, and you can start selling for me?' I don't really know that many people. I don't know if I can do this. So he says, 'Just stand right there. Stand with me.'"

Ramon wiped his face with a napkin and sat back in his chair. "So here I am selling drugs in a suit. But I'm thinking about getting more money to purchase cocaine so I can support my habit. But you know curiosity . . . I want to smoke this. I want to see what's causing all of these people . . . I mean what's the buzz? Why are all of these people lining up? I want to see what's making people so crazy over this thing where I'm selling and making money. Because back in them days it was nothing, nothing to make a thousand to $1,500 a day."

Ramon saw, in a modern-day version of Horatio Alger's myth of the American dream, a chance to "make it." The reality of the American dream is that people from poorer communities often have to take big risks in order to make big money. Fly high or crash—there's not much in between. Drug hustling is one means to those ends. Balzac wrote, "Behind every great fortune there is a crime," which is even more starkly true of the drug trade. There is also a Wild Western appeal to making money in such a way: the idea of cutting a trail where there is none.

THE HEYDAY

Ramon explained the unprecedented amount of money he used to make. "Easily five thousand is standard for doing hand to hand. So multiply that by five guys, and I'm taking 60 percent [$15,000 a week] just for making the packages. So you can see the lure invested. Even if you're not a user, even if you're a family man, you see the lure of the return on your investment. I started 6:45 a.m. every morning."

I asked about that long line. "How many people in a day did you see coming in and out?"

Ramon brushed some food off of his shirt and thought for a moment. "I can't put a number on it. A dollar amount? At the peak in a day . . . fifteen to twenty thousand a day."

"That's with [Dominican] Ramon supplying you? Or were you going to get your own?"

Ramon continued, "That's me going uptown. That was . . . peak time. But then if you multiply the numbers . . . well, let me scale that back a little because there are costs. There's like, in any business, there's a cost. So pocketwise—after expenses—then that would have to come back to six or seven thousand, and I'll tell you why. Anytime you do cash business, numbers don't add up. You can have an honest cashier, but it never adds up. There's always something missing. Then there are costs. The more money I pay, the more insulated I become. I don't have to go on the street anymore, I can just go someplace and just deliver a package. But that costs."

Ramon initially worked the corners in the Times Square area, selling small bags of crack, but he quickly went on to hire people under him so he could sell them faster. "Moving indoors" would require him to pay expenses: "salaries" for his street workers, "rent" to find space to cook the drug, and "wholesale" prices for raw cocaine.

Ramon described some of the details. "So I have to go to someone's house. And I have to pay that house to allow me to stay there a little while. You know what I mean? So I have to pay for a person to come get it. So, six thousand to seven thousand dollars easily. Me at my peak, I would say that. That was nothing. I mean on a bad day, I was making six hundred to seven hundred—on a bad day. That's if I'm not even working hard."

What did Ramon spend his money on? "Hotels. Parties. Thinking that I could become like my connect and have my own business. Thinking I could buy quantities of cocaine and go to Broadway, because back in them days the Dominicans ran Broadway and Amsterdam between 130th to 180th Street. That was . . . phew! They were selling cocaine like you needed a license. Literally like they had a license. I mean, police weren't ready for this overwhelming thing . . . I couldn't even make it to that level. But the level that I was on, I mean, there was periods of time when I was on Thirty-Ninth Street and Ninth Avenue, I'm talking about we were selling crack like it was a regular store.

"I could tell you that I would stand in front of a store, and store owners would come out and say, 'Sir, could you please take your business to another area. Could you move from my store?' Because wherever I went, I was going to interrupt the business of your store. Know what I mean? The clientele coming to me and the clientele coming to your store were two different people. So wherever I stood, store owners used to tell me, 'Could you please . . . ' I mean I was blocking—I wasn't healthy for your business. It was either one of two things, because you had the stores with nothing on the shelves. They either complied with the activity, or if they didn't you could see their business was impacted and they were just trying to survive, because they knew better than to call the police. So what are you going to do as a business owner? You could stay there and not do business. Or get with the program."

As the NYPD did not have a strategy for dealing with the drug back then, New York in the 1980s was something of a Wild West. Murder rates were at historic highs, theft and robbery peaked in the late 1980s, and drug dealers made tremendous amounts of money. I asked Ramon about the role of the police and what would happen if they were called. Ramon laughed. "I don't think the store owner would be there much longer. His business would be impacted, or his life would be in jeopardy. Because if the guy [drug dealer] had a crew, and he gave a signal or a message that this particular store owner was involved in calling the police or involved in getting them arrested, or interfering with the regular traffic flow, this person could eventually wind up—" He paused, carefully calculating his words. "They would get impacted somehow. One way or another you're going to get impacted. If it isn't you, then it would be one of your friends, someone that you know, someone close. Because you are now under observation. There would be some physical consequences." He explained that store owners who challenged the drug dealers were often met with violence. "Unless you had big balls and you were willing to stand up. And I didn't know a lot of store owners willing to do that, that were able to with no fear stand up to people."

In a study on how to reduce violence and crime in the most dangerous Chicago neighborhoods, Robert Sampson, Stephen Raudenbush, and Felton Earls came up with the theory of collective efficacy.[9] They discovered that it was not police presence or public policy that curbed criminal behavior but rather the collective efforts of neighborhood residents and their intolerance of criminal activity. Of course, collective efficacy is difficult to employ because it requires all residents simultaneously to "fight back" crime.

In some neighborhoods, people are standing up now because they are tired of drug dealers and drug activity, but in our opinion they mistakenly consider drugs and drug dealers to be the primary cause of their community's dire circumstances. In fact, much of the drug problem is blown out of proportion by media exaggeration, disinformation, and what the sociologists Craig Reinarman and Harry Levine, in their book *Crack in America,* called antidrug extremism.[10] Reinarman and Levine argued that the "drug scare" drummed up by government officials in the late 1980s and early 1990s was used to justify draconian drug policies. But much of the crime seemingly related to the drug trade had more to do with the national economy generally. Drug dealers and crack sellers were basically acting and reacting to a lack of employment opportunities and wholesale abandonment of their communities by the state. Crack selling provided an opportunity (albeit an extralegal one) that people in ghetto communities took advantage of; a survival mentality settled in these neighborhoods. Instead of responding with more social programs, the state imposed harsher punishments and tactics like "stop-and-frisk," mass arrests, and incarceration.

VIOLENCE IN THE GAME

I asked how dangerous the drug game could get. Ramon paused to think for a moment. "The game is always deadly and dangerous, but when cocaine first came into the country, there was so much money being made that . . . if you owed somebody money, it was nothing to say just make it up. But then as the economy started changing, and people started changing, because remember we're talking about a change of hands: Colombians, Cubans, Dominicans, so as the environment began to change—and it was always deadly in Colombia. When it first came here big time with the Cubans, you know, there was so much money being made. The game was always deadly, but there was always money, so it was nothing to owe somebody and make it up. But as it went from [powder] cocaine, to freebase, to crack, that transition started the viciousness and deadliness of the game. It amassed itself. It was out in the open."

Movies often depict drug dealers as involved in endless corner disputes that always play out violently, ending in murder or maiming. I challenged the stereotype by asking Ramon, "I get the impression that you could say 'You stand over there. And I'll stand here. And everybody's cool.' You give me the impression that it was so good that everyone could just pick a spot." This reminded me of Lee and the water hustle (chapter 5). Every other street light, there's a new crew because no one can hold down every light, and there is plenty of business to be had.

Ramon agreed. "At one time it was like that. When I first started selling crack, you identified your crew by the color of the [crack] cap. Blue caps. Black caps. Red tops. The cap on the bottle. So you identified the quality of the drug by the color of the cap." Ramon began to impersonate a crack user. " 'Man, black top got it! Yo, that's flavor! Yo, that's bells!' You know, 'ringing bells.' So when I first got on the block there was like, black top, yellow top, white top, red top, orange top . . . There was a whole bunch. All the same price. Everybody was selling at the same price: ten dollars. It was against the code to try and sell it for less because then you were driving everyone else's price down."

Ramon explained that dealers respectfully stayed out of one another's way because there were plenty of customers, but with more demand came more supply, and these street policies began to change. "Just like anything else, the popularity rose, and more people started coming in, there were more choices to make, now rather than have like twenty people cop in like ten minutes, and it's now being spread out. And I'm not having that."

Ramon balled his fists up, "Black Top Crew—being the crew who we were—we took over not only Thirty-Ninth Street and Ninth Avenue, but we started reaching out and expanding. And you couldn't enter our territory, because if you did, there was a price to be paid. Plenty of people got shot, plenty of people got hurt, plenty of people got killed. For me to say that I witnessed a lot of it, by the grace of God, did I do with my own hands? No. But was it happening around me? There was a time in that area . . . that area's called Hell's Kitchen. It was very fitting. There were a lot of people back in the days being found decapitated. A lot of prostitutes in that area were being found murdered. It was real vicious, and it reared its head. And by the grace of God, I never had to go there. Did I know? And did I witness? That was just a regular thing."

I wondered how widely spread the violence was at the time. "What were the boundaries of this territory at its peak?"

Ramon rubbed his hands together. "At its peak? The best way I can say it is, we stayed on Ninth Ave. We went from Thirty-Ninth and

Ninth to Thirty-Fifth Street [the southern border] to Forty-First Street [the northern border]. So it was like six blocks, seven blocks up and down the avenue. But we had another spot in the Washington Heights area. But that was like graduating, because now when you go there, you're talking ounces and kilos now. We're not talking crack. We're talking kilos. Washington Heights was a step up. You were in the elite of the game."

THE MAKING OF CRACK COCAINE

Thus far in our interview, Ramon had described the street-level side of dealing crack cocaine. Using the metaphor of a restaurant, the street is the dining floor where customers are seated. He would receive the "food" (drugs) already made, and all he had to do was serve it. He believed that one could "graduate" from wait staff to kitchen staff by finding a supplier of powder cocaine. In his case, that kitchen was in Washington Heights (one hundred blocks north of his "Black Top" territory), where he eventually found a supplier.

"I would cook it [crack] myself. Absolutely. What would happen was I would go to 145th and Amsterdam or Broadway. Cop an ounce or two and cook it. Baking soda and water; that's all that was needed. What you do is, baking soda and water separates anything that's not cocaine and it becomes an oil. You're talking about a powder, baking soda and water. And when you put heat to it, it solidifies the oil that's in the powder. It extracts the pure cocaine and turns it into an oil; everything else disappears. Then what happens is, you let out the water and let the oil dry. And that's crack."

Crack cocaine was less adulterated in the 1980s than it is today, as drug dealers often put other chemicals into the mix, including lidocaine, inositol, speed, and "comeback" (benzocaine and mannitol). These chemicals would be mixed in during the cooking process to add bulk, and they would bond with cocaine hydrochloride and "come back" as one product and other compounds. But even before the creation of the hard, rocky substance consumed on the street, producing cocaine in its powder form involves a complicated process.

Step 1: Cocaine is extracted from coca leaves in processing plants. *Erythroxylon truxillo* or *erythroxylon novogranatense* are the most prominent varieties of coca leaves and yield the most cocaine. The leaves are refined in common "jungle" labs, located in mountainous regions with densely overgrown vegetation and trees and often inaccessible to outsiders. The coca leaves are soaked in gasoline inside metal drums. Sometimes this occurs in a *pozo* lab (a pit in the ground where the coca leaf is macerated and turned into coca paste), which uses acidic solutions.

Step 2: The gasoline containing cocaine alkaloids is drained from the metal drums and filtered into a barrel with diluted acid. The gas is drained off from the acid layer, and sodium bicarbonate or ammonia is added to the solution to make cocaine base.

Step 3: The cocaine base is filtered through a cloth.

Step 4: The remaining substance is dried, resulting in a pure form of cocaine base.

Step 5: The cocaine base is dissolved in a solvent such as ethyl acetate, acetone, or ether and then heated in a "baño Maria" (a steam bath where a substance is heated but does not make contact with the boiling water). Another solvent, such as ethyl ketone, is added to the boiling liquid, along with concentrated hydrochloric acid, which results in the crystallization of cocaine hydrochloride. Excess solvents are taken out of the cocaine hydrochloride at this stage, first by hand and then by using a hydraulic press.

Step 6: The solvents are finally removed in a microwave oven, which creates the basis for powder cocaine.

The Final Steps: The power cocaine makes its way through the drug-traffic pipeline into the United States. Once it reaches its destination—such as Ramon's "kitchen" in Washington Heights— crack is typically made by dissolving the cocaine hydrochloride in a mixture of water and baking soda, as he described. This solution is boiled until the cocaine forms an oily substance that drops out of the solution and settles at the bottom of the container. Finally, excess water, sodium chloride, and other impurities can be removed after cooling the oil to a rocklike substance. The resulting product is crack cocaine in its purest form.

This brick of crack cocaine can then be cut and chopped up into custom-sized pieces and sold for two-, five-, and ten-dollar chunks. Some may assume this processing dilutes the power of the drug; on the contrary, it is actually a more concentrated form of cocaine. Ramon reiterated, "And now you have this little bit of crack. But when you take a hit of that cocaine . . . Phew! That's why when a person takes a hit of crack, it was . . . power. Absolutely, it's more concentrated. So, when you would take a hit of crack and did it more than once, you were done."

THE LURE OF THE DRUG

Ramon had so many customers, he could barely keep up with the demand. He was fascinated by how quickly people would come and what they would do to get the drug. And like many dealers, his curiosity got the best of him, and eventually he tried crack himself. "And it was like the genie was out of the bottle. Trouble, concerns, problems were all corrected. Absolutely, it was the panacea. It was the cure for any problem that I was going through. I understood why they were lined up now. And I was an advocate for this particular drug."

Crack users become so highly addicted to that trouble-free feeling that they seek it out indefinitely. Some users call it "chasing the ghost" or chasing the feeling of the first high. And as Terry Williams once wrote, crack addiction "know[s] no class, racial or ethnic boundaries."[11]

Ramon saw the drug convert the most educated, classy people into bottom feeders. He once knew a person who played percussion for the New York Philharmonic. "His name was written on drumsticks. I forgot his name. And I remember clearly one day this guy coming downstairs in front of his building . . . I helped condemn the building he was in. I was directly responsible for that. It was an image in my mind that I will never forget." Sadness washed over his face as he recounted the life wasted. "He came downstairs. He was smoking crack. I wound up staying in his apartment. And we made it happen there for a while. And later, much later, I remember one day it was pouring rain and saw this white guy standing across the street. I didn't recognize him so I went across the street, and it was him: the guy from the New York Philharmonic. In the pouring rain I could see that he was crying. He was standing in front of the building where he was evicted. And pouring down rain, I saw tears coming down his face, from the sadness. I lived with this dude for a while, and I didn't even recognize him."

Ramon mentioned that he "shut the building down," so I asked what he meant. Ramon explained the daily running of the business. "Now, the guy that sold it to me, I became his underling. Now I hired two or three guys. I had two or three guys working for me. We was the Black Top Crew. So I wound up going into his apartment, and we wound up living there. And eventually we condemned that building. Altogether it was a five-story walkup, three apartments on each floor. But the traffic was so insane. Twenty-four hours a day, seven days a week. To the point where individuals next door were smoking crack in the hallways. To the point where homeless people went . . . because this drug crack, it'll consume you. I mean it will take everything from you. It will take your dignity, your pride. It'll take you." Ramon shook his head. "To a person that uses heroin, it's like riding a horse and buggy compared to crack. Crack is like a rocket ship. Because with heroin, even the heroin addict still can have some sort of responsibility. For instance, a heroin addict, if he knows a place where he can get money, so he can get his next fix, then he will be responsible enough to go get that because his body is so addicted to it. But you could promise someone smoking crack a million dollars, and if he's smoking crack he's not going to show up."

Ramon's body shivered as he recalled how powerful the drug was. "It's the panacea. It's the cure-all because it's better than a million dollars. At that moment, it's just the greatest thing in the world. I know that because I gave up a lot to be in that world." There are tales in New York City of men offering sexual favors to other men, women selling their children into prostitution, and people selling all of their assets just to get a hit.

Ramon explained why crack had so much more of a devastating effect on individuals and communities than cocaine. "Why would I want to spend time getting to that other feeling [of sniffing powder cocaine]. Whoever named it, named it right: crack. It's literally what it makes you do. It cracks you. What happens is . . . the first hit that you take you'll never get back. So you're chasing the ghost. You'll chase it to the point where your heart will go into cardiac arrest. People have actually died from this. People actually starve. People actually sell their children. People actually go into prostitution. You're talking women who could be the top . . . " Ramon clapped his hands together. "Prime example: Whitney Houston. Look at a person so gifted. But here's the curse: she had so much money. Addiction doesn't care about how much money you got; the more money the better. The more education you got the better. Because when you have all of this education and you become addicted, you figure it out. Just like any other addict, you justify why you do it. 'I'm not like those people.' And I remember saying that. I was going to work. I was working at AT&T. I was going to work, and I used to live off Sound View Avenue [in the Bronx] off the 6 train. I remember these guys on the corner. And I had my briefcase and suit and I said, 'I'll never be like those guys.' And years later, I was just like those guys. On the corner—six or seven o'clock in the morning—drinking beer, didn't get any sleep, asking people for change. I will never forget that."

Ramon believed that the crack epidemic hit the Puerto Rican community in New York the hardest. Unlike his Dominican supplier (who never used the drug), Ramon believed that Puerto Ricans were affected the most. "When I finally came out and left that world, I did a little research and found out we [Puerto Ricans] were number one in all of the wrong things. As far as Latinos go? We're number one in unemployment. We're number one in not getting educated. We're number one in prison. We're number one in the welfare line. We're number one in the treatment programs. We're number one in getting incarcerated. We just continue to be number one in everything bad. So I was ashamed at the time to say that I was Puerto Rican. It was just amazing how this particular guy, Ramon [his supplier], he came over here and he was strictly business. He took care of business. And I made him a lot of money! I can remember clearly, Christmas of '84 or '85, I had a Macy's shopping bag full of money. And that was regular."

In a certain sense, I was drawn to Ramon—the straightforwardness of his interview and the central idea that his story illustrates: that jobs are not enough. This has profound economic implications especially when considered against the background of materialism and consumption that is largely intrinsic to our culture.

It's all big business, and no one cares about the larger moral implications. Some will resort to any means (legal or not) to reach a standard of living that is well beyond their normal earning power. Minimum-wage jobs are simply not enough. The sociologist Saskia Sassen warned of the effect of globalization on large cities and the rise of the informal economy.[12] In *The Global City*, Sassen argued that the corporatization of world goods and the concentration of control of those goods into the hands of a few would eventually bolster the black market because the common man would seek fairer prices for these items. Illicit goods and services are needed by many, but as we saw in chapter 6, their production and purchase are often targeted by law enforcement.

All of this intersects, too, with the underground economy in New York and the absorption of immigrants into the drug trade (at various levels) or the "bancas" (policy houses; see chapter 7) because capitalism has cut a wide path in the so-called Third World. The constant stream of new folks arriving in America to seek financial opportunity is another byproduct of capitalist globalization, which continuously feeds and refreshes the hustler class in New York.

Ramon's story portrays how young black and Latino people have few good choices for making a living in the city, or so it seems. Ramon spoke candidly about how Dominicans controlled the cocaine and crack trade in Washington Heights, but the sociology of young men of color who decide to sell drugs or engage in other petty nonviolent crime has to be teased out overtly. It is, on the one hand, about choice and about a lack of choice, unemployment in ghetto communities, racism, media extremism, and a criminal-justice system out of control. Ramon indicates that the money he earned in the drug trade felt very much like winning the lottery: he still had no vision beyond living day to day. At the time he only focused on what used to be or what he could be, never on his present situation. As Alibi once said: "A 'used-to-be' is like a 'never-was.'"

Like Ramon, many young people believed (and still believe) they could achieve the American dream by selling illegal drugs. His is a sobering account of how he became engulfed in the game and got stuck there until it ate him up.

THE END OF THE PARTY

Like all hedonistic pursuits, the fun eventually runs out; the amusement park has to close. Ramon described how the life began to end for him. He then lived in an apartment on Thirty-Ninth Street. "First thing, would be to take a hit of crack. That's breakfast. That would be the first thing to stimulate the day. Then get dressed, go outside and pick up a package. Or come outside and wait for my connect to come. Know what I mean? By package I mean something that was already made. Each package has ten bottles. Ten bottles represents a hundred dollars. Back in the day it was a sixty-forty split. He'd get 60 [percent]; I'd get 40 [percent]. So making four hundred to six hundred dollars a day was nothing. Ten packages was nothing. That was a slow day. That was no effort whatsoever. That was just stepping outside. I would make four hundred. There were times where I actually sold twenty to thirty packages. By ten o'clock at night . . . let's say I started at 6 a.m. that morning. I'd finish at ten o'clock. By 7 a.m. the next morning I would be broke."

I thought I misheard him. "Wait. Back up. What do you mean, you'd be broke?"

"I literally would be broke. I would finish early in the evening. And I would start smoking and partying, inviting people. And going down the ho stroll and making deals, purchasing things. So I'd be making $1,200 dollars by ten p.m. By 7 a.m. I would be broke. The next day I'd start all over again. But then it got to the point where—I didn't mention to you whether I brushed my teeth or bathed. I didn't say none of that stuff. Because that wasn't important. Meals were a treat or a rarity. You know what I mean? When the addiction finally consumed me it was rare to eat. I would rather spend money on the drug than eat. And eventually my using got in the way of selling."

Ramon dealt with the game on many levels, and eventually he found himself on the losing end. With pain in his eyes he lamented, "In the long run it's not worth it, just the karma, the spirit that you send out. You can't sell death to support life. It's going to come back to you some-how. If it doesn't come back to you directly, it's going to be someone you love, someone you care about. And I've seen it across the board. It doesn't matter who you are. What level you are on. You cannot sell death to support life. It will come back."

His way of living began to disrupt the business of his Dominican connection; that's when the violence associated with the trade entered Ramon's situation. "If you mess with people's money," he said, there are consequences to pay."

Those consequences usually involve three factors: territory, repu-tation, and honor. Territory refers to the specific spaces controlled by groups and individuals; those spaces represent profit or income. Most drugs are distributed on consignment, with the explicit understanding that once those drugs are sold the consigner will be reimbursed. If the money is not paid back, the consigner's reputation could be damaged—unless the consigner retaliates with violence. Not much in the way of honor is left in the drug business, but violating trust means retaliation and revenge. It is considered an offense to your reputation in the street culture to violate these principles, and to breach this tradition is usually a cause for violence.

Ramon believed that during crack's heyday he was safe from violence because everyone was making money and therefore had less reason for retaliation. He stared over my shoulder at 125th Street, recalling, "Because here I am being an underling at one time, managing four or five people, to where I couldn't be trusted with any more packages. My connect eventually just—for lack of a better term, instead of murdering me—he just stopped giving me packages. At one time I was a superstar. I was making this guy . . . he would come to work at nine or ten in the morning, by nine to ten o'clock at night . . . just me alone I made him four to five thousand, six thousand. Just me! But remember, there's five, six, seven of me. Know what I mean? So I went from that, to him having mercy on me instead of murdering me, and he just stopped giving me work, so he doesn't have to do vicious things to me. I would spend it [money] before he showed up. That's manipulating each package. Each package had ten bottles. I would go into each and take out a little bit from each. Put it [the bottle] back [in the package of ten]."

Ramon's habits began seriously to compromise his earnings and threatened to destroy the entire operation. "Then the customers started complaining. And Dominican Ramon's going 'Yo wassup?!' To the point where I started taking actual packages from him. And then I promised to make it up to him because I made money. To the point where I owed money and he was like, 'Yo, pay me for this.'" Ramon slammed his hand on the lunch table. "For some reason, God had mercy on me, because it wasn't him, because he didn't have mercy on no one. Because I've seen some work done where people were actually getting shot, getting hurt because they're not complying with money that was supposed to transpire."

Ramon became what he desperately did not want to become: a loathsome stereotype of the poor drug-addicted Puerto Rican male. His assessment of himself is visceral, and his pain is raw and unforgiving. There are no excuses here. Ramon recognized his own agency, his personal role, in creating his situation, and he laid his cards on the table.

THE TRANSFORMATION

When Ramon's connection let him go, he tried to survive in the game as a dealer but eventually failed. Ramon did not stop using and dealing until he had an epiphany. According to the sociologist Norman Denzin, "epiphanies are interactional moments and experiences which leave marks on people's lives. In them, personal character is manifested. They are often moments of crisis. They alter the fundamental meaning structures in a person's life."[13]

Ramon's epiphany required him to hit rock bottom. "You know, purchasing, cooking my own, but the addiction overcame me to the point where I became homeless. Then I started getting arrested, and then one day . . . they used to deputize New York City police officers two days a week as federal officers. So any arrest that they would get would become a federal case. Especially crack, because crack became an epidemic in this country." Ramon was fortunate to never be arrested by federal officers, as that would have resulted in several years in federal prison. But one day Ramon had a religious experience. "I had a spiritual encounter. I used to sell drugs, and I would pray to God to 'get me out.' There were drug dealers, my coworkers at the time were looking at me like I was crazy. I would actually kneel and pray to God to 'deliver me from this' because I didn't know how. I didn't know nothing about treatment."

One day Ramon claimed that his prayers were answered. "I heard a voice, as clear as I'm talking to you now. And it told me to go to Jacobi Hospital [in the Bronx], and I knew nothing about Jacobi Hospital at the time. And I went to Jacobi Hospital and started the process of treatment. When I was doing that, this program [the drug rehabilitation program at Jacobi Hospital], and this is a program that pays for someone's training while they are in treatment. So I made a list of everything I wanted to do, crossed it out, and narrowed it down to two things. I was going to go to culinary school or become a counselor. And I wound up becoming a counselor at Beth Israel [Hospital] going on twelve years. I work at Promesa [inpatient rehabilitation] part time. I work at a facility.

I work at the DOME [Developing Opportunities through Meaningful Education, Inc.]. I got my book cleared. Since then I've gone to several churches. Several places have asked me to be a speaker. Men of Color summit, I was a keynote speaker. So that's it."

His treatment was not as easy as it seemed. "Prison . . . I went into prison. Came out. And went right back into selling. And when I got into it . . . the addiction takes over. It's not like once an alcoholic, always an alcoholic. No. I don't believe in that because I am a totally new person. The problem with treatment is that it only satisfies the external behavior of the individual. It only takes care of the external part. If you truly want change, you have to go within and change the spirit. Because where the heart lies, lies the person. Most people relapse because the heart has not changed. I used to tell people, 'my mother died and it wasn't even a thought.' My mother died, my brother died, my best friend died, and it was the last thing on my mind. It never entered my mind. I will never use again. People say, 'never say never.' That's bullshit. I will never go back into the pits of hell."

THE GAME TODAY

I asked Ramon about this heyday in the crack game compared to dealers today. "Well, we all know cocaine was accepted and common, but no one said anything. It was accepted. Like the guys on Wall Street. The crack epidemic was so free because no one had any knowledge of the ramifications, the collateral damage, the unintended consequences that crack was going to have. I mean, of all the drugs, we know every addiction is dangerous and deadly. But the impact of the crack epidemic, we're seeing it now with our kids. I was seeing the crackhead moms having kids. They're grown now, and they're having kids. And now this is what we're seeing: the collateral damage, the ripple effect of the crack epidemic. This country . . . no one knew about the collateral damage of this particular drug. You know, we knew about heroin. We knew about speed. We knew about amphetamines. We knew about LSD. We had a little knowledge of that. But we had no clue as to what the crack epidemic was going to do. And we didn't know. The reason it was so free, first of all . . . small to conceal, the enormity of the money being made. Just like any drug, when there is a lot of money being made, you're paying someone. You know, someone is making money somewhere. To turn a blind eye . . . "

I asked, "Would you be successful today if you sold drugs?"

His brow furrowed. "I do not think I would, no. Reason? Fear factor. Back in the days at least there was a little trustworthiness. There was this code of not talking. If I got busted for selling, it would be very rare for me to turn in the person who gave me the package or the person I worked with because there was a certain code. But now fear is prevalent on the planet. Fear is a very motivating factor. You see it on all levels from law enforcement on down to road rage; people beating each other up on the trains. Today there is no code that no longer exists. And so you got this snitching culture out there now."

I'd always heard that outlaw culture demonized snitching; Ramon was saying the opposite. I wanted to hear more about this. He said, "You get arrested, and you're going away for ten to fifteen years. You snitch. That's a fact."

He continued: "I wouldn't make it today because of the global economy, because unemployment is so high, because so many people are doing it. The chances of you succeeding . . . the biggest drug dealer that I was aware of was Pablo Escobar. I mean this guy had more money than anybody. Now so many people are doing it . . . now people are shooting each other over weed, when that was the drug that was nothing. Back in the days you would hurt somebody if they owed you two hundred to three hundred, or two thousand to three thousand. Now they killing each other for a dollar! The game has changed. And that's all over. Now any time you try to sell drugs, you are putting yourself on a Broadway stage. Ninety-five percent of the police work surrounds this. Just watch the body language, and you can tell who's the client, who's the dealer, who's sending the package, who's got the money. So, there would be no chance for me."

I asked why he didn't just sell something more clandestine, like marijuana or even powder cocaine. "Crack . . . the money made was just too massive. People would rather sell crack than an ounce of cocaine. You could take an ounce of cocaine and pay—because I think an ounce back in the day was $1,200 to $1,500—from that ounce . . . from that $1,200 investment, I could now make five thousand dollars. The risk of course increased nine-thousand-fold; because now you have to be out there. Because when you're dealing with crack you're dealing with the elements. You can't even imagine some of the things that would transpire: women offering themselves. Men offering sexual favors. Women offering their children. I remember a Cadillac salesman—who used to work on Fifty-Ninth [Street] and Tenth Ave.—he was coming to cop some stuff, and he was trying to trade the suit on his back for a purchase of drugs! Above and beyond what people would have done just to get a hit. It's the only drug that makes sense that something like that would happen. It's evil. It's just pure evil."

Ramon eventually beat the odds and removed himself from the crack game, but this required an extraordinary intervention. Some estimate that 80 percent of users never recover; this is one of the reasons it is considered a dangerous drug. But a drug's dangerousness depends on several things: (1) purity (potency), (2) route of administration (how the drug is taken into the body, i.e., sniffing, smoking, or injecting), and (3) dosage (how much of the drug is consumed) at one time.[14]

Crack cocaine is said to be devastating to those who try it even once, but there are many who smoked crack and found it wanting, too powerful, or not to their liking. The neuroscientist Carl Hart is a perfect example of the countermyth of drug use, as he articulated in his book *High Price: A Neuroscientist's Journey of Self-Discovery That Challenges Everything You Know About Drugs and Society*. Hart, a professor at Columbia University, grew up in cocaine-plagued southern Florida during the 1980s and admitted to using cocaine, marijuana, selling drugs, and engaging in petty crime. Later, as a tenured professor he argued that drugs are essentially the scapegoat for larger social issues, including race and poverty:

There is a belief, for example, that crack cocaine is so addictive it only took one hit to get hooked, and that it is impossible to use heroin without becoming addicted. There was another belief that methamphetamine users are cognitively impaired. All of these myths that have been perpetuated primarily by law enforcement, and law enforcement deals with a limited, select group of people—people who are, in many cases, behaving badly. But to generalize that to all drug users is not only short-sighted and naive, it's also irresponsible. The impact of that irresponsible behavior has been borne primarily in Black communities.[15]

Drugs have been used as a scapegoat for decades (in the guise of drug scares or drug panics), blamed as the cause of more widespread social problems. Further, drugs have historically been linked to minority groups who are seen as threatening in one way or another. In the 1980s, crack was seen as the drug of the "'un-' population": un-employed, un-educated, un-domiciled, un-civilized. Crack users became the special target of the criminal justice system, and they filled prisons to the brim. Members of poor and minority communities who desperately needed sustenance and support readily took hold of an extralegal opportunity structure because that was the only game in town: no jobs, no prospects from the state, no other chances to catch the American dream.

Ramon was different—he actually had a job in the formal economy but decided to give it up for the more lucrative world of drug dealing. What does this suggest? Do these men and women decide that crime may just, in fact, pay, and thus exercise a certain free will to pursue criminal activity in the form of hustling because they simply can make money faster than any legitimate job within their reach can offer? Is the pursuit of hustling a question of not being able to find a job, or is it a matter of moving beyond what the psychologist Kenneth Clark in *Dark Ghetto* called "menial jobs?"[16] What is important here are both the sociological as well as the economic implications of understanding that the inability to get a job is not the sole reason that these men go into the drug trade or the world of hustling.

The hustler is lionized in rap music and now on the stage—the person to aspire to—and for some, the drug dealer holds the same appeal as the Wall Street broker: the person who makes money by any means necessary. Hustlers are not just ghetto or working-class icons. They are just as American as apple pie or grits on Sunday morning. What are the other options between being a poor "nobody and nothing" and finding one's way out? A few hip-hop artists, such as Shawn Carter (Jay Z), Curtis Jackson (50 Cent), and Calvin Broadus (Snoop Dogg) walked this path and became heroes because in America, money matters, and, to a large degree, it does not matter how you obtained it.

TEN

NYPD AND THE FINEST CONS

The government should neither participate in nor be a party to, crime nor break the law in order to enforce it.
—Gary Marx, *Undercover: Police Surveillance in America*

There are eight million stories in the naked city; this has been one of them." This now famous line from the 1960s crime drama *The Naked City* suggests the wide variety of illicit tales left untold in a city of (at the time) eight million residents. Although it is considered to be the "safest big city in America" today, New York City was infamous for its high crime in the 1980s. Stories such as the tale of Bernard Goetz—who shot four teenagers on a Manhattan train after they allegedly attempted to mug him—became a part of New York City lore. Anyone could be a potential victim; anyone could be a hero, anywhere in the city. Although he was eventually convicted of possession of an illegal weapon, Goetz became a champion for some.

New York City was—and still is, in some places—a tough town. The police department tripled in size during Mayor Rudolph Giuliani's two terms. Between 1993 and 2005, reported crime in New York declined by 46 percent;[1] arrest and incarceration rates began to skyrocket. New York City police officers, heralded as heroes, ushered in a new era of safety and (almost) worry-free city living. But crime scholars have noted that the number of police on the beat or the force has no causal connection to the reduction in crime. Frank Zimring, a noted criminologist who has been researching crime since the 1970s, has shown that 80 percent of crime reduction in the city—such as robbery and burglary—could not be attributed to policing changes.[2]

Thanks to this increase in street policing, however, much of the visible con game culture—such as the ubiquitous three-card monte players, who enjoyed a heyday in the 1980s—was pushed off the streets and into the darker corners of the city. Giuliani rebranded a long list of nominally tolerated social behaviors—such as vagrancy, panhandling, and selling cheap homemade goods—as "quality-of-life crimes," adding to the city's arrest and conviction totals while simultaneously "cleaning up" sidewalks, vestibules, and parks—and, some worried, trampling personal freedoms. The offenses Giuliani targeted often demoralized community residents and particularly affected business people because they were seen as creating physical disorder. The game of three-card monte, for example, required cardboard boxes and playing cards, which were usually discarded in the street once the game was done. But more importantly, it encouraged many locals and tourists alike to gather on the street to watch, often blocking sidewalks, littering, getting into street fights, and causing other "disturbances of the peace," which rubbed many middle-class sensibilities the wrong way.

Some critics saw this criminalization of minor offenses as a war against the poor, with the police leading the vanguard. Loic Wacquant illustrated how government began attacking the least advantaged in our society in the name of safety in *Punishing the Poor*:

> Out of a proclaimed concern for efficiency in the "war on crime" . . .
> this discourse overtly revalorizes repression and stigmatizes youths from
> declining working-class neighborhoods, the jobless, homeless, beggars,
> drug addicts, and street prostitutes . . . designated as the natural vectors

of the pandemic of minor offences that poison daily life and the progenitors of "urban violence" bordering on collective chaos.[3]

One could argue that the poor were forced to resort to these so-called offenses because they were searching for creative ways to make a living during a time of deindustrialization, unemployment, and economic downturns.

Some experienced police officers have firsthand knowledge and a clear memory of these times, as I (Trevor Milton) discovered one summer afternoon at a Manhattan playground. While I was watching my son, I entered into a chance conversation with a retired police officer named Frank (a pseudonym), who was watching his grandkids. The small talk about kids and then eventually about the work we both did led to his telling me about his recent retirement from the police department. I told him I was writing a book about con games.

Frank said he had come across thousands of hustles and cons in his day, and in a situation qualitative researchers call "ethnographer's luck" asked if we could meet again and talk about his experiences. He explained the various cons that police officers engage to get food and other things free from stores and position themselves for lucrative jobs (security and otherwise) both on and off the books.

I wondered why a retired police officer was willing to talk to me. Is one of the tricks of the trade of ethnographic research to find people who are retired from their profession, who would be more willing to talk because they feel that they have less to lose? His tales of NYPD theft and precinct turf wars sounded like something one would see in a movie; actually to hear a police officer corroborate these stories as reality was another matter.

We arranged to meet one on one in a Manhattan park, where there would be no distractions. (He seemed to feel better meeting in an outdoor space as opposed to a place more enclosed like a restaurant.) Frank—roughly mid-forties, short but muscular—liked to show off his chiseled arms with a short-sleeved NY Giants t-shirt. Born and raised in the Bronx, he had a typical New York swagger and frequently flashed his gap-toothed smile as we sat on a park bench and watched pass-ersby. I asked him about the most recent cons he had come across. He stretched his legs out onto the walking path before answering. Then his low baritone voice began to fill the park.

THIEVING HUSTLES

"One I was thinking of the other day was guys stealing from one pre-cinct and selling in another." He sat up straight and started drawing imaginary lines with his hands. "So you have the borderline between precincts. Some precincts border others that are more middle to lower class. So like black and Hispanic neighborhoods. And the adjoining pre-cinct would have more of an upper-class clientele . . . or residents. In the lower-class neighborhoods, they have bodegas. In the upper-class neigh-borhoods, they have delis."

I chimed in, "And grocery stores."

"And grocery stores. Yup, yup. So these . . . not bums . . . I think they are more opportunists than anything. They go to the ghetto neigh-borhoods—the bodegas—and they take orders. And with those orders, they go to like the Duane Reades [in upscale neighborhoods], and they steal exactly what the bodegas want. They come back, and they already have it sold already." Frank folded his arms. "So it's not a matter of a crackhead saying, 'Hey, I'll sell this to you for 50 cents.' No. It's 'Here's your merchandise. I brought you your merchandise. You set the price.' And that's it. It's a done deal."

I questioned, "I get the impression it's like young kids, like nineteen or twenty years old."

"No."

"So these are like old men?"

Frank shrugged his shoulders, "Some, yeah. If I had to get an age range. I'd say between eighteen and forty."

I hesitated before my next question. "So do you think these guys are like—I'd hate to use this word—but like fiends [addicts]?"

Frank waved his hands. "No! No, they're not. Some of them are not drug related, at all. That's just their hustle."

"So you mean like . . ." I pointed to a drugstore across the street. "Take this Duane Reade for instance. I feel like I wouldn't be able to steal from there, even if I had the skills for it."

With one arm still folded, Frank pointed to the street. "Okay. There's a Duane Reade where there is a train stop at the back entrance, which is an entrance that the public can use. The main entrance is on Broadway, but you have to go around the block to enter the train. Now, if you had somebody working with you, to know when the train is coming, right? The Enfamil baby formula—which is very expensive—is always in the back. But this back door is left open. The store opens at 8 a.m., and security doesn't get there until 9 a.m."

I furrowed my brow. "What?"

"Exactly! They've [Duane Reade] been told many many times [to beef up their security in the morning]. And the only person watching the door is a pharmacist. And he's not jumping over a counter to save Enfamil." We both laughed.

"And someone is looking down the [train] tunnel?"

Frank shook his head. "Someone is sending some kind of signal saying, 'The train is coming.' They have a black bag. They pack it up. There's one shelf that has all the Enfamil. And each of those cans is like thirty dollars. They come with the bag, they drop it on the floor." He mimicked an arm dragging across a shelf. "They go fdddrrrromp! Fix it, grab it. Walk right out the store. You know? The shelf is here, and the pharmacist is here. So the pharmacist can't see you until you get near the door. They see you walking out, but the door's right here. So, he's gone. He runs down the steps. Hops on the train, and he's gone."

I joked, "They might want to lock that door."

Frank laughed and slapped his knee. "They've been told that, and they say because of the neighborhood it's in, the people that shop there are more likely to feel confined if that door is locked."

Much of what Frank described sounded like crimes of opportunity rather than premeditated malice. As we have discussed throughout this book, the criminologists Derek Cornish and Ronald Clarke proposed in their "rational choice" theory that even an average person could become a criminal if the right opportunity offered an undeniable reward in the right moment.[4] Since the 1990s, the NYPD has been utilizing this principle by attempting to reduce criminal opportunities and increasing punishments for all kinds of offenses, thereby in theory driving the average person to think "it's not worth the trouble." But for every preventative measure, there is a loophole, and con artists and hustlers seek these out.

Frank illustrated this fine line between opportunity and punishment by discussing department-store scams. "There's a DSW [shoe store] and a Burlington Coat Factory in Union Square. There's a homeless guy—this one I know for a fact—and homeless kids who live in the park. And there are people that come up to them—regular people—who come up to them and they take orders. They take orders for what the people want from DSW."

"And people know to approach these kids?"

"Yeah. They walk up to them and say, 'This is what I want.' I don't know how they—the kids—know the exact article of clothing." Frank did not disclose what type of commission they receive in exchange.

Aware of the rules intended to curb theft, I wondered if these kids understood the difference between petty larceny and grand larceny. Petty larceny is a class A misdemeanor, which is punishable by a small fine; grand larceny theft (theft of goods worth five hundred dollars or more) is a class B felony—punishable by up to three years in prison. I kept this in mind with my next question. "So are they smart enough to stop at $490, or do they just go for it?"

Frank giggled. "I don't think they're smart enough; I just think the orders are not big enough. I think that they take what they can because there's not enough room to fit that much in. I don't think it's a matter of planning; I think it's a matter of luck. And chance. Unless you are stealing a very expensive item or from a specialty store. You know? DSW is not going to have a thousand-dollar jacket."

I slouched on the bench, staring at the nearby cityscape. "That's funny to me because stealing from a clothing store is like stealing from a bank. Like I wouldn't be able to get away with it nowadays. But I guess there's always some loophole, or there's some area where you can slide in."

Frank flashed his gap-toothed grin and threw me a curveball. "Well, if you want to go to the bank-robbing end of it, they do that, too."

Bank robberies in Manhattan had been making news headlines at the time, but they still seemed technically impossible to me. "What do you mean?"

Frank slapped me on the back, leaving what I imagined was a mild bruise. "And you would think in Manhattan it would be hard to rob banks, but they do it!"

From my vantage point, it appeared that banks were the ultimate examples of the logic of the rational-choice perspective: given the bulletproof glass, the armed guards, the surveillance cameras, the marked bills, the silent alarms, the quick police response, and even the dye packs in the bags of money, no rational person would never attempt to rob them. Yet, regularly, someone robs a bank in Manhattan and gets away with it.

Frank smirked and put his hands in the air. "They do it all the time. And what they do is, they don't get greedy. They don't put on a mask and hold a gun. They walk in with usually a cap and glasses and walk up to the teller, but before that, the street hustle is this: before they do that, they must have some sort of police scanner or something . . . they know how many people are working. How many police cars are out there. They know. And they know what frequencies each police precinct's radios are working with. I'm positive. Because the way they run—"

I wasn't sure what he was getting at. "So, they are spaced out far enough from the precincts?"

Frank grabbed a nearby stick and started drawing a diagram into the dirt next to the bench. "So it's always like two precincts. Some, very rarely, will use three precincts. So if I transmit over my radio that someone just robbed a bank at this corner, my precinct and an adjoining precinct will get that call." He drew a vertical line in the dirt and marked two x's to the left of the line. "They'll hear it. But, if the borderline is the next block—say our precincts are divided by east and west and we both stop north to south on each side of the line—they will rob this bank and run that way." He pointed to the right of the line.

I confirmed his meaning. "Running away from the second precinct."

"Running *toward* the precinct that is not receiving the call coming over the radio. It will eventually come over their frequency, but it will take five minutes—which is enough time for people to get where they are trying to get, and then they are gone. Their getaway car and their getaway plan is on that side of the block. They do it a lot. So you'll notice that the calls—the banks that are getting robbed are on the edges of bordering precincts that don't transmit to each other."

I thought for a moment about past news reports about bank robberies.

Frank continued, "And it can't be coincidental. And in addition to that, before they go into the bank, they'll make a bogus phone call on something happening on the other end of the precinct." He pointed to the other side of the park. "Over there. So everyone is rushing to fly over there. And by the time we get back here to get a description, he's gone. Because he's already in this precinct which does not transmit to this third precinct, and now he has double the time. And he'll get like a ten-minute run. Or a fifteen-minute run."

Stroking my chin. "That's pretty smart. So you say they don't get greedy, so they grab what?"

Frank dropped the stick and sat back into the bench. "They just take whatever is there. They take—like the most I've ever heard is like $24,000."

Much of the con-artist activity Frank explained fit the ideology of rational choice. Police surveillance (or lack thereof in certain spots) and public policy allow opportunities for criminal behavior, and the aforementioned perpetrators oblige. But this also reflected a sign of the times. New Yorkers live under ever-increasing amounts of surveil-lance and a strict penal code. Getting away with a crime involves seeing the cracks in the foundation of the law, or knowing how to get over on someone who can open a door for you, or knowing someone that will allow you to get away with it in the first place.

COP CONS

In his book *Undercover: Police Surveillance in America*, the sociologist Gary Marx argued that police and state officials should be held to a higher standard than the average citizen: "The state should not teach bad morals lessons or engage in conduct that shocks the conscience."[5]

Of course, police officers are not shielded from criminal opportunities and are not immune to greed and corruption. The New York City Police Department has a long list of allegations of corruption and brutality and cons and hustles of their own. In 2014, 106 former NYPD and New York City Fire Department employees were caught in one of the largest disability fraud cases in the city's history. Since 1988, these officers conned the city out of $400 million in tax dollars by faking disabilities. Another cohort of cop con artists claimed to have suffered from "crippling emotional damage" after being first responders to the terrorist attacks in downtown Manhattan on September 11, 2001. It was later found out that many of the recipients of disability benefits had never even been to Ground Zero.

Former NYPD officer Joseph Esposito—who advised officers and firefighters how to fake disabilities in exchange for a fee—was dubbed the ringleader of the fraud and eventually pled guilty to first-degree grand larceny and agreed to cooperate with the Manhattan district attorney.[6] Even the "finest" and "bravest" citizens of New York are susceptible to crime if the right opportunity comes along.

I asked Frank if he would volunteer any stories of police corruption. "So is there such a thing as a police con? Or a police hustle?"

Frank smiled so big that I couldn't see his eyes. "Of course." He slouched in the bench and folded his arms, allowing some of the memories to come to him. "Well, the con is like, the con is the classic good guy/bad guy. That's the con. That's the biggest one. Basically, anytime you say anything to a police officer, it's on the record. It's never off the record. The biggest con that police officers have is . . . say you get pulled over . . . they call it a 'spontaneous utterance.' Spontaneous utterance is exactly what it sounds like . . . "

"On my part as the driver?"

"It's the person in the car. It's the person stopped on the street. When they say something—unprovoked—that can harm them in a case. So basically—and this is everywhere—worldwide. Spontaneous utterance is something that can be used against you in a court of law. You know it's a part of one's Miranda rights."

"My understanding then is that without the Miranda, then it's inadmissible in court."

Frank smiled. "Except for spontaneous utterance."

"So that's a lot of gray area."

"Right! In other words, the biggest con that the police department has is getting you to say . . . getting you to admit guilt without specifically asking you a question. Like, 'Did you do it?' "

"To me that sounds like that has to happen before the arrest."

Frank straightened up in his seat. "No, no. If I have probable cause to arrest you, okay? Let's give the example of shoplifting. Security caught you but didn't catch you on camera. Security caught you stealing something. But you didn't pass the register. You only put it in your bag. And now security stops you and says, 'Yeah, he was going to pass the register.' But you were right at the register, so it's like an iffy thing. I mean, you put it in your bag and you were about to walk out. And you the thief are basically saying, 'Hey, I was here to buy stuff, and I put it in my bag and I forgot to pay. And as soon as they stopped me, I was turning around to pay.' So that's like an iffy area because—"

I interrupted, "Can that be counted as an utterance?"

"Yes, but . . . but what you were saying is that you 'weren't stealing,' you were 'coming back to pay.' Now . . . your nerves are all in a bunch. And you're thinking, 'I'm not going to say anything. I'm not going to fuck this up.' So what I do is, I come in. I calm things down. I'm like, 'Don't worry about it. Shoplifting is fucking nothing. It's stupid. You know.' Frank motioned to a fake chair, 'Just have a seat . . . Hey you want a cup of water? You want this?' " Frank stood and shifted around as if he were adjusting an imaginary police duty belt. "I wait. And then later on, I get to know you because I have to ask you questions.

And so then I'm like, 'This is stupid. This guy last week got caught stealing. And you know? It's the same charge whether you admit it or not. I told the guy last week' . . . So I'm lying at this point . . . 'It's the same charge. And you know what the guy did? He told me the fucking truth. And you know what I did for him? I let him out. I fucking let him out because you know what? I was thinking, this guy is honest. He's telling the truth.' And then you go . . . " He pointed at me.

I laughed. "Ding! Light bulb!"

"You're thinking, 'This guy is a good guy. He let this other guy go. I think I'm going to tell him that I did it.' And then, boom! That's it. You're done. Because once you say that—now, I didn't ask you a question. I didn't ask you if you took the stuff."

"Oh, because otherwise an attorney needs to be there. Or a confession."

"Well, yeah. In other words, you need to be Mirandized. So that term spontaneous utterance is actually written in our manuals and in the law. Spontaneous utterance is admissible in court . . . before you get Mirandized. So that is a con. That is a con that police use all the time."

I smirked. "I get it. So the judge asks, 'Officer did you ask him?' "

" 'No.' "

" 'No?' "

" 'Nope.' . . . I mean there's dirty cops who lie, but you know . . . That's not a con, that's . . . "

I laughed. "Well, now you're conning the judge."

"That's just a lie." Frank held up his hands submissively. "But there's ways to get around it. Unless you are a seasoned criminal, I mean, seasoned criminals are not stupid. But the average criminal, is not, you know [that smart]."

It was interesting to hear Frank's quick admission that officers use the language of the law to their advantage, even if they are doing something unethical. The NYPD has had an image problem for decades. Many New Yorkers view members of the NYPD at best as dishonest and at worst as outright corrupt. For example, at the time of my interview with Frank, the NYPD was caught in the midst of a ticket-fixing scandal. It was found that there was a "systematic practice citywide"[7] of making traffic tickets disappear for offending police officers and their friends.

I decided to continue questioning Frank. "Do you know of situations where officers use their uniforms to their advantage? Use their badge to their advantage?

Frank laughed and stomped his feet on the ground. "Yes! There's officers who do things that are against our policies, very against our policies. One where you walk into—I've seen this before—one where you walk into, say, a restaurant. It's kind of the unwritten rule that you will get a discount on your food."

"For free?"

"Some . . . Now, that's one thing. The problem is, is when they don't. They don't do—it's called 'do the right thing'—when people don't do the right thing . . . If they charge them full price in a restaurant—I don't know if that's a con or a hustle—but they [the cops] will go back and hit the place." Frank explained that if an officer feels slighted, he will send his underlings back to look for code violations, something most restaurants are incredibly afraid of, because the grading system can make or break a restaurant.

Frank continued, "There's a lieutenant at my job—and I don't know how he gets away with this." Frank leaned in closer and lowered his voice. "There was a hotel that opened up. Now this hotel was built from the ground up. Talk about millions and millions of dollars. This lieutenant walks up to the head of security—who he doesn't realize is a retired police inspector—he walks up to him, and because the hotel opened up in what he considers to be his backyard, he walks up to him and says, 'Hey, this is what I'm going to do for you. I'm going to make sure you don't get summonses. I'm going to make sure that you're taken care of. The whole parking thing. Inside, you're not going to get visits.' And so the head of security told me and said, 'What the fuck is up with this guy? I could have taken his job.'

"So the cop says that to him, and the security guy says, 'Do you have any idea who I am?' He said, 'No, why?' He said, 'I'm a retired inspector . . . from such and such precinct.' And the conversation ended there." Frank laughed. "He was 'this is who I am. Get the fuck out of my face.' And that was the end of it. He left and he never spoke with him again. But . . . on the flip side of that, there are people who have been under his command, and this guy has been with a girl-friend . . . he's married, so this is a girlfriend of his . . . drinking and eating. And they haven't done the right thing [i.e., the restaurant has not offered him a discount]. So he's on duty, drinking [alcohol] and eating, and he's called his cops—those under him—to come in and find violations with the restaurant. In other words, he's sitting down eating, and he says, 'Hey, so let me get the bill.' Here comes the bill. The bill's the full boat. So he looks at it, pays it, puts it back. Five min-utes later, his guys come in, shut down the place for like hours . . . and if you shut down the place for hours on a Saturday night, the place is losing a lot of money. He gave them all these summonses, violations, this, that, and the other."

I was shocked. "I mean, I feel like it's a hustle if the message is out. Like, 'That's Officer so-and-so, make sure he gets a free meal. Or he'll fuck with us.'"

"Well, what this guy doesn't understand is that he's not liked by these owners. And this is why I don't understand why he's still employed. I don't understand why he still has his job. And the only conclusion I can come to, is if and when he's getting in trouble, he has what's called a hook—someone higher up that he knows—which means what they're doing is shutting down the phone calls."

I added, "He must be somebody's favorite."

"Yeah. Somebody's favorite who's connected. And maybe he's con-nected to the officer." Frank sat for a moment, trying to think of other examples.

I coached him along. "How about something where people got stuff on the side. But it's advantageous to be an officer in order to do that stuff on the side."

Frank leaned back and spoke without hesitation. "The security business."

"But that's sounds legit to me . . . unless you are talking about something off the books."

He scoffed. "Well there's that too. Say you're a cop. And you are a lieutenant or captain or whatever, and I work here."

Frank pointed toward the park, then in the general direction of some restaurants. "And I always go to lunch there, and right next to it is a building that has security. After some time working here, I make friends, I make connections, and I say, 'Okay, well, I'm going to get a job there.' And the hustle is finding a job off the books and also securing yourself a position in an agency when you retire."

He mentioned that the head of security at a major university was a retired deputy inspector. "Now you cannot tell me that he did not secure that job before he retired. He stuck his tentacles into that school and he got there. All the security underneath him are ex-NYPD officers. That's a perfect example. That guy used his position in the NYPD to secure a position after he retired. That's against NYPD regulations. But because he was deputy inspector, nobody looked into it. Nobody cared to look into it."

I asked, "And his qualifications are?"

"Could he have legitimately retired from the NYPD?" Frank threw up his hands. "And could he have submitted his application to the school and received the position? Yeah . . . Did it happen like that? No."

The Mud Truck

As I was scribbling down some notes, Frank pushed my shoulder. "I got another one for you, another example. The mud truck."

"The what truck?"

"The mud truck. It's like a coffee and hot-chocolate truck. That was the favorite of a lieutenant I knew. That was his favorite place for coffee and what not. One day, the Department of Traffic gave him a summons and kept on giving him a summons. He secured his space where he was parking, and that's the spot where the mud truck is. It was across the street from Starbucks. Starbucks kept calling, saying 'he's not parked legally, you have to give him a summons.' "

"Oh, that's competition, yeah."

"Because the truck was the favorite of the lieutenant, and it was a known fact, you don't write this mud truck a summons. What did they do? They got smart and called the Department of Traffic, which he has no direct control over. Department of Traffic started writing summonses. The Department of Traffic was there one day, and he got wind of it, and he sent one of his cronies to go over to correct the situation. He had an argument with a Department of Traffic officer because he was writing a ticket for a car parked illegally. So this officer was supposed to be promoted to sergeant, and he never was. And he's still in the process of getting in trouble. That is one example of how it happens all the time. It happens all the time. Every day. Every day."

Ticket Fixing

I began to wonder if the current police cons were any different from those back in New York City's 1980s crime heyday. Many of the laws have changed since then; have the cons and hustles changed in the age of the Internet?

Frank answered, "So, the latest thing on the edge of what's going on in the police department is the whole ticket thing."

"Do you mean ticket quotas?"

"Not ticket quotas. Ticket fixing. Ticket fixing has been around since the beginning."

In 2011, the New York Police Department was knee deep in a fraud investigation. Ten officers were charged with ticket fixing, and six officers were charged with "unrelated corruption accounts."[8] This eventually led to the investigation and disciplining of more than three hundred officers, with one lieutenant losing his job and his pension.

Frank explained that ticket fixing is mostly done through favors between officers and their relatives and friends. "You get a summons.

You're driving and you pass through a stop sign and you get pulled over, because you're talking to your wife on the phone and you don't realize it, and you get a summons. You call me and say 'Hey, I got this summons and blah blah.' And I say, 'No problem.' I take the summons and call the guy that gave you the ticket. 'He's a friend of mine, blah blah blah,' and they take care of it."

Still unsure of the procedure, I asked, "You mean they write something on the sheet of the ticket?"

Frank pretended to tear a piece of paper in half. "No, they rip it up before they even give it to you. They way this happens is, either they take care of it right there, or they take care of it at court. You show up at court, plead not guilty, and the officer is asked by the judge, how do you plead against this person? And he says, 'I don't recall this case.'"

Frank shook his head. "[Then Mayor Michael] Bloomberg changed the whole way that the tickets are done. And what he did was, every summons has a barcode and a number on it. Before, we would have a pack of summons, and you returned the pack, but you could determine the total number of summons. So if you returned a pack that had nineteen, then it was nineteen. If you returned seventeen, then you returned seventeen. That's the way it went. So if your summons never made it back, then that's the way it was. So what Bloomberg did was to make everything scanned in. So now he can take it from his office. So he can take the summonses and check from when things were written to when everything was returned. 'Why is this one summons not returned?' So in other words, there's no more ripping up summonses anymore. That's gone."

Frank leaned in closer. "Now, to adjust, people are calling up their friends and saying 'fix the summons for me' and someone going to court and saying, 'I don't recall.' So he said, 'When you go to court—traffic court—and you testify and say, 'I don't recall,' then you get found not guilty, I go sign out and go back to my office, and then someone from internal affairs is saying, 'I want to see your memo book'—your memo book is where you write everything down—'I want to see your memo book, and I want to see your summons.' What they do is they have your memo

book and your summons and they go through it. And they see something to fuck you with. And if anything is missing out of those things,
then they give you what's called a Command's Discipline, which is an
official writeup, and they take ten vacation days away from you."

The Hot-Dog Unit

We spoke for a minute about the changes in policing and how it has
affected con artists and hustlers. I assumed that the increase in size
of the police force had to have affected them. "It seems to me that the
laws . . . the tripling of the police force since the 1980s has chased a lot
of stuff indoors."

Frank laughed and waved his hand dismissively. "The 'tripling of the
police force since the 1980s' is all a sham."

I was surprised to hear him rebut a fact widely touted by the city.
"Are you saying that's not true?"

"The tripling of the police force does not affect crime. I cannot
say it does not affect all crime but it does affect some crime . . . there
have been so many units." (The New York City Police Department has
approximately 34,500 officers placed in more than three hundred separate units.)

Frank joked, "I think there's so many units, there's a hot-dog unit."
He laughed. "The thinking with the units is, I get into power, and then I
get my boys in. And I got to hook you up . . . now I rise up in rank where
I'm in charge—in some way shape or form—of creating a new unit. You
don't want to do anything. You're my boy. I create the 'hot-dog unit.'"
We both laughed. "And I put you in charge of the hot-dog unit. And
then you have six other boys that are your boys. So they all get into the
hot-dog unit together and they do nothing."

He looked up and glanced at the now more crowded nearby benches,
stood up, and motioned for me to stand. "Walk with me. I'm going to
tell you a story." We began to walk down a wide path. "I knew this guy
in another precinct—two guys—that got into a unit together. One was

the R&P [radio and patrol] coordinator—which is an official position. The R&P coordinator's official position is to make sure all of the cars are up and running and efficient in that precinct. This guy was Italian." At the time, Frank explained, the tour system allowed officers to make their own hours. "Because usual tours [now] are like 7 a.m. to 4 p.m., 4 p.m. to 12 p.m., and 12 p.m. to 8 p.m. And then they had two odd tours, like 10 to 6 and 8 to 4."

The gravel under our feet crunched just loud enough to mask what he was saying from passersby. "Before Sean Bell, people were allowed to work odd tours." Sean Bell, a twenty-three-year-old African American, was murdered by both undercover and plainclothes New York City officers in 2006; afterward, the officers involved were questioned about their schedules and use of force. "So, if you're a supervisor and you hate me—and you don't even realize that I'm at work—can you fuck with me? No, right? So if you as the supervisor come in at 7, all I have to do is change my tour to start at 5. So I'm long gone."

"So as long as you work eight hours, you can work any eight hours?"

"You could take any eight in the past. That was in the past. So what this guy did was, he had a tour that was like 1 a.m. to 9 a.m. Like, who the fuck is working at that time?"

I was surprised. "What was he into during those hours?"

Frank stopped walking and grabbed the back of my arm. "What he did was, he was building his house in Rockland County. Upstate."

"Overnight?"

"No. He would call in, and then he would sleep. He would be sleeping. He would call up at 1 a.m., 'Yeah, I'm present for duty'. And they would put him on the book."

"So technically, on paper, he was in the city somewhere. But who's going to look for him at one in the morning?"

Frank slapped me on the back. "Right, exactly. And around five or six o'clock he would stroll in . . . He was good. I'll give it to him, he was good. He would buy pizzas for the guys in the garage. So you know, if this guy brings in a car, you're getting fed today. So what are you going to do? You make sure his car is right. This guy had his cars on point all the time. So nobody fucked with him, but not because the cars were right, but because he was who he was."

Frank shook his head. "He built his house and got paid to do it. I never saw the guy more than, like, three times."

"Did he get caught?"

"Nope. The guy had a hook."

Our walk came to an end at Frank's SUV, and so too did our candid conversation. I thanked him for his time. He smiled, shook hands, and patted me on the back. He made it clear that no one is immune to greed and entitlement. In fact, it was one of the many things that gives New York City its character. But this was just one version of police life in the NYPD. There are 35,000 police officers in New York City, each with their own story. This has been one of them.

ELEVEN

WALL STREET CONS

You got 90 percent of the American public out there with little or no net worth. I create nothing. I own. We make the rules, pal. The news, war, peace, famine, upheaval, the price per paper clip. We pick that rabbit out of the hat while everybody sits out there wondering how the hell we did it.

— Gordon Gekko, *Wall Street* (1987)

Wall Street is the fabled place where rags-to-riches stories can happen every day. If drug dealing can be the most dangerous hustle, Wall Street can be the most lucrative. It is a world where testosterone and complex finance meet, where the money is large and the cons even larger.

Single financial-services firms can pull the strings of the global economy, and traders can strip a person of forty years' worth of life savings in an instant. Investment bankers make an average of $153,005 annually: that's six times the amount of the average worker in the United States.[1] Whereas a crack dealer can make five thousand dollars a week, a chief executive can make $1.6 million per week.[2] And where there is the opportunity to make this type of money, there is the motivation for cons.

The bottom line for executives is to accumulate wealth, often by any means necessary. The same goes for investors. Wall Street stockbrokers are the go-betweens: the runners, the movers and shakers that find clients and invest their dollars in order to earn more money. The deception lies in how this trading is (legally) run. Brokers do not trade money; they trade derivatives—contracts between two parties that specify the value of a trade and how it's going to be paid. Derivatives are promises and nothing more.

The New York Stock Exchange (also known as the Intercontinental Exchange) calls itself "the architects of the world's markets."[3] It is the largest stock exchange in the world, with an estimated $16.6 trillion of value in all of its exchange notes and a daily trading value of $169 billion.[4] This is a fast-paced, cutthroat universe. Immortalized by characters such as Gordon Gekko in Oliver Stone's *Wall Street* (1987) or the real-life Jordan Belfort of Martin Scorsese's *The Wolf of Wall Street* (2013), brokers are often portrayed in the media as unconscionable sociopaths who will do anything for an extra dollar, but in a society that celebrates the acquisition of wealth by any means, we see them more as heroes than villains. We appreciate their unquenchable thirst for wealth even if we detest the extremes to which they will go to make it. As the fictional Gekko said, "The point is, ladies and gentlemen, that greed, for lack of a better word, is good."

Many of these brokers and executives are New Yorkers; they are masters in the art of deception, like Alibi or Daniel, and tireless salespersons with the same drive as Lee or Otis. They just happen to dress in more expensive suits. They are a part of what the sociologist C. Wright Mills called the "power elite."[5] With their level of financial capital comes power: the power to boost a national economy—and the power to destroy it.

THE ORIGINS OF THE GREAT RECESSION

Since the 1920s, Wall Street has played a role in most economic depressions and recessions, including the most recent Great Recession, which began in October 2008. An overabundance of derivatives, wild speculation, and subprime mortgage lending (in which borrowers are typically unable to pay back the loans)—and a healthy dose of greed—led to one of the most rapid financial collapses in American history. According to the Consumer Education Foundation: "By [the time of the crash], the amount of financial derivatives in circulation around the world—$638 trillion by one estimate—was more than ten times the value of all the goods and services produced by the entire planet. When all the speculators tried to cash out, starting in 2007, there really wasn't enough money to cover all the bets."[6] As a result, banks began to collapse, and investment screeched to a halt. The American economy took a huge blow, resulting in a loss of more than 1.8 million American jobs in the first three months of 2009 alone.[7]

Many financial experts suggest that this collapse was aided, in part, by the 1999 repeal of the Glass-Steagall Act of 1933, which imposed limitations on the activities different types of financial institutions could engage in. The original limitations stated that commercial banks could not act as investment banks by dealing in securities and relying on deposits. Neither could commercial banks act as insurance companies. Since the 1980s, the financial industry had lobbied to change the law. As David Simon wrote, "In 1999, the financial services industry spent a record $417 million [on lobbying] to have the Glass-Steagall Act of 1933 overturned."[8] That finally occurred in 1999 with the passing of the Gramm-Leach-Bliley Act. This new law eliminated the restrictions of Glass-Steagall and allowed commercial banks to merge with other financial institutions and become financial holding companies. The rise of Citigroup—and other financial conglomerates—was an immediate result of the repeal. It is worth noting that Gramm-Leach-Bliley was heavily endorsed by Robert Rubin (at the time, secretary of the

Treasury), who then resigned as secretary of the Treasury in 1999 and became the head of Citigroup. By late 2008, after the share price of Citigroup dipped below a dollar, he had disappeared from the public arena.

The abolition of Glass-Steagall stimulated greedy behavior by blurring risks (with overinflated derivatives), increasing financial uncertainty (by gambling with individuals' life savings), adding complexity (in order to trick consumers into subprime loans), and most importantly swallowing up capital. After its abolition, bankers could make investments and gamble with people's retirement funds, mortgages, and life savings—and they took full advantage. Greed became the name of the game, and con artists came out of the woodwork to get their piece. Things became more perverse as financial-services firms began to accumulate toxic debt. Banks began to lend out what were known as NINJA mortgages (No Income, No Job, no Assets), and in 2004, Henry Paulson (then CEO of Goldman Sachs but who would later become the U.S. secretary of the Treasury) successfully lobbied the U.S. government to exempt the top five banks from the "net capital rule," which was established in 1975 to require banks to hold enough liquid capital to pay all of their debtors. Many viewed this act as the final nail in the coffin.

The amount of financial fraud that occurred between 1999 and 2008 was unthinkable, and the regulatory agencies created to supervise and restrain financial excesses did little to stop it. Consider the notorious Bernie Madoff, who founded Bernard L. Madoff Investment Securities LLC in the 1980s. The Securities and Exchange Commission (SEC) is supposed to supervise firms like Madoff's but failed to detect his financial manipulations as he defrauded middle-class investors out of $65 billion. He was eventually caught with his hands in other people's bank accounts, investment portfolios, money markets, and hedge funds. (The proverbial "cookie jar" is too inadequate a metaphor to describe the hundreds of individuals and institutional investors who were defrauded.)

According to the anthropologist Karen Ho in her book *Liquidated: An Ethnography of Wall Street*, "Even the mainstream media was very critical of the myriad insider trading scandals, stock market manipulations, and the 'human cost' of corporate takeovers, and many writers explicitly identified Wall Street practices and elite privilege as the causes of human suffering."[9]

This is a complicated world by design, one in which Joe Average is blind to the invisible hand that is moving the markets, where government regulators create thousand-page documents to prevent fraud, and where attorneys make their careers off of finding the loopholes. The economist Adam Smith first used the phrase "invisible hand (of God)," assuming that individuals try to maximize their own good and get richer in the process. Smith originally wanted to emphasize the positive unintended consequences of an individual's actions on society. Through trade and entrepreneurship, society as a whole is better off. But we've come to use the phrase to illustrate the negative consequences of individual greed on society.

THE PONZI MAN

In the 1920s, a thirty-eight-year-old Boston man named Charles Ponzi is said to have made $2 million a week in what later became the defining moniker for a confidence scheme and that would carry his name into infamy: the Ponzi scheme. This visionary project—or underhanded plan—was used with such skill that it took on storied proportions. Charles Ponzi guaranteed investors that they would make "50% profit within 45 days,"[10] an outright lie. He would pay out the "profits" of old investors with money from new investors. The journalist Mitchell Zuckoff, in *Ponzi Scheme: The True Story of a Financial Legend*, describes the brash young Charles Ponzi operating at his office. Hundreds stood in line to give him money to invest.

> Investors slid their cash to one of the young tellers. Often they were three particular girls: Angela Locarno, her sister Marie Locarno, and their friend Bessie Langone. In return for cash, the investors received promissory notes, receipts really, that guaranteed the original investment plus

50% in forty-five days. The receipts bore Ponzi's ink-stamped signature, which led many to call them simply "Ponzi notes."[11]

In the law professor Arthur Lett's *Swindling and Selling* he states:

> A Ponzi can, after all, be viewed as an adaptation of a chain or pyramid with a structure such that information moves downward pyramidically while wealth moves back and forth between the hub of a wheel and points on an ever-enlarging rim. In theory, it's a very simple scheme. Mr. Ponzi promises that if a mark will give him $100 today, he will give the mark $150 a month and a half hence. And he does. On the first of June, say, A, B, C, D, each give him $100. He thus needs $600 to deliver to them on July 15th. But on July 1st, six other guys, E, through J, each give him $100, and their return, $900, isn't due until August 15th. So when July 15th rolls around, Mr. Ponzi gives A through D the $600 E through J gave him, and by the time he owes E through J their $900, at least nine other marks have appeared to kick in their $100 each.[12]

Of course, when the largest amount of money is collected, the perpetrator of the con is supposed to disappear; often times, that meant go to jail.

What Charles Ponzi did at the turn of the century, and what con artists on Wall Street and pretty much everywhere else in America do today, is to seduce people with claims of steady dividends higher than they would normally get from conventional investments. It seemed (and still seems) too good to be true, and it was. As was said by the master con artist of yesteryear, Joseph "Yellow Kid" Weil, "They wanted something for nothing and I gave them nothing for something."[13] The Chicago-born Weil was an equal-opportunity confidence man— swindling both rich and poor of money—and was said to have collected over $8 million between 1903 and his death in 1976.

The Ponzi plan perfected by Bernard Madoff claimed to pay investors steady dividends of 8 to 12 percent over a period of twenty years. No doubt the "dragging element" (its apparent longevity of gains) of this long con made it attractive to clients and took away any doubts that the confidence they had in him might be misplaced. Federal investigators believed Madoff's Ponzi scheme began in the 1980s and worked for so long because investors rarely (if ever) asked to cash out.

Madoff admitted during his trial that he would deposit investors' monies into a Chase account and that he "used the money in the Chase Manhattan bank account that belonged to them or other clients to pay the requested funds"[14] when clients asked to cash out. This scheme fell apart with the economic collapse of 2008, when investors wanted to cash out their money rather than watch it go down the drain. Madoff was said to be $7 billion behind in redemption payments in the first week of December 2008 alone.[15]

These entrepreneurial con artists have been around even before Charles Ponzi. John D. Rockefeller's father, William, was a con man who called himself a "botanical physician" and a "snake oil" salesman, a term for those who sold phony elixirs such as cancer cures and baldness prevention. In the next section, we will meet a man who spent time on the "Street" and knows a thing or two about Ponzi schemes because he is the penultimate Wall Street insider.

AN INSIDE MAN

In order to grasp the complexity of this world, Trevor Milton had the pleasure of talking with a Wall Street insider, J.T. Gartner (pseudonym), a sixty-seven-year-old man and retired stockbroker. Humble and restrained, he's not a typical broker, but he did have a seat on the American Stock Exchange for thirty years.

I met J.T. at his large yet unpretentious home in southwestern Connecticut, where his wife served a roast-beef dinner. There was light snow on the ground outside. I removed my shoes out of courtesy, and they offered me slippers. It was a cold night and a long drive, so the warm food and compassionate hospitality was welcome. J.T. was retired from Wall Street, but he had plenty to say about it. He had specialized in equities, options, futures, and bonds: all investment tools with various rates of fixed returns or high-risk/high-yield returns.

I entered the discussion wanting to know about the nature of stock traders and their ability to run cons. What were the best slams? How many Bernie Madoffs were out there slithering down the downtown streets of New York? J.T. immediately told me that my focus should not be so much on the individual traders but rather on the financial firms that push them to trade.

I started asking questions about the financial crash of 2008. "After the crash, it looks like Wall Street never skipped a beat, and a lot of financial services firms are hoarding money waiting for the recession to end. The idea was that the bailout money [$700 billion given to banks through the Emergency Economic Stabilization Act of 2008] was designed to pour money back into the economy to create jobs, et cetera, but it looks like the banks and services firms are waiting around for the recession to end before they give out loans."

J.T. finished chewing, wiped his mouth with a napkin, and then pointed his fork toward the table. "I disagree with you. First of all, it's really very complicated. The Federal Reserve buys the paper, the bonds. The Federal Reserve deposits it into the banks. And the banks receive a quarter percent of interest on the money on deposit at the Federal Reserve."

The Federal Reserve—also known as the "Fed" or the "central bank"—was created in 1913 to be a safety net for the national financial system in case of crisis. Controlled by a board of (privately selected) governors—and fed currency by the U.S. Department of Treasury—its job is to oversee monetary policy and to lend money to private banks in times of recession or depression in order to maximize employment and stabilize the economy.

J.T. smiled as he explained that private banks have to uphold their end of the bargain but often do not. "Why loan the (Treasury) money out when they can earn a quarter percent risk free? Because the cost of money for them is less than a quarter of a percent. The banks make a lot of money; all of those billions. A quarter percent of $65 billion is like $175 million a month." He calculated these numbers without pause and without averting his gaze. "I don't know what the balance sheet is, but it's like $2 trillion in reserve is $5 billion a year earned in interest." Accurate to the dollar, he shrugged his shoulders and continued to eat. "Whatever it is, it's a lot of money."

The biggest banks—those labeled "too big to fail"—earned record dollars in 2009 as national employment hit its highest rate (10.2 percent) since 1982 and the economy grew more unstable. Expert economists and presidential advisors held tight to a Freidmanesque[16] style of economic policy—one that advised government to cut taxes and invest in the business sector—which largely meant giving money to the wealthy and hoping that it would eventually trickle down to the middle and working classes in the form of jobs and affordable goods. In one of Barack Obama's first acts as president, he signed the American Recovery and Reinvestment Act, which gave the banks another $831 billion in order to encourage loans and stimulate job growth. The banks simply took the money, sat on it, earned interest, paid it back, and said, "thanks!"

Those too-big-to-fail banks got even bigger. According to the sociologist David Simon in *Elite Deviance*: "Even now, three out of the four largest banks in America (J. P. Morgan Chase, Bank of America, and Wells Fargo) are now larger than before the bailout . . . These four big banks now issue two-thirds of all credit cards, half of the mortgages and control nearly 40 percent of all bank deposits."[17] In his book, Simon chronicled both illegal and legal acts of powerful financial institutions and their detriment to society.

The biggest loser since 2009 has been Keynesian economics, the theory that recommends raising taxes and investing in workers. Every attempt by the Obama administration to create jobs directly through federal funding has been shot down by a conservative U.S. Congress, and banks have taken stimulus money and gone laughing all the way, well, to the bank.

J.T. would have liked to see a more Keynesian approach to fixing the crisis. "Let's suppose the Federal Reserve reduces its payment to the banks, they would lend it out. If they would lend it out, interest rates would rise because it would stimulate economic activity. But this would bankrupt the government. So they're locked. The velocity of money is very low. The money is tied up, then the government would be bankrupt. All the revenues received would be going to paying the interest on the debt."

I tried to imagine a world where the U.S. government filed for bankruptcy. "What happens to the banks if the government goes bankrupt?"

J.T. continued to move the food around his plate. "Interest rates would go up, and then economic activity would stop."

"Then it's another recession."

"Yeah. One of the reasons is that the total indebtedness of the country is like 225 percent of the GDP. In other words, the indebtedness of all the people, and all of the businesses and the state—which is the total U.S. indebtedness—is so great." The U.S. government has been in the habit of borrowing money for decades—for military and social programs alike. As of this writing, it still owes $16.8 trillion. And private debt (money owed on credit cards, student loans, mortgages, etc.) is estimated at $60 trillion for the nation.

J.T. shrugged his shoulders. "So we're locked in." He sees the solution as simple but politically impossible. "So what the Democrats are saying—which I subscribe to—the right thing for the country is to tax the wealthy and do meaningful infrastructure, but the wealthy are not going to tolerate that. And it's hard to do legitimate infrastructure in the political climate we have, which involves a lot of corruption. So we're fucked."

The political strategy for fixing the U.S. economy between 2009 and 2013 followed the Republican playbook: favoring economic austerity (reduced spending in order to reduce the deficit) and lowered regulations (so the wealthy can increase their wealth), in the hopes that this will create jobs. A catchphrase during Mitt Romney's 2012 presidential campaign run was to "try not to scare job creators." In 2015, the national unemployment rate has dropped to 5.5 percent, but this can largely be attributed to government investment in those job creators.

As J.T. finished eating, he laughed at the idea. "Yeah, but that [job creation] is not going to happen, and the reason that's not going to happen is because of globalization." A byproduct of globalization is the outsourcing of many of the new jobs created. During the industrial age, a wealthy manufacturer could literally create tens of thousands of jobs overnight once sales started to pick up. As the political scientist Naomi Klein pointed out in *No Logo*,[18] "Such menial tasks [were] farmed out to contractors and subcontractors whose only concern is filling the order on time and under budget (ideally in the Third World, where labor is dirt cheap, laws are lax and tax breaks come by the bushel)."

Wealth tends to trickle out rather than trickle down. According to J.T., "This has drained the legitimate jobs of this economy, so that's not the solution. Which brings up the third facet of this: we no longer live in a society that has legitimate opportunities for everybody to live a life like you want to live. So in other words—you've heard the statistics—85 people own 50 percent of the wealth of the globe. So like the Waltons and the Saudis . . . The wealthiest 1 percent own 50 percent of the wealth or something like that." Again, J.T. acted like he was unsure of his numbers, but he was completely accurate.

We finished our meals, and J.T. motioned for me to walk to his study. We walked upstairs, down a long hallway, and into a room with several humming computers. He buttoned his leaf-green sweater and sat in his favorite chair before continuing to talk about the plight of the American worker. "There aren't legitimate jobs for all the people that would want to work. When they say 'Anybody who wants a job can get a job' . . . well, if you're a fifty-five-year-old engineer with a house and a mortgage and two kids in college, how are you going to survive on a McDonald's salary?"

Repo Men

I asked more about the daily operations on the Street. J.T. wanted to make a clear distinction between "upstairs" (where executives watch over their investments and dictate investment goals to brokers) and "downstairs" (where the brokers trade derivatives, stocks, and bonds). He explained that floor traders—as portrayed in movies about Wall Street—are somewhat a thing of the past. "The floor is electronic. The floor has very little relevance to the subject that you are trying to address. In other words, the amount of fraud that goes on with what I call 'floor operations' is relatively small, although the robot trading is a problem. The floor operations have a problem for two reasons: the lack of liquidity when the robots get into trouble and the repo market. The repo market—"

I asked, "Like repossession?"

J.T. laughed. "It *is* repossession. It's the place where banks trade overnight money. There are fifty significant banks in the country. The repo market [repo is short for 'repurchase agreement'] is worldwide, with counterparties. And what they have is . . . everybody keeps a ledger of who they owe and who owes them. Now let's suppose a bank, any bank, has a problem. It affects all the banks. If they stop trading with all the banks, that bank can't pay all of its obligations. It's like Atlanta in the snowstorm [in January 2014]: they can't trade anymore and the system crashes." J.T. used Atlanta—a city not known for snowfall—as an example of a city that shut down because of snowfall in 2014. "If the repo market—which is the most liquid—if that freezes up, we're all gone. In other words, it would take five hundred years of litigation to untangle the mess."

The repo market is a form of short-term borrowing for dealers in government securities. The dealer sells the government securities to investors, usually on an overnight basis, and buys them back the following day.[19] J.T. continued, "If for some reason there is a glitch in the repo market, things can get messy."

This world is extremely complicated yet very fragile. The smallest transactions can snowball into an avalanche. An inordinate amount of speculation is built on the hope that people will not try to cash out on their investments. Value is created out of thin air, but one blow to public confidence can suddenly lay bare all the smoke and mirrors. This was illustrated by the film director Curtis Hanson's adaptation of the economic collapse of 2008, *Too Big to Fail*. In the movie, U.S. Treasury Secretary Henry Paulson (played by William Hurt), painted a sobering picture:

> There's not a bank in the world that has enough money in its vaults to pay its depositors. It's all built on trust. . . . If [the big banks] pull back on interbank lending it's over within hours. From there it goes, too fast to stop, and not just one bank; the whole system. And average people wondering, "is my money safe?" They start pulling their cash. And after that: lines outside the bank, smashed ATMs. A couple of weeks: there's no milk in the store.

I read this quote to J.T., and he nodded in agreement. "That's right. It's like blood flowing in the body, and if there is an interruption in the blood flow, then there are problems."

The biggest con artists on Wall Street are not the downstairs stockbrokers—or the computers that have been built to replace them— but the financial-services firms and the executives that solely focus on the bottom line and making money by any means necessary. J.T. explained, "The real issue is the dividing line between what's legitimate and honest and fully disclosed and the stuff that isn't and that is half truths and outright dishonesty. So in other words, there's a number of ways to meet the letter of the regulations without intent.

"Let me give you an example. Let's suppose you're a public company, and you want to keep your revenues up. So now you're going out to raise more money. If you're a manufacturer, like a computer company, when it builds a computer and puts it on the loading dock, it considers that a sale. Another way is to get your wholesalers to buy extra merchandise for you. That's 'stuffing the pipeline.' But all of those are ways to minimize your work in progress and maximize your sales. Lehman Brothers did that with money.

"They would borrow $50 million on the 29th of the month just to show it on its books and then return it to its lender on the 1st of the next month. Somehow the accountants allowed this, so there was the illusion of all this cash on hand." Lehman Brothers and other institutions like it would borrow money at the end of each month to create the appearance of having liquid cash—and therefore healthy viability—to attract investors. The stage was set, the one-day bulk of cash was the prop, investors come, and the slam is successful.

J.T. rubbed his hands together. "All of the people that are involved in the global companies and know their business, they have an immense advantage when they want to take advantage of the unsophisticated." And sometimes the unsophisticated can be traders and seasoned investors themselves.

A "Golden Opportunity"

J.T. told me story of how he was once conned out of his own money. "Through some friends, I met a retired accountant for a gold-mining company. The company had been in business for twenty-five years, in an exploratory mode—and probably spent $100 million developing their property—and some money people came in and took over the company. The accountant is a Scotchman that is as straight as can be. He will tell the truth and fully disclose everything. Straight, but not sharp."

The investment seemed so good that the president of the company had put his own money into the investment. "This is a legitimate deal, but it had a hook. So I decided to invest. This guy is operating the company, but I never met the real money behind the company. He was operating the company 100 percent correctly. After I had made my investment, the money people came in and put $15 million into the company. Positive sign, right? They got warrant and interest rates on their money. And then a month and a half later, they announced an acquisition of a property from Newmont Mining, which included a mine and a mill in the deal.

"Great deal. Because they found out that they would finance this purchase, $83 million for this second purchase. They would finance this by selling a gold interest to another company and to another entity for a third of the money, and to another lender for 11 percent plus warrants, and they would have a public offering for the other third. Like $27 million. They had that all in line."

The "money people"—as J.T. called them—saw the value in the mining company and immediately began speculating on the company's future value. The con is turning those speculative future earnings into immediate present money. For example, if a company is actually worth $10 million—but it is projected to be worth $100 million in ten years—some will sell shares of that $100 million or sell the company outright for $100 million, grossly above the actual present value.

In the case of the mining company, "The stockbrokers raised $27 million for them, and I could see it coming. The next day, they took their $15 million out of the company. Leaving themselves with the warrants [an option to buy it back later] . . . at the end of this process, they ended up with 20 percent of the company, or the increase in the value of the company. They put in $15 million. They took out $15 million. At no risk to them because of they knew all of the parties involved. Now this is applauded in business." All built on trust, promise, with no risk.

Stockbrokers (floor traders) may do something very similar. J.T. explained that some brokers are masters of the "pump and dump." This is the stereotypical stockbroker con, where the broker artificially inflates the price of a stock in order to sell it at a higher price. The investor purchases the stock—and maybe enthusiastically purchases a lot of the stock—and then loses his or her money, but the broker has already made a commission: a typical slam.

J.T. explained it more precisely. "You have a company that makes available 500,000 shares. The 500,000 can come from selling stockholders. If you have a stock that's selling at $2, they'll sell it at $1.50. The brokerage house will get its brokers to talk up the stock, and it will jump to $2.50 or $3 a share. They would distribute the 500,000 shares, and then the stock would fall back to $2." Now the company has made $1.5 million, and the broker can earn up to a 50 percent commission: $750,000 for something that was worth only $1 million.

A profit of $750,000 is certainly a good day's work, which is why brokers like Jordan Belfort (who was depicted in *The Wolf of Wall Street*) are so motivated to make sales. J.T. explained that "[Jordan] is like a horse that the stock is running to, which allows the company to sell retail to unsophisticated people." And ran he did because money is addictive. Some researchers suggest that traders develop what's called a "cocaine brain," which may be sometimes fueled by actual cocaine but is mostly stimulated by a biological need for greed. As explained in a *Business Insider* article: "Researchers have discovered that making money, such as is done by investors, stimulates the same part of the brain that using cocaine stimulates. The more you have, the more you want until it kills you, or you learn to control it."[20]

For some on the Street, fiduciary responsibility (defined as a broker's legal obligation to inform, manage, and protect an investor's money) goes out the window when commissions are titillating. As is said by the character Mark Hanna (played by Matthew McConaughey) in *The Wolf of Wall Street*: "So if you've got a client who bought stock at $8 and now it's at $16 and he's all fucking happy, he wants to cash in and liquidate, take his fucking money and run home, you don't let him do that . . . because that would make [the money] real. The only thing real is our commission."

The stakes are even higher as we move into the second decade of the twenty-first century. E-companies like Google, Facebook, and Apple dominate the market. As J.T. said, "They don't make anything, and they don't employ that many people." And for companies that make intangible products, there is even more room for speculation and price inflation. We have nothing to compare it to, no way to calculate their value with empirical certainty, and therefore have to trust the "experts."

These new behemoths have abandoned the notion of making a product and instead have—as Naomi Klein would say—focused exclusively on their brand. They "made the bold claim that producing goods was only an incidental part of their operations."[21] We live in a world where a company like Facebook could be valued at 4 cents a share or at $42 a share (on its initial public offering in May 2012) based on that magical guessing game. J.T. shrugged his shoulders when talking about these companies. "You're touching on a sensitive subject because I prefer to live in the real world. And I live in the twentieth century."

Reducing Opportunities

J.T. felt that the only way to fix all these problems would be to roll back some of these regulations. "We should reintroduce Glass-Steagall. No bank should have control over the investment banks. The investment banks should be able to raise money as equity or mezzanine financing from commercial banks. But no banks should be able to control the investment bank. They should be subject to monitoring. The amount of money they put in should not be able to bring down the bank."

J.T. felt that he spent his entire career being honest and responsible, which limited the amount of money he made. Those around him tore into investors and evaporated working people's life savings. The current financial system allows banks to loot the public, even though there are rules designed to prevent it. J.T continued, "The point is that, there are all sorts of accountants, lawyers, investment banks, rating agencies . . . the whole panoply of participants in the system which are looking for opportunities to give the veneer of legitimacy, either by outright fraudulent statements or half-truths. The business man is not interested in doing things legally. To a businessman, what he wants to know is 'do I have an arguable assertion to make to justify my actions?' Not that I know in my heart that this is the right way to do it. 'Am I infringing on someone's patent?' This one says 'yes,' this one says 'no.' I'm going to go that way. There are some that know it's wrong but are able to create the veneer of legitimacy."

J.T. believed that the regulatory system cannot keep up with those crossing the line but that if the U.S. government truly wanted to prevent fraud, they could. He asked, "Have you ever heard of Carnivore?" Carnivore was a surveillance system created by the FBI in 1997 to monitor a targeted user's Internet traffic. It would later be renamed DCS1000 and then NaruInsight, and it is currently used to monitor criminals and terrorist threats. J.T. emphasized, "if Obama is serious about regulation, he should use this system on financial-services firms."

J.T. believed that eventually something would have to give, and we as a society will regret all of this greed. "What a lot of Republicans don't seem to understand is that there is a difference between a millionaire and a hundred-millionaire or a billionaire. And this is a new phenomenon. There is an order or magnitude of the opportunities available. Who's the guy that started CNN? [Ted] Turner, right? Well he cashed out, and now he has miles of property around the country. More than he can ever use. And people should just take what they need.

"That being said, Malthus was right. We will be like bugs in a Petri dish and eat up all the resources." Thomas Robert Malthus, an eighteenth-century scholar, successfully predicted in 1798 that the world population would double every twenty-five years and that this could lead to the depletion of the world's resources. J.T. closed the notebook in front of him; he prepared to turn in for the night. He gave me one more gem before I left his home and began my journey back to New York City. "This cannot go on forever. We have too many people that are cut out of the opportunities and too many that hoard all of these resources for themselves. One day they'll learn."

END NOTE

What do J.T.'s colleagues have in common with the other con artists we've met in these pages? While they move in different circles—from crack houses to police stations, from ghettos to Wall Street—they are all more alike than you might first think. Each one is a shrewd opportunist; each makes the most of the chances he or she sees. They all have more than their fair share of innate attributes, such as street smarts, cognitive reasoning, and charm, which they use to their utmost when running down a con. They understand the social norms and rules of the environments they live in (Wall street, bancas, street corner, crack house) and capitalize on any weakness or tolerance for extralegal activities that they can find.

Cornel West opined that American culture has elevated "market" values such as greed, money, and power to the center of our culture and pushed "nonmarket" values such as compassion, love, and caring to the periphery. This elevation of "social larceny," if you will, has disordered our society, in our opinion. A democratic, civil society cannot stand if money and "mo' money" becomes the primary mark of distinction among its citizenry and inequality the fault of those without any. This brings us to one of the most important themes in our treatise: hypocrisy, the pretense of claiming the moral high ground or belief that one's own behavior is exempt from the laws of society. All of the con artists in this book are guilty of this to some degree. But then, the rest of us are, too. Hypocrisy rages in our city, in our country, and in our selves.

Hypocrisy and greed are double cousins, as greed fuels the con man's pursuits, whether we are discussing Gordon Gekko (from *Wall Street*) or Daniel or Alibi. Greed leads to recklessness. Consider the risks taken by Lorena in her pursuit of rent-free living, or by Bernie Madoff, or by Ramon, who continued his hedonistic pursuit of pleasure and money until it burned him. Conning is as addictive to a con artist as skydiving is to a thrill seeker and as second nature as any professional athlete fighting off injury in order to continue playing the sport he loves. Whether it be on the back streets of the outer boroughs, Canal Street, or Wall Street, hustlers hustle and con artists con because that is what they do. It is not only Wall Street traders that risk becoming addicted to money; all hustlers and con artists do at some point. All they have to do is ask, "how can I get more?"

We believe it fitting to end our narrative with Alibi, as he attempts one last con in the city.

Before Alibi left New York for good, I (Terry Williams) was able to have one more encounter with him. Alibi had gone down to Kenner, Louisiana, and during this sabbatical period I happened to meet the daughter of a famous New York City lawyer who was an apprentice to a filmmaker who was a close friend of mine. She (let's call her Eliza) wanted to make her own films. One day, during a casual conversation, I mentioned that I was working on a life story of a con man. Eliza asked if I could get this con man to let her film him in the act of conning someone.

I told her this would be hard to do because to film evidence of illegal activity might prove to be a real problem for the con artist. In addition I had many ethical issues to contend with, to say nothing of the problems I already had with Alibi and his crew. I decided simply to approach Alibi to see what he had to say about it. Surprisingly, he agreed to do it if there was money to be made. I told him the filmmaker was a documentarian and not likely to pay much but that maybe he could get a small fee.

I discussed the possibility of payment with Eliza, but she too said there would not be much, since she had very little to offer. Alibi was out of town at this time but coming back to New York for a visit any way. I told him he could meet with Eliza but that he would have to negotiate his own deal with her once he arrived.

We had a meeting, which was rather awkward since Alibi said very little and answered Eliza's questions in a curt "yes" and "no" manner. Afterward, Eliza asked if I thought Alibi would really participate in the filming, and I said I thought he would. As a matter of fact, I had asked Alibi that very same question, and he assured me that he was willing.

The day came, and we headed for Times Square, where Alibi was to meet another member of his crew. They were to run the Murphy on a complete stranger. The Murphy, as discussed in chapter 4, is a very old con game with variations every generation.

Our station would be across the street from the famous Grace Building, an elegantly curved structure between Fifth and Sixth Avenues on Forty-Second Street. At the appointed time we would be situated in Bryant Park, across the street, filming the entire con. It was clear after some time had passed that the con was not going to take place; Alibi was not able to get a stranger to stop. Instead, he obviously had asked some of his buddies to pretend they were strangers. At the end of the day, he asked for several hundred dollars for the attempt and said that was worth his and his friend's effort. Eliza refused to pay, and Alibi asked instead for plane fare back home; that too was refused.

There is an old fable of a scorpion and a frog. The scorpion asks the frog to carry him across a river. The frog is hesitant because he is afraid he will be stung by the scorpion. The scorpion assures him that he won't sting the frog, because if he does, they would both drown in the river. So the frog agrees to carry the scorpion on his back across the river. Midway across, the frog feels a sting. Indeed, the scorpion has stung him. As they sink into the water, the frog asks why the scorpion would do this. The scorpion simply replies that it is in his nature; he cannot help himself.

Like the scorpion, Alibi tried to con us even though we had been associates for years. I may have been a friend to him. I may have been family. But it was in his nature to con, and no one was off limits. Not even me.

As long as we have need and greed, as Gore Vidal put it succinctly, we will have con games and con actors who find ways to make a living in our thriving metropolis.

EPILOGUE

Since we are essentially a nation of hustlers rather than makers, any attempt to set limits or goals, rules or standards, is to attack a system of free enterprise where not only does the sucker not deserve that even break but the honest man is simply the one whose cheating goes undetected.

—Gore Vidal

The con artist is a keen observer of human behavior and life on the street—and the sidewalk, the park bench, the coffee shop, and the corner. To know when and how to get a stranger to stop in a busy city like New York—and to relieve her of her valuables without overt violence—takes a great deal of careful talking, listening, and looking. But to earn her trust to "help" a person she has never seen—as in the hotel con in chapter 4—is even more remarkable. The con artist does that on a regular basis, by constantly watching and learning. Some of this knowledge of street life and culture comes through apprenticeship, by sitting at the knee of a master trickster, but a great deal cannot be learned that way because society and culture are constantly changing. Only by observing, reading, and interacting in the "now" can this knowledge be gotten.

Take for instance, the cell phone. Thanks to our nearly constant use of cell phones on the street, a certain level of distraction has become the norm. If you are in a text trance, you are not paying attention. And while everyone is busy texting, the con artists are having a field day—since a distracted person is the perfect mark.

Ricky Jay the illusionist captures the ultimate irony and paradox inherent in the existence of the con game: "You wouldn't want to live in a world where you couldn't be conned."[1] His logic is simple: that would mean "a world where no one could be trusted," not your friend, not your neighbor, not your lover, not your parents, not your government, no one. This would be devastating to a civil society. As you have seen in the preceding pages, the essence of the con is deceived trust, and trust implies the confident belief that another person will not fail you. The con phenomenon is something we have been captivated by for many years, not only because it is interesting in its own right but also because its very essence—the fragile dynamics between the conned and the con—is a mystery we all want to explore.

Con games are part of the social fabric of New York City. They are as common as a scuffle on Forty-Second Street, a bump from a stranger on a crowded sidewalk, or the broken smile of a street mendicant. And they are eternal. Changes in the street ecology (because of new building development or increased police pressure, for example) may scatter the street games and markets, but only temporarily. Perhaps the biggest New York City hustle of all is that of the real-estate developers, who assure us that "upscaling" is the way to solve the city's social problems. West Forty Second Street, for example, may have been gentrified, but the underground markets will continue to flourish elsewhere. The uptown ghetto, also currently gentrifying, may be a place today but a state of mind tomorrow.

The opportunity for profit will continue to attract the best street players to the underground economy. They are part of the social fabric of the city, and they will not disappear but rather multiply. Why? Because the old saying that "crime doesn't pay" is just not true. It does pay—for the rich and the powerful, for well-connected white males, for corporations—and it always has. It pays because greed is embedded in our social DNA. It is part of our collective desire to attain that elusive American dream no matter what it might cost ourselves, our community, our culture, or our world.

In conclusion, we will attempt a bit of futurology. What will the city look like by the year 2030? What will Harlem resemble, or Bedford-Stuyvesant, or the South Bronx? Much of the answer depends on the attention that we pay to life on the street and, more importantly, on the changing role of employment, crime, leisure, and entertainment in the daily life of New Yorkers. Consider the emerging technology being used by the police, such as *Robocop*-type surveillance, monitoring, drones, and the like, which will probably increase intensely and have a powerful effect on street life and behavior. If our inability to create jobs for the unskilled and homes for the indigent continues, new generations of ever-younger faces will arrive on the hustling scene, as they will if we cannot solve the economic and social issues faced by deprived new majorities and new immigrants. If our incarceration rates remain incomprehensibly high, hordes of ex-inmates, without the rights or means to make a regular living, will rely upon their con skills as the only way to survive when they are released back onto the street. The demand for commercial sex and pornography, especially of the more violent sort, and the demand for marijuana, other drugs, and whatever new forms of chemical stimulation are out there by 2030 will also affect the fabric of the city. We all want a deal. We all want a bargain, and as long as we all want something for nothing we will always be vulnerable to get nothing for something.

WHERE ARE THEY NOW?

As we've noted throughout this volume, hustling is hard work. It's logical to wonder if the con artists and hustlers we've profiled here have the durability to keep on for the long haul and continue to make a living.

Or does every hustle have an expiration date? Is conning and hustling only a conduit to quick, fast money that is easily spent—or can the winnings ever congeal into a steady income?

Years after the initial interviews, we followed up with our con artists to view their end game. We were very curious to see where they landed. Would the dramatic economic ups and downs between 2008 and 2014 have crushed their game? Would social and economic forces push them toward more legitimate work? Had they been arrested or imprisoned? Or had they found a permanent home hustling in New York City? Here is a quick rundown of their activities to date.

Alibi: Last heard from in 2012. Whereabouts at this time unknown.

Mrs. Wilson: whereabouts unknown.

Herlene: whereabouts unknown.

Skip: last seen [2006] in a crack house on 133rd Street.

Ace: whereabouts unknown.

Otis: whereabouts unknown.

Lee: teaches modern dance in a city middle school.

Daniel: left Canal Street, went back to school, and now manufactures and sells electronic products.

Maria: continues to work in the numbers racket.

Lorena: has disappeared, her whereabouts unknown. Her former landlord, Angelina, is still in the realty business.

Ramon: teaches youth about the negative effects of drugs in alternative-to-incarceration programs.

Frank: retired from the New York City Police Department.

J.T.: still lives in his home in Connecticut.

We realize how a few of those we wrote about have chosen another path and found the inner strength and perhaps social means to move on to less precarious endeavors. We are not aware of all their motivations for getting out of the hustling game, but it is clear that mentorship played a role in Ramon's, Daniel's, and Lee's lives: they all had someone who took them aside and "pulled their coats" to teach them a new way of living.

NOTES

INTRODUCTION

1. Alibi Jones is not his real name but a pseudonym chosen for this text.
2. New York State Penal Code, §155.05.
3. Thomas Picketty, *Capital in the Twenty-First Century*, trans. Arthur Gold-hammer (Cambridge, Mass.: Harvard University Press, 2014).
4. Karen Halttunen, *The Confidence Man and the Painted Woman* (New Haven, Conn.: Yale University Press, 1982), 6.
5. Loic Wacquant, "Inside the Zone: The Social Art of the Hustler in the American Ghetto," in *The Weight of the World: Social Suffering in Contemporary Society*, ed. Pierre Bourdieu (Stanford, Calif.: Stanford University Press, 1999).
6. Henry Mayhew, *London Labor and the London Poor* (London: Penguin, 1851).
7. C. R. D. Prus and Robert C. Sharper, *Road Hustler: The Career Contingencies of Professional Card and Dice Hustlers* (Lanham, Md.: Lexington, 1977).
8. YPD Crime.com, "New York Laws," http://ypdcrime.com/penal.law/article 165.htm#p165.25.

9. Pool is not considered a game of chance because the skill factor dominates the chance factor.

10. Joseph Henchman and Scott Drenkard, "Cigarette Taxes and Cigarette Smuggling by State," *Tax Foundation* (March 19, 2014), http://taxfoundation .org/article/cigarette-taxes-and-cigarette-smuggling-state.

11. Betty Lou Valentine, *Hustling and Other Hard Work: Life Styles in the Ghetto* (New York: Free Press, 1980), 43.

12. Ibid., 25.

13. Prus and Sharper, *Road Hustler*, 2.

14. Ronald V. Clarke and Derek B. Cornish, "The Rational Choice Perspective," in *Explaining Criminals and Crime: Essays in Contemporary Criminological Theory*, ed. Raymond Paternoster and Ronet Bachman (Los Angeles: Roxbury, 2001), 23–42.

15. These two uses quickly emerged following an earlier use as "territory" or "land." The TLFI dictionary (available on the linguistic portal of the CRNS) indicates citations in 1283 for the former and in 1549 for the latter.

16. Sarah Daynes, "The Social Life of Terroir Among Bordeaux Winemakers," in *Wine and Culture: Vineyards to Glass*, ed. R. Black and R. Ulin (New York: Bloomsbury, 2013), 15–32. *Terroir* would make an interesting addition to the examples given in Meillet, "Comment les mots changent de sens," in *Linguistique historique et linguistique générale* (Paris: Champion, 1965), 1:271. Meillet argues that the fundamental force that spurs a change of meaning in words is found with their movements between particular language of specialized groups and the general language of the broader society.

17. As in the phrases "*un accent du terroir*," "*les produits du terroir*," "*gout de terroir*."

18. As a visiting scholar at the Russell Sage Foundation, Terry met Robert Merton, who was a foundation scholar there. Merton gave him a paper he'd written about "serendipity in research," i.e., discovery by chance of data that are not actually being sought. These data helped formulate ideas related to the fortuitous events Terry kept encountering during his research, and he wanted somehow to incorporate this notion of chance into the narrative. Merton wrote a book with Elinor Barber on serendipity in 1958, *The Travels and Adventures of Serendipity*, on the origin of the word, which had originally been coined by Horace Walpole in 1754.

19. John Edgar Wideman, *Brothers and Keepers* (New York: Henry Holt, 1984).

20. Hakim Hasan, afterword to *Sidewalk*, by Mitchell Duneier (New York: Farrar, Straus and Giroux, 1999).

21. Teun Voeten, *Tunnel People* (Oakland, Calif.: PM, 2010).

1. ALIBI: PORTRAIT OF A CON MAN

1. William James, *Principles of Psychology*, vol. 1 (1890).
2. St. Clair Drake and Horace R. Cayton, *Black Metropolis: A Study of the Negro in a Northern City* (Chicago: University of Chicago Press, 1945).
3. Jane Jacobs, *The Death and Life of Great American Cities* (New York: Random House, 1961), 6.
4. Mitchell Duneier, *Sidewalk* (New York: Farrar, Straus & Giroux, 2000), 8.
5. Jacobs, *The Death and Life of Great American Cities*.
6. Edwin Sutherland, *The Professional Thief* (Chicago: University of Chicago Press, 1937), 56.
7. Ibid.

3. THE CON CREW

1. Terry M. Williams and William Kornblum, *Growing Up Poor* (San Francisco: Lexington, 1985), 74.
2. Alejandro Portes, "Social Capital: Its Origins and Applications in Modern Sociology," *Annual Review of Sociology* 24 (August 1998): 1–24.
3. Jane Jacobs, *The Death and Life of Great American Cities* (New York: Random House, 1961), 58.
4. E. B. White, *Here Is New York* (New York: Harper Brothers, 1949).
5. http://www.all-art.org/Architecture/24c.htm.

4. THE CON GAME AS STREET THEATER

1. Tamotsu Shibutani, *Social Processes: An Introduction to Sociology* (Berkeley: University of California Press, 1986).
2. Erving Goffman, *The Presentation of Self in Everyday Life* (New York: Anchor, 1959).
3. Ibid.
4. Erving Goffman, *Behavior in Public Places: Notes on the Social Organization of Gathering* (New York: Free Press, 1966), 113.
5. Ibid., 112.
6. Erving Goffman, "Cooling the Mark Out: Some Aspects of Adaptation to Failure," *Journal for the Study of Interpersonal Processes* 4 (1952): 451–463.
7. Ibid.
8. George Herbert Mead, *Mind, Self, and Society from the Standpoint of a Social Behaviorist* (Chicago: University of Chicago Press, 1934).

5. PETTY STREET HUSTLES

1. Henry Mayhew, *London Labor and the London Poor* (London: Penguin, 1851), 2.
2. Ibid., 30.
3. Mitchell Duneier, *Sidewalk* (New York: Farrar, Straus and Giroux, 1999).
4. New York City Administrative Code, subchapter 27, §20-453 requires that all people selling goods in public must first obtain a vendor's license.
5. J. Agnew and D. Livingstone, eds., *Handbook of Geographic Knowledge* (London: Sage, 2011).
6. Betty Lou Valentine, *Hustling and Other Hard Work: Life Styles in the Ghetto* (New York: Free Press, 1980), 56.
7. Terry M. Williams and William Kornblum, *Growing Up Poor* (Lanham, Md.: Lexington, 1985).
8. Trevor B. Milton, "Class Status and the Construction of Black Masculinity," *Ethnicity and Race in a Changing World* (Spring 2012): 17–34.
9. Elliot Liebow, *Tally's Corner: A Study of Negro Streetcorner Men* (Lanham, Md: Rowan & Littlefield, 1967).

6. CANAL STREET AS VENUS FLYTRAP

1. Kenneth T. Jackson, *The Encyclopedia of New York City* (New Haven, Conn.: Yale University Press, 1995).
2. Edwin H. Sutherland, *The Professional Thief* (Chicago: University of Chicago Press, 1937), 140.
3. Anticounterfeit laws in New York City have pushed those selling counterfeit and knockoff goods into more clandestine methods for selling these goods. Unsuspecting and innocuous "whisperers" literally whisper the names of popular brands tourists walk past in order to draw them into a sale.
4. New York Penal Code §165.71, "Trademark Counterfeiting in the Third Degree": A person is guilty of trademark counterfeiting in the third degree when, with the intent to deceive or defraud some other person or with the intent to evade a lawful restriction on the sale, resale, offering for sale, or distribution of goods, he or she manufactures, distributes, sells, or offers for sale goods which bear a counterfeit trademark, or possesses a trademark knowing it to be counterfeit for the purpose of affixing it to any goods.
5. http://www.nyc.gov/html/dca/html/licenses/094.shtml.
6. HR 2033 was originally introduced as a bill to the Senate in 2007 by New York Senator Charles Schumer, but it has yet to pass.

7. Lynsey Blackman, "The Devil Wears Prado: A Look at the Design Piracy Prohibition Act and the Extension of Copyright Protection to the World of Fashion," *Pepperdine Law Review* 35, no. 1 (March 2012): 106–160.

8. Marc Beja, "Brooklyn Man Busted with 44,000 Bootleg DVDs and CDs," *AM New York* (June 2012), http://www.amny.com/urbanite-1.812039 /brooklyn-man-busted-with-44-000-bootleg-dvds-and-cds-1.3795305.

9. Blackman, "The Devil Wears Prado," 113.

10. Paul Stoller, *Money Has No Smell: The Africanization of New York City* (Chicago: University of Chicago Press, 2002).

11. Administrative Code 20, 465-20, states: "No general vendor shall engage in any vending business on any sidewalk unless such sidewalk has at least a twelve-foot wide clear pedestrian path to be measured from the boundary of any private property to any obstructions in or on the sidewalk, or if there are no obstructions, to the curb. In no event shall any pushcart or stand be placed on any part of a sidewalk other than that which abuts the curb. b. No general vendor shall occupy more than eight linear feet of public space parallel to the curb in the operation of a vending business and, in addition, no general vendor operating any vending business on any sidewalk shall occupy more than three linear feet to be measured from the curb toward the property line." See more at http://codes.lp.findlaw.com/nycode /ADC/20/2/27/20-465#sthash.L9yE10XB.dpuf.

7. THE NUMBERS GAME

1. Louise Meriweather, *Daddy Was a Number Runner* (New York: First Feminist Press, 1986).

2. St. Clair Drake and Horace R. Cayton, *Black Metropolis: A Study of the Negro in a Northern City* (Chicago: University of Chicago Press, 1945), 478.

3. The material presented here is drawn from a paper and fieldnotes based on research by Mario Serrano Marte from a visit to a "Spanish" policy operation. Names have been changed.

4. These roles are also described astutely in Don Liddick's *The Mob's Daily Number: Organized Crime and the Numbers Gambling Industry* (Washington, D.C.: University Press of America, 1999).

8. NEW YORK TENANT HUSTLES

1. Furman Center, "Profile of Rent Stabilized Units and Tenants in New York City" (June 2014), http://furmancenter.org/files/FurmanCenter_FactBrief _RentStabilization_June2014.pdf.

2. B. Carter, "Landlords Say Newark Man Refuses to Pay Rent, Then Ties Them Up in Court," *Star Ledger* (May 15, 2011).

3. New York City Public Advocate, "Landlord Watch List," http://pubadvocate .nyc.gov/landlord-watchlist.

4. Ronald V. Clarke and Derek B. Cornish, "The Rational Choice Perspective," in *Explaining Criminals and Crime: Essays in Contemporary Criminological Theory* (Los Angeles: Roxbury, 2001), 23–42.

5. John P. Avlon, "Sue City," *Forbes* (July 14, 2009).

6. Stephanie Cohen, "The City's Most Litigious Lady," *New York Post* (January 17, 2010).

9. A DRUG HUSTLE: THE CRACK GAME

1. Trevor B. Milton, *Overcoming the Magnetism of Street Life: Crime-Engaged Youth and the Programs that Transform Them* (Lanham, Md.: Lexington, 2012), 8.

2. David Amsden, "The One-Man Drug Company," *New York* (April 17, 2006).

3. Steven D. Levitt and Sudhir A. Venkatesh, "An Economic Analysis of a Drug-Selling Gang's Finances," *Quarterly Journal of Economics* (August 2000): 755–789.

4. Jeremy Haken, "Transnational Crime in the Developing World," in *Global Financial Integrity* (Washington, D.C.: Center for International Policy, February 2011).

5. Robert Mann, "The Drug Laws That Changed How We Punished," *National Public Radio*, http://www.npr.org/2013/02/14/171822608/the-drug -laws-that-changed-how-we-punish.

6. New York City Department of Health, "Illicit Drug Use in New York City," *NYC Vital Signs* 9, no. 1 (February 2010).

7. New York City Police Department, "Tear End Enforcement Report," http:// www.nyc.gov/html/nypd/downloads/pdf/analysis_and_planning/2013 _year_end_enforcement_report.pdf.

8. Terry Williams, *Crackhouse: Notes from the End of the Line* (New York: Penguin, 1992).

9. Robert Sampson, Stephen Raudenbusch, and Felton Earls, "Neighborhoods and Violence: A Multilevel Study of Collective Efficacy," *Science* 277: 918–924.

10. Craig Reinarman and Harry Levine, *Crack in America: Demon Drug and Social Injustice* (Berkeley: University of California Press, 1997).

11. Williams, *Crackhouse*, 35.

12. Saskia Sassen, *The Global City: New York, London, Tokyo* (Princeton, N.J.: Princeton University Press, 1991).

13. Norman Denzin, *Interpretive Autoethnography: Qualitative Research Method* (Los Angeles: Sage, 2014), 52.

14. Gina Kolata, "Drug Researchers Try to Treat a Nearly Unbreakable Habit," *New York Times* (June 25, 1988).

15. Kristen Gwinne, "Everything Americans Think They Know About Drugs Is Wrong: A Scientist Explodes the Myths," *AlterNet* (June 13, 2013), http://www.alternet.org/drugs-addiction.

16. Kenneth Clark, *The Dark Ghetto: Dilemmas of Social Power* (Hanover, N.H.: Wesleyan University Press, 1989).

10. NYPD AND THE FINEST CONS

1. Todd Zeranski, "NYC Is Safest City as Crime Rises in U.S., FBI Say," *Bloomberg News* (June 12, 2006), http://www.bloomberg.com/apps/news?pid=10000103&sid=a.

2. Franklyn Zimring, *The City That Became Safe: New York's Lessons for Urban Crime and Its Control* (New York: Oxford University Press, 2012).

3. Loic Wacqant, *Punishing the Poor: The Neoliberal Government of Social Insecurity* (Durham, N.C.: Duke University Press, 2009).

4. Derrick B. Cornish and Ronald V. Clarke, *The Reasoning Criminal: Rational Choice Perspectives on Offending* (New York: Springer-Verlag, 1986).

5. Gary T. Marx, *Undercover: Police Surveillance in America* (Berkeley: University of California Press, 1988).

6. Lia Eustachewich, "Ringleader of 9/11 Pension Scam Lands Generous Plea Deal," *New York Post* (August 27, 2014), http://nypost.com/2014/08/27/ringleader-of-911-pension-scam-lands-generous-plea-deal/.

7. W. Rashbaum and A. Baker, "Authorities Move to Charge Sixteen Officers After Widespread Ticket Fixing," *New York Times* (October 27, 2011): A22.

8. Ibid.

11. WALL STREET CONS

1. Kenneth Rapoza, "How Much Do Wall Streeters Really Earn?" *Forbes* (March 13, 2013).

2. Mario Gabelli of GAMCO Investor's Inc. received an annual salary of $85 million in 2013.

3. https://www.intercontinentalexchange.com/about#architects.

4. http://www1.nyse.com/about/listed/nya_characteristics.shtml.

5. C. Wright Mills, *The Power Elite* (New York: Oxford University Press, 1956).

6. Robert Weissman and James Donahue, "Sold Out: How Wall Street and Washington Betrayed America," *Consumer Education Foundation Report* (March 2009): 10.

7. Ibid., 12.

8. David R. Simon, *Elite Deviance*, 10th ed. (Upper Saddle River, N.J.: Pearson, 2012).

9. Karen Ho, *Liquidated: An Ethnography of Wall Street* (Chapel Hill, N.C.: Duke University Press, 2009), 149.

10. "Ponzi Payment," *Time* (January 5, 1931), http://content.time.com/time/magazine/article/0,9171,930255,00.html.

11. Mitchell Zuckoff, *Ponzi's Scheme: The True Story of a Financial Legend* (New York: Random House, 2005).

12. Arthur Lett, *Swindling and Selling* (New York: Free Press, 1976).

13. J. R. "Yellow Kid" Weil and W. T. Brannon, *"Yellow Kid" Weil: The Autobiography of America's Master Swindler* (Oakland, Calif.: AK, 2010).

14. Jonathan Stempel, "Madoff Trustee Sues JPMorgan for $6.4 Billion," *Reuters* (December 2, 2010).

15. David Voreacos and David Glovin, "Madoff Confessed $50 Billion Fraud Before FBI Arrest," *Bloomberg News* (December 13, 2008).

16. Milton Friedman and Anna Schwartz, *A Monetary History of the United States, 1867–1960* (Princeton, N.J.: Princeton University Press, 1963).

17. Simon, *Elite Deviance*.

18. Naomi Klein, *No Logo* (New York: Picador USA, 1999).

19. http://www.investopedia.com/terms/r/repurchaseagreement.asp.

20. Courtney Comstock, "Headline from the South: Is Wall Street a Cocaine Factory?" *Business Insider*, http://www.businessinsider.com/headline-from-the-south-is-wall-street-a-cocaine-factory-2010-5#ixzz36nzP7q7I.

21. Klein, *No Logo*, 4.

EPILOGUE

1. Clyde Haberman, "Straight Talk from a Professor of Flimflam (but Don't Ask His Age)," *New York Times* (April 21, 2013).

GLOSSARY

Babysitter	a person who watches over drug shipments
Backstage	place or space where con artists plan and rehearse their next con
Bait and switch	to set up a con
Banca	place that takes bets and pays out winnings in a numbers game
Banker	a person who provides cash for numbers winners
Beat artist	anyone who sells bogus drugs and other items including drugs
Bodega	Corner store, deli
Bookie	a person who works in the "rackets" determines odds and pays off bets.
Booster	a shoplifter
Botanica	place where people buy religious objects, candles, etc. for those who practice Santeria and Catholic rituals.
Bottom woman	the main companion of the pimp
Brick layer	a street-walking prostitute
Bricks	sidewalk or street

Buffer	a young woman who sells her sexual labor (oral sex) for drugs
Bullshit	to lie
Button man	a contract killer
Call girl	prostitute whose appointment is made over the phone
Cake	money or cash
Cams	bootleg DVDs filmed in movie theaters with a handheld camcorder
Can-man	homeless people who retrieve cans from the street
Cannon	a master con man or a superior pickpocket
Catch basin	a bucket or metal tray designed to retrieve lost items that have dropped down a sewer drain.
Chicken	boys in game rooms who sell sex
Chicken hawk	man who preys on young teenagers to perform various sex acts
Clip joint	place where people are conned
Clocking	making a lot of money in a short amount of time
Collection agent	a person who collects money from policy operations
Con artist	a person who swindles
Confidence man	a person who runs cons (short and long).
Conked hair	to straighten "kinky" hair with chemical treatments
Connect	a supplier of illicit drugs
Controller	a person who takes receipts from runners and customers or provides money for bankers in the numbers rackets
Cook	a person who cooks crack cocaine
Cop (verb)	to purchase drugs
Courier	a person who delivers drugs
Cutter	a person who adulterates drugs
Cutting corners	to cheat
Dealer	a seller of drugs

Dipper	a pickpocket
Dog	an affectionate term or a negative expression
Drag	an extended con
Duke man	a pickpocket's helper
Escort	a person who rents intimacy
Fam	family
Fast ho	a woman who performs quick sex
Fast money change artist	a con that preys on bank tellers
Fence	a person who sells stolen goods
Financier	a person who bankrolls deals
Flash	to display one's riches for the public to see
Flat-footed hustler	a street hustler
Fluffer	a woman who performs oral sex on performers before the sex show
Freebaser	a middle-class crack user
Freelancer	a person who works at any time
Fronting	pretending to be something that you are not
Gamester	someone on the make
Gimme guy	a buyer who wants everything in the store
Girl pimp	a madam
Grift sense	a sixth sense for pickpockets; also called a conman's sense
Gorilla	a strong-arm man
Gray market	legal goods, typically sold on the streets illegally
Grind	to work hard while barely making ends meet
Hacker	computer genius; a person who breaks into computers unauthorized
Hitman	a killer
Hitter	a person who shoots heroin or cocaine into others
Ho	a prostitute
Hook	(a) the part of a con that makes it successful; (b) a highly ranked police officer willing to do favors for underlings

Hot merchandise	Stolen merchandise
Independent ho	a sex worker without a pimp
Juggler	a person who wheels and deals
Loan shark	a bookie
Long con	a scam taking hours, days, months, or years
Lookout	a person who watches for the police
Loosie	a single cigarette sold by itself after being removed from a full pack
Manager	a person who looks after the books
Mark	a target of a con; the person to be fooled
Mechanic	a pickpocket's helper
Mixer	a person who mixes drugs
Monte player	a street con artist
Mr. Bates	a businessman
Mule	a person who smuggles drugs
Narco trafficker	a person who smuggles drugs
Numbers man	a person who works in the policy game
Nutcracker	a homemade alcoholic beverage made of liquor and fruit-flavored frozen slush
Office worker	a person who works in a drug house
On the pad/nut	a police officer paid to look away from criminal activity
Papi	an older male
Phone ho	a sex worker who talks sex over the phone
Pick-up man	a person who delivers money or drugs
Pipero	a small pipe
Pitcher	a person in the three-card monte game or who sells drugs
Policy station	place where numbers game is run
Popcorn pimp	a poor pimp with weak game
Pound	a handshake involving the clasping the back of someone's hand rather than the palm
Regular girl	a low-end sex worker
Rehash	to disguise used merchandise as brand-new

Runner	a person who sells drugs or runs numbers
Sage opportunist	criminal with an acquired skill set
Scale boy/girl	a person who measures drugs for sale
Screeners	Bootleg DVD copied from studio-quality originals
Sex worker	a prostitute
Shade	to block a vic or mark's view
Shill	a person who works the three-card monte scam
Short con	a con taking only minutes
Short-story writer	a check forger
Shrimped	to be conned out of money that was invested
Side hustle	money made outside of regular employment
Skeezer	an attractive woman in the drug trade
Slam	to close a deal/to con a mark successfully
Slam team	freelancers for hire on Canal Street used to slam wealthy tourists and businesspersons
Slide	a lookout in the three-card monte card game
Slum jewelry	fake jewelry
Smoke taster	a person who ingests marijuana to determine potency
Smuggler	a person who smuggles
Spiker	a person who injects drugs intravenously
Spot owner	a manager of a drug-selling location
Stall or stick	a person who maneuvers a mark into position
Steerer	a person who brings customers to buy drugs
Swimmer	one who retrieves drugs from the ocean or river
Talk trick	a person who enjoys sex by phone
Taster	a person who ingests adulterated crack before packaging for sale
Terroir	landscape or complex physical space necessary for a successful con game
Thug (gangster)	a person who survives off of violent illegal activities
Ticket puncher	a hired killer

Tool	a pickpocket's helper
Tout	a person who brings buyers and sellers together
Tunnel trick	man who pays for oral sex in the Holland Tunnel or Lincoln Tunnel
Tunnel whore	woman selling oral sex to Holland Tunnel or Lincoln Tunnel commuters
Vic	victim
Whisperer	African (Senegalese) street seller of knockoff goods
Whiz mob	a pickpocket gang
Whore	also "ho" sex worker, prostitute
Wire	a pickpocket's helper
Writer in a spot	a person who writes policy numbers

BIBLIOGRAPHY

Abraham, Roger D. "Rapping and Capping: Black Talk as Art." In *Black America*, ed. John Szwed. New York: Basic Books, 1970.

Agnew, J., and D. Livingstone, eds. *Handbook of Geographic Knowledge*. London: Sage, 2011.

Amsden, David. "The One-Man Drug Company." *New York* (April 9, 2006). http://nymag.com/news/features/16653/.

Anderson, Elijah. "The Code of the Streets." *Atlantic Monthly* 273, no. 5 (1994): 81–94.

Baker, Paul. "The Life Histories of W. I. Thomas and Robert Park." *American Journal of Sociology* 79 (1973): 243–260.

Benjamin, Walter. *Illuminations: Essays and Reflections*. New York: Harcourt Brace Jovanovich, 1968.

Blackman, Lynsey. "The Devil Wears Prado: A Look at the Design Piracy Prohibition Act and the Extension of Copyright Protection to the World of Fashion." *Pepperdine Law Review* 35, no. 1 (March 2012): 106–160.

Blee, Kathleen M. *Inside Organized Racism: Women in the Hate Movement*. Berkeley: University of California Press, 2003.

Bourdieu, Pierre. "The Forms of Capital." In *Handbook of Theory and Research for the Sociology of Education*, ed. J. Richardson. New York: Greenwood, 1986.

——. *The Logic of Practice*. New York: Polity, 1990.

Bourgois, Philippe. *In Search of Respect: Selling Crack in El Barrio*. New York: Cambridge University Press, 1996.

Carr, P., L. Napolitano, and J. Keating. "We Never Call the Cops and Here Is Why: A Qualitative Examination of Legal Cynicism in Three Philadelphia Neighborhoods." *Criminology* 45, no. 2 (2007): 445–480.

Clark, Kenneth. *The Dark Ghetto: Dilemmas of Social Power*. Hanover, N.H.: Wesleyan University Press, 1989.

Clarke, Ronald V., and Derek B. Cornish. "The Rational Choice Perspective." In *Explaining Criminals and Crime: Essays in Contemporary Criminological Theory*, ed. R. Paternoster and R. Bachman, 23–42. Los Angeles: Roxbury, 2001.

Coleman, James S. "Social Capital in the Creation of Human Capital." *American Journal of Sociology* 94 (1988): S95–S120.

Cornish, Derrick B., and Ronald V. Clarke. *The Reasoning Criminal: Rational Choice Perspectives on Offending*. New York: Springer-Verlag, 1986.

Daley, Robert. *The World Beneath the City*. Philadelphia: J. B. Lippincott, 1959.

Daynes, Sarah. "The Social Life of Terroir Among Bordeaux Winemakers." In *Wine and Culture: Vineyards to Glass*, ed. R. Black and R. Ulin, 15–32. New York: Bloomsbury, 2013.

Denzin, Norman. *Interpretive Autoethnography: Qualitative Research Methods*. Los Angeles: Sage, 2014.

DiIulio, John. *Body Count: Moral Poverty and How to Win America's War Against Crime and Drugs*. New York: Simon and Schuster, 1996.

Drake, St. Clair, and Horace R. Cayton. *Black Metropolis: A Study of the Negro in a Northern City*. Chicago: University of Chicago Press, 1945.

Duneier, Mitchell. *Sidewalk*. New York: FSG, 1999.

Eustachewich, Lia. "Ringleader of 9/11 Pension Scam Lands Generous Plea Deal." *New York Post* (August 27, 2014). http://nypost.com/2014/08/27/ringleader -of-911-pension-scam-lands-generous-plea-deal/.

Foucault, Michel. *Discipline and Punish: The Birth of the Prison*. New York: Vintage, 1977.

——. "Structuralism and Structures of Knowledge." *Essential Works of Foucault, 1954–1984*, vol. 3: *Power*. New York: The New Press, 1994.

Friedman, Milton, and Anna Schwartz. *A Monetary History of the United States, 1867–1960*. Princeton, N.J.: Princeton University Press, 1963.

Goffman, Erving. *Behavior in Public Places: Notes on the Social Organization of Gathering*. New York: Free Press, 1966.

——. "Cooling the Mark Out: Some Aspects of Adaptation to Failure." *Journal for the Study of Interpersonal Processes* 4 (1952): 451–463.

——. *The Presentation of Self in Everyday Life*. New York: Anchor, 1959.

Gwinne, Kristen. "Everything Americans Think They Know About Drugs Is Wrong: A Scientist Explodes the Myths." *AlterNet* (June 13, 2013). http://www.alternet.org/drugs-addiction.

Halttunen, Karen. *The Confidence Man and the Painted Woman*. New Haven, Conn.: Yale University Press, 1982.

Haken, Jeremy. "Transnational Crime in the Developing World." In *Global Financial Integrity*. Washington, D.C.: Center for International Policy, February 2011.

Hasan, Hakim. Afterword to *Sidewalk*, by Mitchell Duneier. New York: FSG, 1999.

Ho, Karen. *Liquidated: An Ethnography of Wall Street*. Durham, N.C.: Duke University Press, 2009.

Irwin, John, and Donald Cressey. "Thieves, Convicts, and the Inmate Culture." *Social Problems* 10 (1962): 145–157.

Jackson, Kenneth T. *The Encyclopedia of New York City*. New Haven, Conn.: Yale University Press, 1995.

Jacobs, Jane. *The Death and Life of Great American Cities*. New York: Random House, 1961.

James, William. *Principles of Psychology*. Vol. 1. 1890.

Joyce, James. *A Portrait of the Artist as a Young Man*. Ed. Chester G. Anderson. Viking Critical ed. New York: Viking, 1968.

Klein, Naomi. *No Logo*. New York: Picador USA, 1999.

Kluckhohn, Clyde. *Mirror for Man: The Relation of Anthropology to Modern Life*. Phoenix: University of Arizona Press, 1985.

Kolata, Gina. "Drug Researchers Try to Treat a Nearly Unbreakable Habit." *New York Times* (June 25, 1988).

Lett, Arthur. *Swindling and Selling*. New York: Free Press, 1976.

Levitt, Steven D., and Sudhir A. Venkatesh. "An Economic Analysis of Drug-Selling Gang's Finances." *Quarterly Journal of Economics* (August 2000): 755–789.

Liebow, Elliot. *Tally's Corner: A Study of Negro Streetcorner Men*. Lanham, Md.: Rowan & Littlefield, 1967.

Lindner, Rolf. *The Reportage of Urban Culture: Robert Park and the Chicago School*. New York: Cambridge University Press, 1996.

Lyon, Larry. *The Community in Urban Society*. Long Grove, Ill.: Waveland, 1999.

Malthus, Robert Thomas. *An Essay on the Principle of Population*. London: J. Johnson, 1798.

Mann, Robert. "The Drug Laws That Changed How We Punished." *National Public Radio*. http://www.npr.org/2013/02/14/171822608/the-drug-laws-that-changed-how-we-punish.

Marx, Gary T. *Undercover: Police Surveillance in America.* Berkeley: University of California Press, 1988.

Matza, David. *Delinquency and Drift.* 1964; repr. New Brunswick, N.J.: Transaction, 1990.

Mayhew, Henry. *London Labor and the London Poor.* London: Penguin, 1851.

Mead, George Herbert. *Mind, Self, and Society from the Standpoint of a Social Behaviorist.* Chicago: University of Chicago Press, 1934.

Meillet, Antoine. "Comment les mots changent de sens." In *Linguistique historique et linguistique générale*, vol. 1. Paris: Champion, 1965.

Merton, Robert K. "Opportunity Structure." In *On Social Structure and Science.* Chicago: University of Chicago Press, 1996.

——. "Social Structure and Anomie." In *On Social Structure and Science.* Chicago: University of Chicago Press, 1996.

Meriweather, Louise. *Daddy Was a Number Runner.* New York: First Feminist Press, 1986.

Mills, C. Wright. *The Power Elite.* New York: Oxford University Press, 1956.

Milton, Trevor B. "Class Status and the Construction of Black Masculinity." *Ethnicity and Race in a Changing World* (Spring 2012): 17–34.

——. *Overcoming the Magnetism of Street Life: Crime-Engaged Youth and the Programs That Transform Them.* Lanham, Md.: Lexington, 2012.

Mumford, Lewis. *The Lewis Mumford Reader.* Ed. Donald Miller. New York: Pantheon, 1986.

New York City Department of Health. "Illicit Drug Use in New York City." *NYC Vital Signs* 9, no. 1 (February 2010).

Paget, Marianne A. *The Unity of Mistakes: A Phenomenological Interpretation of Medical Work.* Philadelphia: Temple University Press, 1988.

Parenti, Christian. *The Soft Cage: Surveillance in America.* New York: Basic Books, 2003.

Park, Robert E. "The City: Suggestions for the Investigation of Human Behavior." *American Journal of Sociology* 20, no. 5: 1915.

Park, Robert E., and Ernest Burgess. *The City.* Chicago: University of Chicago Press, 1925.

Picketty, Thomas. *Capital in the Twenty-First Century.* Trans. Arthur Goldhammer. Cambridge, Mass.: Harvard University Press, 2014.

Prus, C. R. D., and Robert C. Sharper. *Road Hustler: The Career Contingencies of Professional Card and Dice Hustlers.* Lanham, Md.: Lexington, 1977.

Putnam, Robert. *Bowling Alone: The Collapse and Revival of American Community.* New York: Simon & Schuster, 2000.

Rapoza, Kenneth. "How Much Do Wall Streeters Really Earn?" *Forbes* (March 13, 2013).

Rashbaum, W., and A. Baker. "Authorities Move to Charge Sixteen Officers After Widespread Ticket Fixing." *New York Times* (October 27, 2011).

Sampson, R., R. Raudenbush, and F. Earls. "Neighborhoods and Violent Crime: A Multilevel Study of Collective Efficacy." *Science* 277 (1997): 918–924.

Sassen, Saskia. *The Global City: New York, London, Tokyo*. Princeton, N.J.: Princeton University Press, 1991.

Shibutani, Tamotsu. *Social Processes: An Introduction to Sociology*. Berkeley: University of California Press, 1986.

———. *Society and Personality*. Englewood Cliffs, N.J.: Prentice Hall, 1961.

Simon, David R. *Elite Deviance*. 10th ed. Upper Saddle River, N.J.: Pearson, 2012.

Stoller, Paul. *Money Has No Smell: The Africanization of New York City*. Chicago: University of Chicago Press, 2002.

Street, David. *Handbook of Contemporary Urban Life*. Ann Arbor: University of Michigan Press, 1978.

Sutherland, Edwin. *The Professional Thief*. Chicago: University of Chicago Press, 1937.

Sutherland, Edwin, and Donald Cressey. *Principles of Criminology*. Lanham, Md.: Alta Mira, 1939.

———. "A Theory of Differential Association." In *Criminology*, 8th ed. Philadelphia: J. B. Lippincott, 1970.

Thomas, William I., and Florian Zaretsky. *The Polish Peasant in Europe and America*. Urbana: University of Illinois, 1996.

Tonnies, Ferdinand. *Gemeinschaft und Gesellschaft*. Ed. Charles P. Loomis. East Lansing: Michigan State University Press, 1957.

Valentine, Betty Lou. *Hustling and Other Hard Work: Life Styles in the Ghetto*. New York: Free Press, 1980.

Van Gennep, Arnold. *The Rites of Passage*. London: Routledge & Kegan Paul, 1960.

Voeten, Teun. *Tunnel People*. Oakland, Calif.: PM, 2010.

Wacquant, Loic. "Inside the Zone: The Social Art of the Hustler in the American Ghetto." In *The Weight of the World: Social Suffering in Contemporary Society*, ed. Pierre Bourdieu. Stanford, Calif.: Stanford University Press, 1999.

———. "The New Peculiar Institution: On the Prison as Surrogate Ghetto." *Theoretical Criminology* 4, no. 3 (2000): 377–389.

———. *Punishing the Poor: The Neoliberal Government of Social Insecurity*. Durham, N.C.: Duke University Press, 2009.

———. "Urban Marginality in the Coming Millennium." *Urban Studies* 36, no. 10 (1999): 1639–1647.

Weber, Max. "Class, Status, Party." In *From Max Weber: Essays in Sociology*. New York: Oxford University Press, 1946.

Weil, J. R. "Yellow Kid," and W. T. Brannon. *"Yellow Kid" Weil: The Autobiography of America's Master Swindler*. (Oakland, CA: AK, 2010).

Weissman, Robert, and James Donahue. "Sold Out: How Wall Street and Washington Betrayed America." *Consumer Education Foundation Report* (March 2009).

White, E. B. *Here Is New York*. New York: Harper Brothers, 1949.

Williams, Terry M., and William Kornblum. *Growing Up Poor*. San Francisco: Lexington, 1985.

Wilson, James Q. *Thinking About Crime*. New York: Basic Books, 1983.

Wilson, James, and George Kelling. "Broken Windows." *Atlantic Monthly* (March 1982): 29–38.

Wilson, William J., and Loic Wacquant. "The Ghetto Underclass and the Changing Structure of Urban Poverty." In *Quiet Riots: Race and Poverty in the United States*. Westminster, Md.: Random House, 1988.

Wirth, Louis. "Urbanism as Way of Life." *American Journal of Sociology*, 44, no. 1 (1938).

Wolfe, Alan. *The Seamy Side of Democracy: Repression in America*. New York: Longman, 1978.

Zeranski, Todd. "NYC Is Safest City as Crime Rises in U.S., FBI Say." *Bloomberg News* (June 12, 2006), http://www.bloomberg.com/apps/news?pid=10000103&sid=a.

Zimring, Franklyn. *The City That Became Safe: New York's Lessons for Urban Crime and Its Control*. New York: Oxford University Press, 2012.

Zuckoff, Mitchell. *Ponzi's Scheme: The True Story of a Financial Legend*. New York: Random House, 2005.

INDEX